BASIC PRACTICE
IN
COURTS, TRIBUNALS AND INQUIRIES

CW01509780

AUSTRALIA
The Law Book Company
Brisbane ■ Sydney ■ Melbourne ■ Perth

CANADA
Carswell
Ottawa ■ Toronto ■ Calgary ■ Montreal ■ Vancouver

Agents
Steimatzky's Agency Ltd., Tel Aviv
N.M. Tripathi (Private) Ltd., Bombay
Eastern Law House (Private) Ltd., Calcutta
M.P.P. House, Bangalore
Universal Book Traders, Delhi
Aditya Books, Delhi
MacMillan Shuppan KK, Tokyo
Pakistan Law House, Karachi, Lahore

BASIC PRACTICE
IN
COURTS, TRIBUNALS AND INQUIRIES

by

Nicholas Fridd, M.A. (Oxon.)
Barrister

with

Steven Weddle, B.A.
Barrister

Simon Levene, M.A. (Cantab.)
Barrister

Robert Fookes, M.A. (Oxon.)
Barrister

LONDON
SWEET & MAXWELL
1993

First edition (1989) – Nicholas Fridd and Steven Weddle (pub.: Waterlows)

Published in 1993 by
Sweet & Maxwell Limited of
100 Avenue Road, Swiss Cottage, London NW3 3PF
http://www.smlawpub.co.uk
Typeset by York House Typographic Ltd, London W13 8NT
Printed by Athenæum Press Ltd, Gateshead, Tyne & Wear

Reprinted 1997

No natural forests were destroyed to make this product.
Only farmed timber was used and re-planted.

A CIP catalogue record for this book is
available from the British Library

ISBN: 0 421 48570 1

All rights reserved.
UK statutory material in this publication
is acknowledged as Crown copyright.

No part of this publication may be reproduced or transmitted in any
form or by any means, or stored in any retrieval system of any nature
without prior written permission, except for permitted fair dealing
under the Copyright, Designs and Patents Act 1988,or in accordance
with the terms of a licence issued by the Copyright Licensing Agency
in respect of photcopying and/or reprographic reproduction.
Application for permission for other use of copyright material
including permission to reproduce extracts in other published works
shall be made to the publishers. Full acknowledgment of author,
publisher and source must be given.

©
Nicholas Fridd
1993

Foreword to the First Edition

by the Rt. Hon. Lord Havers of Edmundsbury

This is a remarkable book — it takes the reader by the hand through practically any court he may visit and tells him exactly what to do and warns the unwary of the pitfalls.

I would have been an avid reader if it had been available when I started at the Bar.

In my view there should be a copy in every set of chambers and solicitors' office.

If there is, there can be no excuse for not getting everything right.

The scope is enormous; it covers all the ordinary courts and the coroner's court and even a consistory court.

I cannot praise it too highly.

M.H.
November 14, 1989

Contents

INTRODUCTION

The purpose of the book

This book is designed to assist an advocate in an unfamiliar court or tribunal.

It offers general advice in respect of each court and tribunal and then gives the advocate a step by step guide to the practice of the court or tribunal.

The book tells the advocate what *usually* happens, what he *usually* says and when he *usually* says it in any court, tribunal or inquiry.

Preparation for the hearing

As a general rule, the preparation for a hearing in the civil courts is more structured than the actual hearing of the case whereas the opposite applies in the criminal courts.

Basic Practice in Courts, Tribunals and Inquiries concentrates, wherever possible, on what happens in court with a background to the pre-hearing preparation.

Practice at the hearing

The advocate should note that practice varies between different courts, tribunals and inquiries and, although allowances have been made for this in the book, the number of variations cannot be exhaustive.

The book is as correct as it can be where the variations of practice will be as many as the courts and tribunals or, indeed, the advocates appearing before them.

The art of advocacy

Basic Practice in Courts, Tribunals and Inquiries is about the form rather than the art of advocacy. If any advice about the art of advocacy can be given, it is summed up in the words of Lord Birkett:

"The primary rules are not many and they are easily mastered. They are to seek simplicity, to avoid verbiage, to use familiar words of plain meaning and to be natural.

It is lucidity that makes speech enjoyable to the hearer; it is grace of speech that makes the spoken word memorable; and grace and lucidity come only from the observance of the primary rules and the willingness to take pains."

Addressing the court or tribunal

Basic Practice in Courts, Tribunals and Inquiries omits references to the titles of the persons who constitute the court (for example, **My Lord** or **Your Worships** or **Sir**) and sometimes refers to the court as **you** for ease of use.

The advocate should always use the correct title (which is set out at the beginning of each chapter or section) as a matter of courtesy.

Acknowledgments

Acknowledgments for the very substantial help and assistance the author has received from judges, court clerks, solicitors and practising members of the Bar follow this Introduction, with the exception of a substantial debt of thanks to Fiona Fridd who shared the typing of this book.

Where it is referred to, the law is correct to June 1993, and includes the proposed amendments to the Criminal Justice Act 1991.

Nicholas Fridd
June 1993

Acknowledgments

The author would like to thank the following persons for their contributions to the following chapters and sections:

Chapter 1: Magistrates' Court
Chapter 2: Youth Court
David Speed, M.A. (Oxon.)
Barrister
Clerk to the Makerfield and Wigan Justices

Chapter 3: Family Proceedings Court
Robert Stevens, LL.B.
Barrister
Deputy Clerk to the Leigh Justices

Chapter 5: Crown Court (3. Seeing the judge)
David Gibson-Lee, LL.B.
Barrister

Chapter 6: Court Martial
Keith Kelleher
Barrister
Formerly Captain in the Army Legal Corps

Michael Duffy
Barrister
Formerly Flight Lieutenant in the Directorate of Legal Services

Trevor Wright
Barrister
Formerly Lieutenant Commander, Fleet Legal Service

Chapter 8: County Court
Steven Weddle, B.A.
Barrister

Simon Levene, M.A. (Cantab.)
Barrister

and in the first edition:

His Honour Judge Russell Vick Q.C.
District Judge Segal

Chapter 9: High Court
Steven Weddle, B.A.
Barrister

Simon Levene, M.A. (Cantab.)
Barrister

and in the first edition:

Honourable Mr Justice Millett
District Judge Segal
Master R.L. Turner
His Honour Judge Russell Vick Q.C.

Chapter 10: Family Proceedings in the County Court and High Court
Judith Parker Q.C.

Brian Alland, B. ENG, M.SC.
Barrister

Steven Weddle, B.A.
Barrister

Robert Stevens, LL.B.
Barrister

Susan Holmes, LL.B.
Barrister

Chapter 12: Court of Appeal (Civil Division)
Chapter 13: Appeals to the High Court and the Divisional Court
Steven Weddle, B.A.
Barrister

Simon Levene, M.A. (Cantab.)
Barrister

Chapter 14: Industrial Tribunal
Guy Prichard, M.A. (Oxon.)
Barrister

Chapter 15: Other Tribunals
Immigration Appeal Tribunal
Martin Wynn Jones
Barrister

Social Security Appeal Tribunal
Guy Prichard, M.A. (Oxon.)
Barrister

Chapter 16: Lands Tribunal
Robert Fookes, M.A. (Oxon.)
Barrister

Chapter 17: Inquiries
Robert Fookes, M.A. (Oxon.)
Barrister

Chapter 18: Coroner's Court
John Wilson, B.A. (Cantab.)
Barrister

Chapter 19: Consistory Court
Nigel Seed, B.A. (Dunelm)
Barrister
Chancellor of the Diocese of Leicester

Chapter 20: Costs (3. Costs in civil cases)
Steven Weddle, B.A.
Barrister

Simon Levene, M.A. (Cantab.)
Barrister

Chapter 23: Etiquette
James Bullen, LL.B. (Lond.)
Barrister

Simon Levene, B.A. (Cantab.)
Barrister

CHAPTER 1

Magistrates' Court

1. INTRODUCTION

Introduction

In no other court does day to day practice vary so widely. This is   **1.01.01**
because of the large number of magistrates' courts and also the volume
of work undertaken by those courts.

The advocate is advised to consult the clerk in an unfamiliar court.

Right of audience

Barrister.   **1.01.02**
Solicitor (and duty solicitor).
Authorised official (for example: local authority employee).
Defendant in person.

Sometimes, any other person, (called next friend or McKenzie
adviser). He should state the reason why he wishes to represent the
defendant and ask the permission of the court, for example:

> **"With your permission, I would like to assist the defendant in
> these proceedings. My name is** (*name*)**. I am a neighbour/friend**
> (*or other*)**."**

Dress

1.01.03   Barristers and solicitors should be respectably dressed.
Defendants in person and other persons may appear in their normal everyday wear.

Mode of address

1.01.04   Lay bench/justices: **Sir** or **madam** to the Chairman (**Your Worship(s)** is sometimes used)
Stipendiary magistrate: **Sir** or **madam**

The hearing

1.01.05   Unless otherwise stated, the hearing of any matter in the magistrates' court takes place in open court.

Seating in court

1.01.06   Although there is no hard and fast rule, the following is a guide:
Where the dock is at the side of the court the defence will usually sit in the rows and/or seats closer to the dock. Otherwise, the defence may sit in the rows, and/or seats, on the right hand side of court facing the bench.

Addressing the court

1.01.07   Any party addressing the court should do so standing (except in the family proceedings court and sometimes in the youth court).

Order of presentation

1.01.08   The order of presentation and speeches follows the title order of the case in the court list.

Witnesses

1.01.09   Witnesses should remain outside court until called to give evidence (except expert witnesses, who will sometimes remain in court, by agreement, with the permission of the court, see **1.07.15**).
The witness should then remain in court until the conclusion of the case or until he is given permission to leave by the court, see **21.01.19–20**.

Appeal

In practice, appeal is to the Crown Court, see **5.06** and **5.07**. For **1.01.10** appeal by case stated to the Divisional Court, see **13.04**.

2. ATTENDANCE OF THE PARTIES

Attendance of the prosecution/applicant

If the prosecution/applicant and/or witness(es) essential to the proof of **1.02.01** that party's case fail to attend court, the defence may apply for the case to be dismissed for want of prosecution, for example:

> **"The prosecution/applicant and/or** (*name of witness(es)*) **does not attend. I have/The court has been offered no adequate explanation for his failure to attend.**
>
> **I therefore apply for this matter to be dismissed for want of prosecution."**

Attendance of the defendant (charge)

If the defendant has been charged and bailed in criminal proceedings **1.02.02** he must attend court. If he does not do so, a warrant may be issued or bail may be enlarged in his absence.

Warrant without bail

A warrant without bail will be issued where the defendant has given **1.02.03** either no explanation or no reasonable explanation for his non-attendance. The court will usually allow the defence a short time in which to make enquiries to establish the reason for the defendant's failure to attend.

The defence should not make an application for bail if no explana- **1.02.04** tion has been given for the defendant's non-attendance.

The prosecution may say:

> **"The defendant does not appear. I ask for a warrant (not backed for bail)."**

The defence may say:

3

"I can give the court no explanation for the defendant's failure to appear."

Warrant with bail

1.02.05 A warrant with bail may be issued where the defence is able to give a reasonable explanation for the defendant's non-attendance.

Enlarging bail

1.02.06 Bail will be enlarged in the absence of the defendant:

(a) Where the defendant has given a reasonable explanation for his non-attendance and there is usually some other evidence (from either the prosecution or the defence) to show that the defendant is unable to attend court (for example, that the defendant is in custody elsewhere).

(b) Where it is convenient for the court (for example, lack of court time) and there is no reason to believe that the defendant will abscond.

1.02.07 The defendant may be excused from attending the magistrates' court before a hearing date and a bail enlargement notice issued.

Attendance of the defendant/respondent (summons)

1.02.08 If the defendant/respondent has been summonsed, he should attend court except:

(a) where he has been invited to plead guilty by letter, or

(b) where it is stated on the summons that the defendant need not do so if he has informed the court that he will be entering a not guilty plea. A date for a contested hearing will then be fixed and notified to the defendant by post.

If the defendant/respondent does not attend court

1.02.09 Where the defendant/respondent has given no explanation or no reasonable explanation for his non-attendance, and the prosecution/

applicant can prove that the summons has been served (on the defendant/respondent):

(a) The case may be heard in the defendant's/respondent's absence. The prosecution/applicant may:
   (i) call oral evidence;
   (ii) read the evidence, if it is in the correct section 9 C.J.A. form, if the prosecution/applicant can prove that copies of the statement(s) have been served (on the defendant/respondent).
(b) A warrant (with or without bail) may be issued where the information is substantiated on oath.

Where the defendant/respondent has given a reasonable explanation **1.02.10** for his non-attendance, the summons may be adjourned.

Where the prosecution/applicant is unable to prove that the sum- **1.02.11** mons has been served, the summons will be marked "not served" and may be re-issued marked "for personal service". A summons may be served by ordinary post.

3. NON-EFFECTIVE HEARINGS

Introduction

Criminal proceedings

Criminal proceedings in the magistrates' court are commenced by **1.03.01** charge or summons. As a general rule, non-imprisonable offences only are commenced by summons.

Where a defendant appears on charge and the case is adjourned, the **1.03.02** defendant is remanded either on bail or in custody to the adjourned date. The date must be fixed. If the hearing on the adjourned date is a non-effective hearing (for example, to fix a date for committal/trial) a bail enlargement notice may be served and the defendant need not attend, see **1.02.07**.

Where a defendant appears on summons and the case is adjourned **1.03.03** there is no need to fix a date for the next hearing, although this is usually done. The case may also be adjourned "for a date to be fixed" or "*sine die*".

In some circumstances (for example, either way offences) the defendant is remanded even if he has appeared on summons, see **1.04.03**.

5

Practice

Identification of the defendant and/or parties

1.03.04   The defendant is usually identified by name, date of birth and/or address. The clerk may say:

> **"Are you (***name***)? What is your date of birth? What is your address?"**

Introduction of the parties

1.03.05   Either party (usually the party making the application for the remand/adjournment) or the clerk may introduce the parties to the court, for example:

> **"I appear on behalf of (***name of party***). The (***other party***) is represented by (***name***).**
> **I have an application for a remand/adjournment. The application is opposed/unopposed."**

Application for remand/adjournment

1.03.06   The party making the application then gives reasons for the application:

Specimen reasons

(a) *First appearance*

1.03.07   **"This is the defendant's first appearance. The defence is asking for (–) days to take instructions."**

(b) *Legal aid*

> **"The defendant has applied for legal aid. The defence is asking for (–) days for the result of that application (and to take instructions)."**

(c) *Advance disclosure*

In either way offences, the defence has the right to advance disclosure of the prosecution case:

> **"The defence is asking for advance disclosure. I believe that (–) days is appropriate."**

See **1.04.07**.

(d) *For a date to be fixed*

> **"The defendant is pleading not guilty and a date will need to be fixed for trial. The time estimate is (–) hours. The issues in dispute in the case are** (*state briefly the issues in dispute*)**."**

See **1.06** Summary trial.

(e) *For committal to Crown Court*

> **"The defendant will be electing trial at the Crown Court."**

Mode of trial will usually be determined at this stage, see **1.04.08–21**. The defence or the clerk may say:

> **"Could/can the election be put?"**

(f) *Remand for old style/read committal*

> **"The defence will be seeking an old style/read committal and a date will need to be fixed. The time estimate is (–) hours. The issues in dispute in the case are** (*state briefly the issues in dispute*)**."**

The advocate should remember that the evidence in an old style committal is written down/typed by the clerk, see **1.05.22–25**, and the time estimate should take account of this.

(g) *Lack of time*

> **"There is insufficient time for the case to be heard today. Could a new date be fixed?"**

(h) *Lack of preparation*

> **"The prosecution/defence has not had time to prepare the case because** (*state reason*)**."**

The court is unlikely to accept an unconvincing reason. The advocate should bear in mind that the court may make an order for wasted costs, see **20.02.31–32**.

(i) *Non-attendance of witness(es)*

> **"A witness essential to the prosecution/defence is unable to attend court because** (*state reason*)**."**

(j) *Non-attendance of defendant*
On charge, see **1.02.02–07**.

On summons only, see **1.02.08(b)**:

> **"The defendant does not appear but nevertheless wishes to contest the summons."**

Argument

1.03.08   If the application is opposed the court may wish to hear argument on the merits of the application. The order of submissions is usually as follows:

(a) Party making the application for remand/adjournment.

(b) Party opposing the application, who may also (in a case of unreasonable delay occasioned by the prosecution/ applicant) apply for the case to be dismissed for the want of prosecution, see **1.02.01**.

(c) Reply by party (a) on any new matters only, raised by party (b) or the court.

Decision

1.03.09   The magistrates announce their decision:

> **"We are/are not prepared to grant this application."**

Remand or adjournment of case

1.03.10   The magistrates determine the next date of hearing (if appropriate):

> **"This case will be remanded/adjourned to** (*date and time*). (*In criminal proceedings*)**: The remand will be on bail/in custody."**

Fixing the date of the next hearing

1.03.11   When fixing the date of the next (or any subsequent) hearing, the advocates should:

(a) Give a realistic time estimate.

(b) Give advance notification to the court office and/or other parties of difficult fixtures.

(c) Apply for a special day (or days) in a case likely to last more than half a day.

4. MODE OF TRIAL

Introduction

Mode of trial proceedings are conducted in either way offences only.   **1.04.01**

Classification of offences	**Court of trial**	**1.04.02**
Summary offences	Magistrates' court	
Indictable offences	Crown Court	
Either way offences	Either magistrates'	
(Schedule 1, M.C.A. 1980)	court or Crown Court	

As a general rule, a defendant appearing before the magistrates' court   **1.04.03**
on summons is likely to be in relation to a summary offence only and
the defendant will not be able to elect Crown Court trial, although
practice varies and, in some areas, either way offences are often
summonsed (usually where the voluntary attendance of the defendant
at court is not in doubt).

Mode of trial will usually be determined at a non-effective hearing,   **1.04.04**
see **1.03.07(e)-(f)**.

The decision will determine whether, at the effective hearing, the
magistrates' court hears the evidence in a summary trial, see **1.06**, or in
committal proceedings, see **1.05**.

Factors to be taken into consideration

When deciding which court is the appropriate court in which the   **1.04.05**
case should be heard, the magistrates' court shall have regard to:

(a) The nature of the case.

(b) Whether the circumstances make the offence one of serious
    character.

(c) Whether the punishment which a magistrates' court would have
    power to inflict would be adequate having regard to the serious-
    ness of the case or, in the case of a sexual or violent offender,
    whether the term of imprisonment that the magistrates' court can
    impose would be adequate to protect the public from serious
    harm from him.

(d) Any other circumstances which make the case more suitable for
    one method of trial rather than the other (for example, the
    complexity of the case).

Practice

1.04.06   The charge or summons is read to the defendant by the clerk:

> **"(***Name***), you appear before the magistrates today charged that** (*the clerk will then read from the charge sheet or summons*)**."**

1.04.07   Mode of trial proceedings are not usually conducted unless the defence has had the opportunity of considering a summary of the evidence (advance disclosure) against the defendant, see **1.03.07(c)**.

Mode of trial may be considered at the defendant's first appearance (where, for example, the defendant intends to consent to summary trial, plead guilty and "get it over with"). In this case, after the charge or summons has been read to the defendant, the clerk may say:

> **"Has the defendant been informed of his right to advance disclosure?"**

The defence may say:

> **"He does not require advance disclosure."**

Representations as to mode of trial

1.04.08   The clerk may say (to either party):

> **"Are there any representations as to mode of trial?"**

Prosecution representations

1.04.09   **"The prosecution ask for summary trial/trial on indictment for the following reasons** (*state reasons, see* **1.04.05**)**."**

1.04.10   The prosecution should outline the facts of the case and draw the court's attention to the factors to be taken into consideration, for example:

> **"The application is for:**
> **(a) Trial on indictment. This is a serious assault involving the use of a weapon. The injuries required** (*state nature of medical treatment, for example 3 stitches*)**.**
> **(b) Trial on indictment. The value of the property stolen is** (*state value*)**.**
> **(c) Summary trial. Although the charge alleges theft of a substantial amount of** (*state value and/or nature of goods*)**, full compensation has been made voluntarily by the defendant."**

Where there is unlikely to be any real dispute, the prosecution need **1.04.11** not give reasons, for example:

> **"This is a charge of theft** (*state nature of goods and value*) **by shoplifting. The application is for summary trial."**

Defence representations

Where there is argument over mode of trial, the defence will address **1.04.12** the court as follows:

> **"The defence would say that summary trial/trial on indictment is more appropriate for the following reasons** (*state reasons*)**."**

The defence may then outline the reasons for the application and draw the court's attention to the factors to be taken into consideration, see **1.04.05**.

The defence will usually only address the court where the prosecu- **1.04.13** tion are asking for trial on indictment and the defence are asking the magistrates to accept jurisdiction, for example, see **1.04.10(a)** and **(b)**:

> **"The defence application is for:**
> **(a) Summary trial. Although the assault involved the use of a weapon, the injury inflicted was not serious** (*give details*)**.**
> **(b) Summary trial. The defence do not agree with the value placed by the prosecution on the property stolen. The defence submit that the value is** (*state value*)**."**

Where there is no argument over mode of trial and the defence **1.04.14** support the prosecution's application, the defence may simply say:

> **"No representations."**

The defendant's right to trial on indictment

The determination of mode of trial does not in any way affect the **1.04.15** defendant's right to elect trial on indictment, see **1.04.17**, although the defendant may be liable to pay the additional costs of the Crown Court trial/plea.

Determination of mode of trial

The court determines mode of trial. The clerk will usually say (to the **1.04.16** magistrates):

> **"Do you accept jurisdiction?"**

The court may retire to consider its decision. The court then announces its decision:

"We accept jurisdiction/We find that this case is suitable for summary trial."

or

"We decline jurisdiction."

Omit **1.04.17** and follow the practice in committal proceedings.

1.04.17 The clerk will then say to defendant (the exact form of words varies from court to court):

"The magistrates have accepted jurisdiction/determined that this case is more suitable for summary trial. If you consent, you may be tried by the magistrates, or you may, if you wish, be tried by a judge and jury at the Crown Court.
However, I must warn you that if you are tried at this court and are found guilty or plead guilty, you may be committed to the Crown Court for sentence if the magistrates, after hearing the facts of the case, are of the opinion that a longer custodial sentence than this court has the power to impose . . ."

either:

" . . . should be imposed on you having regard to the seriousness of the offence . . . "

and/or (in the case of a sexual or violent offence):

" . . . is necessary to protect the public from serious harm from you.
Do you understand that? Where do you wish to be tried?"

1.04.18 In practice, committal after "having regard to the seriousness of the offence" is unlikely but may still take place.

1.04.19 It sometimes happens that a defendant does not understand the clerk's speech which is often recited at high speed. The advocate should explain the effect of this speech to the defendant before the hearing.

Election

1.04.20 The defendant may say (or, **1.04.21**):

"This court."

The clerk will usually then say:

"Do you plead guilty or not guilty?"

If the defendant pleads guilty, see **Chapter 7** Sentencing. If the defendant pleads not guilty, see **1.06** Summary trial.

The defendant may say: **1.04.21**

"The Crown Court."

See **1.05** Committal proceedings.

Change of election

The magistrates' court will usually permit a defendant to change his   **1.04.22**
election from trial on indictment to summary trial (if the magistrates
have accepted jurisdiction).

The magistrates' court will usually only permit a defendant to change   **1.04.23**
his election from summary trial to trial on indictment after consideration of the following:

(a) Whether the defendant obtained or was able to obtain legal
    advice before making his election.
(b) The length of time before the application to change his election.
(c) The age of the defendant.
(d) The mental ability of the defendant.

The defence may say: **1.04.24**

**"I apply for the defendant to be permitted to change his election,
for the following reasons (*state reasons, if* 1.04.23 *applies*)."**

If the court grants the application, the defence may say: **1.04.25**

"Could the election be put again?"

The clerk will repeat **1.04.17**.   **1.04.26**

5. COMMITTAL PROCEEDINGS

Introduction

The function of committal proceedings is for the magistrates' court to   **1.05.01**
determine whether the prosecution are able to present sufficient evidence (a prima facie case) for the court to commit the defendant for trial
to the Crown Court.

If, after consideration of the evidence and any submissions, the court is of the opinion that there is sufficient evidence to commit the defendant for trial to the Crown Court, the court shall commit him for trial. If the court is not of that opinion, it shall discharge the defendant.

Committal proceedings may be conducted by a single examining magistrate.

Forms of committal proceedings

1.05.02 Committal proceedings may take three different forms. These are usually called:
- Old style committal
- "Read" committal
- Section 6(2) (MCA 1980) committal

Old style committal

1.05.03 An old style committal is usually held where the defence is of the opinion that, after cross-examination, the evidence of the prosecution witnesses will disclose no satisfactory case to answer.

An old style committal (usually a "read" committal) must be held if the defendant is unrepresented.

1.05.04 Sometimes, where the only evidence against a defendant is given by a witness whom either party (usually the defence) believe may not attend court, either party may ask for an old style committal to see if that witness attends.

If the witness attends court, the defence may agree to a section 6(2) committal, see **1.05.17–20**. If the witness does not attend court, the defence may ask for the defendant to be discharged, see **1.05.13–15**.

"Read" committal

1.05.05 A "read" committal will usually be held where the defence is of the opinion that the statements served on him disclose no satisfactory case to answer and it would not be in the defendant's interest to test that evidence in cross-examination.

A "read" committal is technically an old style committal. The practice is the same as an old style committal except that the prosecution reads and/or summarises the statements of the witnesses and produces the relevant documentary exhibits.

Section 6(2) committal

A section 6(2) committal is held where the defence is of the opinion   **1.05.06**
that the statements served on him disclose a case to answer.

Avoiding committal proceedings

Transfer to the Crown Court

In some serious fraud cases and some (usually sexual) cases involving   **1.05.07**
children, committal proceedings may be by-passed by the prosecution
giving notice of transfer of the case to the Crown Court. In such a case
the defence will be able to make any submissions that could have been
made on committal at a preparatory hearing in the Crown Court (except
for the dismissal of the transferred charges), see **5.02.11–12**.

Voluntary bill of indictment

The prosecution may apply to a high court judge for a voluntary bill   **1.05.08**
of indictment, usually where one defendant has been committed to the
Crown Court after committal proceedings and the prosecution wish to
join another defendant before trial. The procedure has become overworked in recent years and should be used with discretion.

Practice

Attendance of the defendant

See **1.02.02**, although committal proceedings may take place in the   **1.05.09**
absence of a defendant where (a) he is disorderly in court or (b) he is ill
and represented by an advocate and has consented to the evidence
being given in his absence.

Identification of the defendant

The defendant is identified. The clerk may say: **1.05.10**

> **"Are you** (*name*)**? What is your date of birth? What is your
> address?"**

The charge

1.05.11   The clerk may then read the charge or summons to the defendant (and/or at **1.05.30**):

> "(*Name*), **you appear before the magistrates today charged that** (*the clerk will read from the charge sheet or summons*)."

Mode of trial

1.05.12   Mode of trial (usually in section 6(2) committals only), may be determined if this has not been determined at a previous hearing, see **1.03.07(e)-(f)** and **1.04** Mode of trial.

    The court is only likely to have set time aside to hear an old style committal where mode of trial has previously been determined or where prior arrangement has been made between all parties and the court.

Discharge of defendant before committal

1.05.13   If, after reviewing the evidence before the hearing, the prosecution are of the opinion that the statements in their possession do not disclose a case to answer, the prosecution may apply for an adjournment in order to obtain better evidence. If the application is refused the prosecution may say:

> **"The prosecution is unable to proceed."**

The defence may then say:

> **"Could the defendant be discharged?"**

The defence may apply for costs, see **20.02.22(c)**.

1.05.14   If the defendant is discharged, he may be re-charged if better evidence later becomes available and further committal proceedings held (or the prosecution may prefer a voluntary bill of indictment).

1.05.15   In a case where the court has indicated that it would consider this course to be unjust and, where it has indicated in mode of trial proceedings that it would accept jurisdiction, see **1.04.16**, the defence may consider inviting the court to allow the defendant to change his election, see **1.04.22–26**.

    The defendant may then consent to summary trial and plead not guilty. The court may then dismiss the charge(s) for want of prosecution and the defendant cannot be re-charged.

The defence should beware because the court will sometimes agree to the prosecution's application for a remand after a change of election.

Reporting restrictions

The clerk will usually ask the defence: **1.05.16**

"Do you want reporting restrictions lifted?"

The defence replies: **Yes** or **No** (usually **No**).

If the defence want reporting restrictions lifted, the court sometimes requires a reason to be given by the defence.

If there is more than one defendant and one of them objects to the lifting of reporting restrictions, the court will hear argument as to whether it is in the interests of justice to do so before lifting reporting restrictions.

If in doubt, the court will usually rule against the lifting of reporting restrictions.

● OMIT **1.05.17–20** in an old style committal or a "read" committal.

Section 6(2) procedure

The clerk asks the defence: **1.05.17**

"Do you consent to a section 6(2) committal?"

The defence will answer: **Yes**.

The clerk will then ask the prosecution if they are prepared for   **1.05.18**
committal. The prosecution may reply:

"I tender the original statements and documentary exhibits to the court together with typed copies (*one typed copy is usually sufficient*)**. The statements** (*usually 2 typed copies*) **were served on the defence on** (*date*)**."**

The court will then determine the witness orders, see **1.05.26**. The   **1.05.19**
clerk will say to the defence:

"Could you tell me what witness orders you require?"

The clerk will then read out the names of the witnesses and (depending on the practice of the court) state how many pages comprise that witness's statement and whether he produces any exhibits, for example:

"Statement of (name) consisting of (–) pages. He produces (–) exhibit(s). Witness order?"

The defence will say: **Full/Conditional (order)**, see **1.05.26**.

1.05.20   After determination of witness orders, the clerk may say:

"Does the defendant object to any statement, wish to call evidence or make any submissions?"

The defence will usually answer: **No**

"In which case, you will shortly be committed by the magistrates to the crown court for trial."

- OMIT **1.05.21–33** in a section 6(2) committal.

The case for the prosecution

Prosecution opening

1.05.21   In an old style or "read" committal the prosecution may open the case. The prosecution opening should contain:

    (a) A brief outline of the evidence to be called, and/or read or summarised.
    (b) A brief description of the issues between the parties.
    (c) A brief summary of any relevant law.

Prosecution evidence

1.05.22   The prosecution may:

    (a) Call the witnesses to give evidence (in an old style committal only).
    (b) Read or summarise the statements of the witnesses (in a "read" committal only).
    (c) Combine (a) and (b) usually by agreement with the defence.

1.05.23   Where witnesses are called, they are usually examined and cross-examined only on the issues on which either the prosecution rely (to establish an essential ingredient of the offence) or on which the defence are seeking to make a submission of no case to answer.

1.05.24   The evidence of the witnesses is written down or typed (on a typewriter or word processor) by the clerk or an assistant. The written document is called a deposition.

After each witness has given evidence, the deposition is read to the witness. The witness is then required to sign each page of the deposition and initial any corrections.

The parties should ensure that they ask simple, straightforward **1.05.25** questions, the answers to which can easily be recorded. Complicated questions lead to answers that cannot easily be recorded and which are often incomprehensible when read out of context.

Witness orders

After each witness has signed his deposition, the defence will be **1.05.26** required to state what witness order they require if the defendant is committed for trial.

Full witness order (fully bound witness): Where the witness' evidence is disputed and the witness is required to attend the trial of the defendant at the Crown Court for cross-examination.

Conditional witness order (conditionally bound witness): Where the witness' evidence is not disputed and the witness is not required to attend the trial of the defendant at the Crown Court.

Submission of no case to answer

At the conclusion of the prosecution's case, the defence may submit **1.05.27** that there is insufficient evidence on which the defendant can be committed for trial. The following is a brief guide:

In practice, the order of submissions is as follows: **1.05.28**

(a) The defence may begin:

> **"I submit that there is no case to answer:**
> **(i) on the ground that the prosecution has failed to establish** (*an essential ingredient of the offence*).
> *and/or*
> **(ii) on the ground that the evidence is so weak that no jury properly directed could convict on it."**

(b) The defence should identify the evidence to which he refers and direct the court to any relevant law.

(c) Reply by the prosecution on mixed law and fact but not on the quality of the evidence.

(d) Response by the defence dealing with any new points raised by the prosecution or the court but not repeating the submissions in (b).

(e) The magistrates may retire to consider their decision.

Decision

1.05.29   The magistrates announce their decision.

> **"We find that there is a case to answer."**

or

> **"We find that there is no case to answer. (*Name of defendant*), you are discharged."**

If the defendant is discharged, the defence may make an application for a defendant's costs order, see **20.02.22(c)**, for example:

> **"Would you make a defendant's costs order."**

Reading the charge

1.05.30   The charge (or summons) is read to the defendant by the clerk (although this may be omitted if the defendant is represented and the charge has already been read to the defendant, see **1.05.11**).

A new charge may be preferred where the evidence called discloses another or an alternative charge.

Caution

1.05.31   In some courts, the clerk may ask the defendant (although there is some doubt as to whether this is the correct procedure):

> **"Is there anything you wish to say in answer to the charge? (*Followed by, very rarely nowadays*: You do not have to say anything unless you wish to do so, but what you say may be given in evidence)."**

The defence will usually answer: **No**.

The case for the defence

1.05.32   In practice, the defence do not call the defendant in committal proceedings and, only rarely, call evidence in support of the case.

The decision to call evidence should only be made after very careful consideration because the defendant's evidence (or the evidence of witnesses) will be recorded in a deposition which may be used for the purposes of cross-examination if the defendant is committed for trial and it will involve disclosing the defendant's defence to the prosecution.

An example of when evidence may be called: There is a technical defence and the defence is able to call an expert who will conclusively refute the prosecution's evidence.

The order of the defence case is as follows: **1.05.33**

(a) Defence opening (but see (c) below).
(b) Defence evidence recorded in deposition form:
    (i) Defendant (if called)
    (ii) Defence witnesses.
(c) Prosecution closing (if defence opened).
(d) Defence submission, see **1.05.27–28**.
(e) Decision, see **1.05.29**.
(f) Witness orders determined (if not determined at **1.05.26**).

Committal to the Crown Court

The examining magistrate(s) will then say (to the defendant):   **1.05.34**

> **"On the charge(s) that has been read out to you** (*or on any other offence disclosed by the evidence*) **you will be committed to stand your trial before the** (*name*) **Crown Court at a date and time to be notified to you."**

There may be argument in some (serious) cases as to which Crown Court the defendant should be committed.

Alibi warning

The examining magistrate or the clerk to the court will then ask the   **1.05.35**
defence (or sometimes the prosecution):

> **"Is the alibi warning appropriate?"**

Either party (usually the defence) may say:

> **"No** *or* **Could the alibi warning be given."**

The alibi warning should be given in any circumstance where either party believes that alibi evidence may be given at the Crown Court.

1.05.36   The examining magistrate or clerk may say:

> **"At your trial you may not be permitted to give evidence of an alibi unless you have given particulars of that alibi to the solicitor for the prosecution now or within seven days. Do you wish to give notice of that alibi today?"**

It is unusual for the defence to give particulars of an alibi at committal proceedings.

Section 41 (CJA 1988) committal of summary offences

1.05.37   Where the defendant is committed for trial for an offence triable either way, the magistrates may also commit him for trial (in effect, for plea only) for any connected summary offences (provided they are punishable with imprisonment or disqualification). The clerk may say (to the magistrates):

> **"Will you also commit him on the charges of** (*state charges*)**?"**

Bail

1.05.38   A defendant who is committed for trial must be remanded to the Crown Court (either on bail or in custody), see **Chapter 4**, Bail. This includes defendants who appear on summons, see **1.04.03**.

Some, but not all, magistrates' courts, consider that committal is a change of circumstance, see **4.03.01**, for the purposes of a bail application.

Legal aid

1.05.39   The defence should apply for legal aid to be extended to the Crown Court if no "through order" has been made:

> **"Could legal aid be extended to the Crown Court? There has been no change in (financial) circumstances."**

6. SUMMARY TRIAL

Introduction

1.06.01   A summary trial is a trial in the magistrates' court of a charge or summons against the defendant.

The court has jurisdiction to conduct a summary trial of either-way offences only where the defendant consents to be tried before the magistrates' court, see **1.04.20**.

Attendance of the defendant

If the defendant has been charged and bailed in criminal proceedings **1.06.02** he must attend court. The defendant cannot be tried in his absence.

He may be tried in his absence where he has been summonsed, see **1.02.09**.

- OMIT **1.06.03–04** unless the defendant pleads guilty by letter.

Guilty plea by letter

A defendant may plead guilty by letter where: **1.06.03**

(a) The offence is summary only, and for which the maximum sentence is not more than 3 months' imprisonment.
(b) The summons was accompanied by:
  (i) A notice explaining the guilty plea procedure.
  (ii) A statement of the facts of the offence.

The practice on the hearing of a guilty plea by letter is usually: **1.06.04**

(a) The clerk informs the court that the defendant pleads guilty by letter (and, in road traffic proceedings, sends the court his driving licence).
(b) The clerk or the prosecution reads the statement of facts.
(c) The clerk (hands the court the defendant's driving licence and) reads the letter in mitigation (if any) sent by the defendant.
(d) Sentence (usually a "tariff" fine, see **7.04.06**).

If the court is considering disqualification and/or imprisonment, the **1.06.05** defendant must attend (although some courts do, in fact wrongly, disqualify in the absence of the defendant where he is represented).

Practice

Identification of the defendant

The clerk will identify the defendant: **1.06.06**

"**Are you** (*name*)**? What is your date of birth? What is your address?**"

Introduction of the parties

1.06.07   The clerk usually introduces the parties to the court.

"(*Name*) **appears on behalf of the prosecution.** (*Name*) **appears on behalf of the defendant.**"

Reading the charge/summons

1.06.08   The clerk will then read the charge or summons to the defendant:

"(*Name*)**, you appear before the magistrates today charged that** (*the clerk will read from the charge sheet or summons*)**.**"

● OMIT **1.06.09–10** where there are no preliminary applications.

1.06.09   Mode of trial (in either-way offences only) will then be determined if this was not done at an earlier hearing.
It is unlikely that the court will have set aside time for a summary trial if mode of trial was not determined at an earlier hearing, see **1.03.07(d)**.

Preliminary applications, *see also* **5.04.07–10.**

1.06.10   Preliminary applications (by either party) may be made before the charge or summons is put to the defendant. The most common preliminary applications are:

(a) Application for an adjournment.
(b) Application to withdraw or discontinue if no plea has been taken (otherwise, see **1.06.13**).
(c) Amendment of the charge or summons.
(d) Application to dismiss where charge or summons is:
   (i) bad for duplicity.
   (ii) defective/not known to law.
   (iii) oppressive.
(e) Applications relating to the conduct of the trial.
(f) Separate trials:
   (i) where the defendant is charged with two or more different offences;
   (ii) where two or more defendants are charged with different offences arising out of the same facts;

(iii) where a juvenile is jointly charged with an adult.

(g) Reporting restrictions, where a juvenile is involved in the proceedings, whether as a defendant or as a witness.

Pleas

If the trial date has been fixed on the basis of an indication of a not **1.06.11** guilty plea and the defendant has not entered a plea to the charge or summons at an earlier non-effective hearing, the clerk may say:

> **"Can the charge(s)/summons be put to the defendant?** *or* **Can pleas be taken?"**

The clerk will then ask the defendant: **1.06.12**

> **"Do you plead guilty or not guilty?"**

If the defendant pleads guilty, see **Chapter 7**, Sentencing.

If the defendant pleads not guilty: **1.06.13**

(a) The court will hear the evidence in a summary trial, or

(b) The prosecution may offer no evidence, see also **5.04.14**. The case against the defendant is then dismissed. The defence may apply for costs, see **1.06.52**.

Conduct of the trial

The order of presentation, examination and cross-examination of **1.06.14** witnesses and speeches follows the title order of the case in the court list.

The usual order of speeches is: The prosecution have one speech only before calling the evidence. The defence have one speech only after the conclusion of all the evidence.

The case for the prosecution

Prosecution opening speech

In the magistrates' court the prosecution usually opens the case **1.06.15** although does not have to do so. If the prosecution decides to open the case, the opening should contain:

(a) A brief outline of the facts.

(b) A brief summary of any relevant law (especially if a technical defence is anticipated).

The prosecution may conclude the opening:

"I now call (*name of first witness*).**"**

Witnesses

1.06.16   The witness is called and identified by the prosecution as follows:

"Are you (*name*)**? What is your address?** (*If relevant*) **What is your occupation?"**

The usual rules as to the examination, cross-examination and re-examination of witnesses apply, see **Chapter 21**, Examination of witnesses.

1.06.17   A witness may be released after having given evidence, see generally **21.01.19–20**. Civilian witnesses, in particular, should be warned not to discuss the evidence with witnesses yet to be called.

Admissibility of evidence

1.06.18   Questions of admissibility are determined by the magistrates and, in the event of evidence being excluded, the magistrates should not consider that evidence when reaching their decision.

The clerk never determines questions of admissibility in the absence of the magistrates.

1.06.19   A witness may be giving, or about to give, evidence to which a party objects. The party may interrupt the witness, as follows:

"I object to this evidence."

1.06.20   If the evidence is clearly inadmissible (for example, hearsay), the clerk may direct the party examining the witness to omit that evidence.

In any other situation and/or where there is likely to be an argument over the admissibility of the evidence, the court will hear the evidence and rule on its admissibility.

1.06.21   The order of submissions is usually as follows:

(a) Either party (usually the defence) identifies the evidence to which an objection is taken.

(b) The party gives reasons for the objection and refers to any relevant law.

(c) Reply by the other party (usually the prosecution).

(d) Response by the party objecting dealing with any new points raised by the other party or the court but not repeating the submissions in (b).

(e) Decision by the court.

Although a magistrates' court is entitled to determine the admissibility of evidence in a "trial within a trial" (*voire dire*), see **5.04.42–43**, this is very rarely done. **1.06.22**

This situation is entirely unsatisfactory and is, in practice, often by-passed. In this case, the defence may refer to the disputed evidence in his closing speech, for example: **1.06.23**

> **"The defendant is then alleged to have said** (*quote the disputed evidence*)**. He admits/denies making that statement which, in any event, I would submit is inadmissible for the following reasons** (*state reasons*) **and I would invite you to exclude it from your consideration of the case."**

This approach has the following advantages:

(a) The disputed evidence is not highlighted.
(b) The prosecution often do not exercise the right to address the court in closing on points of law, see **1.06.45**.

Evidence of witnesses not attending court

Where the evidence of a witness is not disputed by the defence, the statement of that witness may be read to the court if a copy of the statement: **1.06.24**

(a) has been served on the defence at least 7 days before the hearing, and
(b) the defence, within 7 days of service, has not served (either orally or in writing) notice objecting to its being tendered in evidence.

If an arguable objection is raised by the defence at the hearing, an adjournment may be granted with a note as to costs.

Where the evidence of the witness is to be read, it is usually introduced by the prosecution as follows: **1.06.25**

> **"The next witness is** (*name*) **in the form of a section 9 statement, the original** (*and copies for the magistrates*) **of which I will hand to the clerk.**
> **The statement was served on the defence on** (*date*)**.**
> **This is the statement of** (*name*) **(who is a** (*occupation, if relevant*)**) of** (*address*)**. The statement is dated** (*date*)**. He states . . ."**

The prosecution will then read the statement. The clerk and the magistrates will be familiar with the declaration (that "the statement is true") which is usually omitted.

Evidence under the CJA 1988

1.06.26   For evidence under the CJA 1988, see **5.04.49–51**, although this is rare in the magistrates' court.

Admissions

1.06.27   A formal admission of facts is rare in the magistrates' court. An admission may be made by either party. It must be made in writing, if possible, on a standard section 10 (CJA 1967) form which may be available from the clerk. If no form is available, the admission may be written on a piece of paper and signed by the party making the admission. The admission is then read to the court, as follows:

> **"The following fact(s) are admitted by** (*name of party making the admission*)**, that** (*read admission*)**."**

The signed admission (and copies for the magistrates) are handed to the clerk.

Other formal evidence

1.06.28   For schedules, maps, plans, photographs, see **5.04.54**.

Close of prosecution case

1.06.29   When the prosecution has called and/or read all the evidence and any admissions have been made, the case is said to be closed. The usual form of words is:

> **"That is the case for the prosecution** *or, more simply*, **That is the case."**

Submission of no case to answer

1.06.30   The law on this subject is complex. The following is a brief guide:

1.06.31   In practice, the order of submissions is as follows:

(a) The defence may begin:

"I submit that there is no case to answer on (*specify the charge or summons*)**:**

(i) on the ground that the prosecution has failed to establish (*an essential ingredient of the offence*)**.**
and/or

(ii) on the ground that the evidence is so weak that the court could not properly convict on it."

The defence must make it clear to the court that a submission of no case to answer is being made in order that it is not confused with a final speech.

(b) The defence should identify the evidence to which he refers and direct the court to any relevant law.

(c) Reply by the prosecution on mixed law and fact but not on the quality of the evidence.

(d) Response by the defence dealing with any new points raised by the prosecution or the court but not repeating the submissions in (b).

(e) The magistrates may retire to consider their decision.

(f) The magistrates announce their decision.

If a submission of no case to answer is upheld the defendant is discharged. The defence may apply for costs, see **1.06.52**. **1.06.32**

The case for the defence

Conduct of the defence **1.06.33**

The order of presentation of the case for each defendant and examination and cross-examination of a defendant or defence witness follows the title order of the case in the court list. The prosecution always cross-examines last.

If the defence is calling witnesses, the witnesses are called after the defendant has given evidence (if the defendant gives evidence), and before the case of the next defendant, in title order of the case in the court list. **1.06.34**

Defence opening

The defence have the right to open the case. In practice, this right is never exercised because the defence would lose the right, without the leave of the court, to close the case. **1.06.35**

The defence would not lose the right to close the case if (on a technical defence) the defence were to open:

"I will be calling the defendant (and/or (*name of any witness(es)*)**) to deal with the following point** (*state point*) **and in due course will refer you to** (*state the relevant Act or authorities*)**."**

This approach enables the clerk to identify the relevant law in advance and to advise the magistrates accordingly.

Evidence of the defendant

1.06.36   The usual rules as to examination, cross-examination and re-examination apply except the defendant must not be cross-examined as to credit namely, whether he is likely, by reason of his bad character, to be untruthful (except see **1.06.37**).

Evidence of character

1.06.37   The law on this subject is complex. The following is a brief guide (and see, **5.04.69–72**).

If the defendant is of bad character and the defence make imputations (in cross-examination) on the character of a prosecution witness, the prosecution may cross-examine the defendant on his bad character with the leave of the court.

Note: The prosecution should give careful consideration to making an application for leave because, if it is refused, the defence may apply for a fresh trial before a differently constituted court.

1.06.38   The only time when the clerk may ask the magistrates to retire and address the parties in court in the absence of the magistrates is to warn an unrepresented defendant that he may be in danger of being cross-examined on his bad character. The clerk will never determine, in the absence of the magistrates, whether the defendant should be cross-examined on his bad character.

Defence evidence

1.06.39   The evidence on behalf of the defence is presented in the same way and subject to the same rules as the evidence on behalf of the prosecution, see **1.06.16–28**.

Alibi

1.06.40   An alibi notice is not required in the magistrates' court, although the court may grant the prosecution an adjournment if the prosecution is genuinely taken by surprise by alibi evidence.

Alibi witnesses are called in the usual way after the defendant has given evidence.

Close of defence case

The usual form of words is: **1.06.41**

"That is the case for the defence."

Evidence in rebuttal

In practice, it is rare for the prosecution to call evidence in rebuttal   **1.06.42**
except in road traffic proceedings, see **1.07.16**. The prosecution must
apply for leave, giving reasons why the evidence was not called as part
of the prosecution case, see **5.04.78**.

Speeches

Defence closing speech

The defence may make a closing speech even if the defendant has not   **1.06.43**
given evidence. The defence closing speech should contain:

(a) A summary of the evidence which will enable the court to find the
    defendant not guilty.
(b) A summary of the relevant law, where the law may be in dispute.

The defence closing speech should not contain: **1.06.44**

(a) A recital of all the evidence.
(b) A repetition of the submission of no case to answer if no defence
    evidence was called.
(c) A detailed explanation of the burden and standard of proof. To do
    this would insult the experience and intelligence of the
    magistrates.

The prosecution may reply only on disputed points of law raised by   **1.06.45**
the defence in his speech.

The defence may respond, with the leave of the court, on any point of   **1.06.46**
law raised, for the first time, by the prosecution or the court but should
not repeat his submissions in **1.06.43(b)**.

Verdict/decision

The magistrates may retire to consider their verdict.   **1.06.48**

1.06.49   When announcing the verdict, the court may say:

> **"We find you guilty/We find the case proved."**

or

> **"We find you not guilty/We find the case not proved."**

(A verdict of guilty to a lesser offence is not available in the magistrates' court).

1.06.50   If the verdict is guilty, see **Chapter 7**, Sentencing.

1.06.51   If the verdict is not guilty, the defendant is discharged. The defence may apply for costs.

Costs

1.06.52   The defence may make an application for a defendant's costs order, see **20.02.22(b)**, for example:

> **"Would you make a defendant's costs order?"**

The effect of the order is that costs reasonably incurred by the defendant are paid out of central funds.

If the defendant is not legally aided, his costs will be his reasonable legal costs, otherwise costs are usually only "out of pocket" (for example, travel) expenses. There is no power to reimburse the defendant for loss of income during the proceedings.

Appeal

1.06.53   Appeal against conviction and/or sentence is to the Crown Court. The notice of appeal must be served on the clerk to the magistrates' court and the prosecution within 21 days.

The hearing of the appeal at the Crown Court is a re-hearing of the case before the magistrates' court.

See **5.06** Appeal against conviction, **5.07** Appeal against sentence, and also **13.04** Appeal by case stated.

7. ROAD TRAFFIC

Introduction

1.07.01   Road traffic offences are usually heard on summons although, sometimes, on charge.

Almost all road traffic offences are summary only and the court will not usually conduct mode of trial or committal proceedings.

If the defendant pleads not guilty, the practice in **1.06** summary trial should be followed.   **1.07.02**

If the defendant pleads guilty or is found guilty, the following common situations are considered: **1.07.03**

1.07.04–22   Special reasons not to endorse
1.07.17–20   Special reasons not to disqualify (for example: "laced drinks")
1.07.23–28   Penalty points disqualification ("totting")
1.07.29–30   Mitigation and sentence.

If, after disqualification, the defence is considering an appeal against conviction and/or sentence, the following situation is considered:
1.07.31–37   Suspension of disqualification

ENDORSEMENT: SPECIAL REASONS NOT TO ENDORSE/DISQUALIFY

Introduction

Road traffic offences are either endorsable or non-endorsable and some carry a mandatory or discretionary disqualification. If endorsable, a road traffic offence may carry a fixed or a variable number of penalty points within a certain range. The details of the offence and the number of penalty points will be endorsed on the defendant's driving licence and notified to the DVLC.   **1.07.04**

Special reasons

If an offence is endorsable or carries a mandatory disqualification, the court must order endorsement or disqualification unless it decides *after hearing evidence* that there are special reasons for (in the case of an endorsable offence) not endorsing or, (in the case of a disqualifiable offence) ordering endorsement but not disqualification.   **1.07.05**

As a general rule, endorsements remain on the driving licence for a period of 4 years, although, for the purposes of what is usually called "totting" (disqualification by reason of exceeding the maximum   **1.07.06** number of 12 points), the endorsement will cease to have effect after 3 years.

What is a special reason?

1.07.07   To be a special reason, the reason must:

(a) Be a mitigating circumstance.
(b) Not amount to a defence to the charge.
(c) Be special in relation to the offence and not the offender.
(d) Be a matter which the court ought properly to consider in sentencing.

Practice

1.07.08 The defendant:

(a) Pleads guilty (either before the court or by post).
(b) Is found guilty on proof of the summons (and service) in his absence.
(c) Is found guilty after a summary trial.

1.08.09   The defendant produces his driving licence, which may be handed to the court by the defence at the beginning of mitigation, for example:

"I produce the defendant's driving licence."

In a simple case not involving special reasons or "totting", mitigation may follow, see **1.07.29**.

1.07.10   The defence may put the clerk on notice that any endorsements on the defendant's licence should not be disclosed at this stage, for example:

"I will be arguing special reasons."

Although the clerk may say:

"The defendant produces a full/provisional clean driving licence."

Defence opening on special reasons

1.07.11   The defence may address the court in opening:

(a) Why it is argued that there are special reasons not to endorse for the offence.

(b) Refer the court to any relevant law.

(c) Outline the evidence to be called.

Evidence

The defence must call evidence of special reasons not to **1.07.12** endorse/disqualify.

The defence will usually call the defendant and may also call expert evidence (usually, in drinking and driving offences where the defence are arguing that there are special reasons not to disqualify, see **1.07.17–20**).

The usual rules as to the examination, cross-examination and re-examination of witnesses apply, see **Chapter 21**, Examination of witnesses.

Expert evidence

If the defence intend to call expert evidence, the defence should **1.07.13** notify the prosecution of its intention to do so a reasonable time before the hearing.

It is recommended that the defence notifies the prosecution in writing and makes full disclosure of the expert's evidence in the form of a section 9 (CJA 1967) statement.

A failure to give notice will entitle the prosecution to seek an **1.07.14** adjournment (usually with costs) to instruct an expert witness for the purposes of:

(a) Assisting the prosecution in cross-examination of the defence expert.

(b) Calling evidence in rebuttal.

The experts to be called by the defence and the prosecution are **1.07.15** usually permitted to remain in court, in order that they may listen to and assess the evidence of the parties.

Evidence in rebuttal

The prosecution may apply for (and is usually granted) leave to call **1.07.16** evidence in rebuttal where there is a discrepancy between the opinions of the expert witnesses.

Example: Special reasons not to disqualify ("laced drinks")

1.07.17   A common example of a special reason not to disqualify on a charge of driving with excess alcohol is where the defendant contends that he consumed alcohol unknowingly, otherwise known as "laced drinks".

1.07.18   The defence must prove, on the balance of probabilities, that:

(a) The drink was laced.
(b) The defendant did not know or suspect the lacing.
(c) That, if the drink had not been laced, the defendant's alcohol level would have been below the legal limit.

1.07.19   The defence should consult an expert on the issues raised in **1.07.18(c)**.

1.07.20   The defence will usually call the following evidence:

(a) The defendant to prove **1.07.18(b)**. If the defendant was substantially in excess of the legal limit, the court is unlikely to accept his evidence that he did not know or suspect that the drink was laced.
(b) The person or persons who laced the defendant's drink or who knew that the drink had been laced, to prove **1.07.18(a)**.
(c) An expert to prove **1.07.18(c)**.

Defence closing

1.07.21   When the parties have called and/or read all the evidence, the defence may address the court, in particular, on **1.07.11(a)&(b)**.

Decision

1.07.22   The court will announce its decision:

"We find/We do not find special reasons."

If the court finds special reasons the reason must be recorded in the court register.

Penalty points disqualification "totting"

1.07.23   After the clerk has seen the defendant's driving licence, he may say (to the magistrates):

(A) **"The defendant produces a full/provisional clean driving licence."**

(B) Or, if the defendant is not liable to "totting" or he is liable to "totting" but the offence is one which carries a fixed number of penalty points, the clerk may say:

"There are (–) relevant convictions, namely (*state previous convictions and penalty points endorsed on the driving licence*)**."**

(C) Or, if the defendant is liable to "totting" and the offence is one which carries a variable number of penalty points the clerk may say (although practice varies):

"There are (–) relevant convictions. I will invite the court to decide on the number of penalty points before reading out the details of these convictions."

Where (C) applies, the defence should not address the court on the **1.07.24** basis that a minimum number of penalty points should be imposed if the only reason for doing so is to avoid the "totting" provisions.

The defence may address the court on the basis that a minimum number of penalty points should be imposed because the circumstances of the offence are not (comparatively) serious.

Where "totting" applies, the clerk may say: **1.07.25**

"There are (–) points on the defendant's licence for (*state particulars of the offences and penalty points*)**.**
That means that the defendant is liable to disqualification.
(*Name of defence*) **do you wish to address the court on disqualification?"**

Mitigating circumstances and exceptional hardship

In practice, to avoid disqualification by "totting" the defence has to **1.07.26** establish, *by calling evidence*, mitigating circumstances.

A mitigating circumstance is special to the offender and not the offence, contrast **1.07.07(c)**.

A mitigating circumstance is not: **1.07.27**

(a) The triviality of the offence(s).
(b) Hardship to the defendant, other than exceptional hardship.
(c) Any mitigating circumstances which have previously been considered by the court.

In practice, mitigating circumstances are almost always exceptional **1.07.28** hardship. The defence may seek an adjournment to call evidence.

Mitigation

1.07.29   The defence may then address the court generally in mitigation, see **7.04.01–15**.

As a general rule, the court will be concerned only with the defendant's financial circumstances for the purposes of a fine (except in cases of repeated offending).

Decision/sentence

1.07.30   The court announces its decision/sentence:

> **"For this offence there will be a fine of £(–)."**

and where disqualification applies:

> **"We order that you be disqualified for** (*state period*)**."**

and/or where endorsement applies:

> **"And (–) penalty points will be endorsed on your licence."**

or (where special reasons are proved):

> **"We order that no penalty points be endosed on your licence/ We do not order disqualification, having found special reasons for not doing so."**

and where "totting" applies:

> **"We order that you be disqualified for** (*6 months/1 year/2 years*)**."**

or (where exceptional hardship is proved):

> **We order disqualification for** (*a shorter period*)**/We do not order disqualification, for the following reason.**

Note: In each case, the reason must be recorded in the court register for the purposes of, for example, **1.07.27(c)**.

> **"And costs of £(–)."**

Appeal: Suspension of disqualification

1.07.31   If a defendant is disqualified from driving, he may appeal to the Crown Court against either the conviction or the sentence and disqualification.

An application to suspend disqualification pending appeal may be made to the magistrates' court when the notice of appeal has been lodged with the court clerk (although some courts will accept an undertaking by the defence to lodge the notice). **1.07.32**

Practice

The defence may address the court as follows: **1.07.33**

> **"Would you consider an application to suspend disqualification on service of the notice of appeal?"**

It is usually considered to be bad practice (and is often counter-productive) to have a pre-prepared notice of appeal ready to serve on the clerk when the court has announced its decision. **1.07.34**

When the notice of appeal has been prepared, the case is recalled. The defence may say: **1.07.35**

> **"I tender the notice of appeal to the court."**

The defence may then address the court on the reasons to suspend the disqualification, for example: **1.07.36**

> **"I rely on the matters I put before the court in mitigation and (*for example*), if I am to address the Crown Court in due course on the defendant's employment, it is essential that the defendant keeps his licence until the appeal is heard."**

The court announces its decision. **1.07.37**

8. LIQUOR LICENSING

Introduction

An application for a liquor licence (or the transfer or renewal of a liquor licence) is made to the magistrates' court (licensing justices). The application is heard on a fixed date which may be obtained from the court office. **1.08.01**

An application for a protection order is made to an ordinary sitting of the magistrates' court, see **1.09** Application for a protection order.

The law on this subject is complex. The following is a brief guide. **1.08.02**

APPLICATION FOR A LIQUOR LICENCE

Introduction

1.08.03 The correct preparation of the application is essential. If a notice required to be served, see **1.08.04–08**, has not been served in time, the application is unlikely to be heard (or may be dismissed).

Preparation

Notice of application

1.08.04 The application is made on a standard form notice which should be signed by the applicant and state:

(a) The applicant's occupation.
(b) The situation of the premises.
(c) The kind of licence for which the application is made (usually describing the liquor to be supplied).

1.08.05 The notice and a prepaid acknowledgement must be served, at least 21 days before the date of the next hearing, on:

(a) The clerk to the licensing justices.
(b) The police.
(c) The fire authority.
(d) The local authority.

1.08.06 The notice of the application must be displayed on the premises for at least 7 days during the 28 days before the hearing.

1.08.07 The notice of the application must be advertised in a local newspaper between 14–28 days before the hearing.

1.08.08 A map of the area and/or plans of the premises (as appropriate) should be sent to the court. The clerk should be consulted on the requirements of the licensing justices.

Objections

1.08.09 Except in cases of the renewal (but not the transfer) of a liquor licence, when 7 days notice of objection must be given, an objector does not have to give prior warning of his objection(s).

Notice of objection (in cases of renewal) is given to:

(a) The clerk to the licensing justices.
(b) The licensee.

In all other cases, the objector(s) may attend the hearing and make his objection(s) without notice.

Attendance of the applicant

Where an application is made for a new licence or for the transfer of a licence, the applicant should attend.   **1.08.10**

If he fails to attend, the application may be dismissed.

Practice

The title of the application is read out by the clerk, for example: **1.08.11**

> **"An application for a justices'** (*state type of*) **licence in respect of** (*title and address of premises*)**."**

The case for the applicant

Introduction of the parties

The clerk or the advocate representing the applicant may introduce the parties. The advocate may say: **1.08.12**

> **"I appear on behalf of the applicant,** (*name*)**, who is the** (*owner/ manager/other*) **of** (*title and address of premises*)**."**

(If the objector(s) are known and/or represented):

> **"(Name), objects to this application/appears on behalf of** (*name*)**, who objects to this application.**
>   **The applicant attends court today."**

Opening

The advocate may briefly open the application. The opening may contain: **1.08.13**

(a) A description of the area, with reference to the map, see **1.08.16**.
(b) A description of the premises, with reference to the plan, see **1.08.18**.

    (c) A description of the character and background of the applicant.

    (d) Any explanation of the kind of licence for which the application is made.

1.08.14   The advocate will usually then produce the formal evidence on behalf of the applicant, namely:

    (a) Proof of service of the written notices of application.

    (b) Proof of the display of the notice of application.

    (c) Proof of the advertisement of the notice of application.

    (d) Any petitions in support of the application.

1.08.15   The advocate may say:

> **"I understand that the originals of the notices are with the court. Perhaps, your clerk could confirm that they are in order?"**

or

> **"I tender written acknowledgement(s) of the application from** (*the police/fire authority/local authority*) **who do not object to this application."**

> **"I tender the notice displayed on the** (*state part of premises*) **between** (*state dates*)**."**

> **"I tender copies of page** (–) **of** (*name of newspaper*) **for** (*date*)**."**

> **"I tender a petition signed by** (–) (*persons/residents/other*) **in support of the application."**

Maps

1.08.16   An ordnance survey map, on the scale of 25 inches to the mile (1:2,500) is usually produced to the court (with copies for any objectors), showing:

    (a) The location of the proposed premises which should be in (or near) the centre of the map.

    (b) Concentric circles at quarter mile intervals around the location of the proposed premises.

1.08.17   The location of the following are usually shown (with suggested colour code):

    (a) The proposed licensed premises   (Red)

    (b) Public houses   (Black)

    (c) Off-licences   (Green)

(d) Licensed premises with a special hours
    certificate   (Yellow)
(e) Any other licensed premises   (Blue)

Colours may be dictated by directions sent out by the court. If not, the advocate should ensure that the plan has a clear colour code index.

The advocate should draw the court's attention to the local need for the licensed premises by using the map. (The advocate should remember that the licensing justices may have better knowledge of the local area than he has).

Plans

An architect's plan of the premises is usually produced to the court   **1.08.18** (for new or converted premises). The advocate should draw the court's attention to:

(a) Fire precautions and/or alternative exits from the premises.
(b) Hygiene facilities for the preparation of food and/or washing of glasses and plates.
(c) Toilet facilities.
(d) Car parking (if appropriate).

Evidence on behalf of the applicant

The applicant is called and identified by name and address. The   **1.08.19** applicant may be examined on the following matters:

(a) Current occupation and occupation(s) during the preceding 6 months.
(b) Experience in the licensed trade.
(c) Good character (or otherwise).
(d) Proof of display of the notice (if not dealt with at **1.08.14**).
(e) Proof of advertisement of the notice (if not dealt with at **1.08.14**).
(f) Local need for the licensed premises.
(g) If the applicant is not experienced in the licensed trade, he may be tested on his knowledge of licensing law, for example:

"What are the Sunday opening hours? When can you serve children?"

Examination in chief may conveniently be concluded as follows: **1.08.20**

"Finally, have you read the list of persons disqualified from holding a licence? And are you so disqualified?"

The usual rules as to the examination, cross-examination (by objectors) and re-examination of witnesses apply, see **Chapter 21**, Examination of witnesses.

Witnesses on behalf of the applicant

1.08.21   Witnesses on behalf of the applicant may be called, for example:

(a) Witnesses to give evidence of local need (including prospective customers).
(b) The architect or surveyor who prepared the plan (if required).
(c) Character witnesses.

Close of the applicant's case

1.08.22   When the advocate on behalf of the applicant has called and/or read and/or produced all the evidence, the case is said to be closed. The usual form of words is:

"That is the case on behalf of the applicant."

The case for the objector(s)

Opening

1.08.23   The objector and/or the advocate on behalf of the objector may briefly outline his reason(s) for objecting to the application:

(a) That there is no local need (which usually means that the objector may lose business or suffer disruption).
(b) If the police object, usually that the applicant is not a suitable person to hold a licence.
(c) If the fire or local authority object, usually that the premises are unsuitable.

1.08.24   In the case of an objection to a renewal of a licence, the objector should prove service of the written notice of objection, see **1.08.09**. If notice of objection has not been properly served, the court may adjourn the application.

Evidence on behalf of the objector(s)

1.08.25   The objector is called and identified by name and address. The objector then states his objection(s).

The usual rules as to the examination, cross-examination and re-examination of witnesses apply.

The objector may call evidence in support of his objection(s).　　**1.08.26**

Speeches

Order of speeches

The parties may address the court at the conclusion of the evidence, **1.08.27** as follows:

(1) Objector(s), usually in the same order as objections.
(2) Applicant.

The parties should confine their speeches to those parts of the application which are in issue.

Decision

The licensing justices may retire to consider their decision.　　**1.08.28**

When announcing the decision, the court may say:　　**1.08.29**

> **"We grant this application, (subject to conditions)."**

or

> **"We refuse this application."**

The court has no power to award costs to either party. For example, a **1.08.30** successful applicant cannot be granted costs against an objector even though the applicant may have been put to considerable expense.

Appeal

Appeal by either party or other aggrieved party is to the Crown Court. **1.08.31** The notice of appeal must be served on the clerk to the licensing justices and any other party within 21 days.

The hearing of the appeal at the Crown Court is a rehearing of the case before the magistrates' court, see **5.09** Appeal in licensing proceedings.

Only the objector(s) who were heard at the magistrates' court or an aggrieved (interested) party may appeal to the Crown Court.

9. APPLICATION FOR A PROTECTION ORDER

Introduction

1.09.01   A person may want to take over licensed premises before he is able to obtain a transfer of the licence from the licensing justices. He should apply to the magistrates' court for a protection order (to "protect" himself whilst operating the licensed premises) until the date of the next meeting but one of the licensing justices.

Notice of application

1.09.02   The application is made on a standard form notice, which should be signed by the applicant and served, at least 7 days before the date of the hearing, on:

(a) The clerk to the court.
(b) The police.

Objections

1.09.03   An objector does not have to give notice of his objection.

Practice

1.09.04   The application is usually heard in the applications list at the beginning of a normal sitting of the magistrates' court. The title of the application is read out by the clerk, for example:

> **"An application by** (*name*) **for a protection order in respect of** (*title and address of premises*)**."**

Introduction of the parties

1.09.05   The clerk or the advocate representing the applicant may introduce the parties. The advocate may say:

> **"I appear on behalf of the applicant,** (*name*)**, who** (*state reason for application, for example: is taking over the lease*) **of** (*state name of premises*)**."**

"The current licensee attends and consents to this application."

or

"The current licensee has given his consent in writing to this application which, is with/I tender to, the court."

Evidence on behalf of the applicant

The applicant is called and identified by his name and address. The **1.09.06**
applicant is usually examined on the following matters:

(a) Current occupation(s) during the preceding 6 months.
(b) Good character or otherwise.
(c) Experience of the licensed trade.
(d) Knowledge of the licensing law, see **1.08.19(g)** and **1.08.20**.

The (outgoing) licensee usually attends and may be called to give his **1.09.07**
formal consent to the protection order.

The advocate representing the applicant may then say: **1.09.08**

"Unless the court has any questions, I apply for a protection order to be made in favour of (*name*)**."**

The advocate does not make a speech.

The magistrate (or clerk) may then say: **1.09.09**

"Are there any (police) objections?"

An objection to a protection order is rare. It is usually made by the **1.09.10**
police on the grounds that the applicant is not a fit and proper person.
The advocate is advised to check in advance.

If there is no objection, the magistrates may say: **1.09.11**

"The protection order is granted."

The court has no power to order costs to either party. **1.09.12**

CHAPTER 2

Youth Court

1. INTRODUCTION

Children and young persons

2.01.01   The youth court has jurisdiction to hear criminal proceedings in respect of:

(a) Children aged 10–13 (inclusive).
(b) Young persons aged 14–17 (inclusive).

For ease of reference, except where the age of the child or young person is relevant, both categories are referred to as "juveniles".

2.01.02   In practice, criminal proceedings involving juveniles will be heard in the youth court except where:

(a) A juvenile is jointly charged with an adult.
(b) A juvenile/adult is charged with an offence and an adult/juvenile is charged with aiding and abetting that offence.
(c) A juvenile is charged with an offence which arises out of circumstances connected with an adult offender.

2.01.03   If the juvenile is found guilty by the adult court he will usually be remitted to the youth court for sentence.

2.01.04   Unlike the juvenile court, which it replaced, the youth court does not have jurisdiction in care proceedings which are now made in the family proceedings court.

Right of audience

Barrister, solicitor, juvenile in person or by his parent, guardian or social worker (an "appropriate adult"). **2.01.05**

Dress

Barristers and solicitors should be respectably dressed. **2.01.06**
The juvenile and any appropriate adult may appear in normal everyday wear.

Mode of address

The youth court is constituted of not more than 3 justices which should include at least one man and one woman. The justices are addressed as **sir/madam** to the chairman (although **your worships** is sometimes used). **2.01.07**

Conduct

The proceedings in a youth court are held informally, often in an ordinary room. The authors can offer no general guidance on seating in court. **2.01.08**
Any party addressing the court should do so standing (unless invited by the court to remain seated).

The court and/or the parties' representatives are under a duty to explain the proceedings in ordinary language to the parties. The child and any witness under 18 years old is generally referred to by his first name. **2.01.09**

Expressions

Conviction: Finding of guilt **2.01.10**
Sentence: Order made upon finding of guilt.

Witnesses

Witnesses should remain outside the court until called to give evidence. The witness should then remain in court until he is given permission to leave by the court or until the conclusion of the case. **2.01.11**

Other special provisions

If the room is an adult court room it must not sit as a youth court within one hour of a sitting of the adult court. This has the result, in practice, of preventing the bench altering proceedings in mid-hearing. **2.01.12**

2.01.13   The youth court is closed except to the following persons who may only be present in court if concerned in the case.

  (a) Members and officers of the court.
  (b) Probation officers and social services officers.
  (c) The parties and their legal representatives.
  (d) Persons authorised by the court (for example, trainee social workers, law students).
  (e) Representatives of the press (although the press may not report any matter which would lead to the identification of the child). In practice, there is little point in the press attending.

2. TRIAL IN THE YOUTH COURT

Introduction

2.02.01   As a general rule, the practice in a criminal trial in the youth court follows the practice in **1.06** summary trial in the magistrates' court.

Attendance of the parties

2.02.02   The juvenile must attend.
          The parents (or guardian) of a child or young person aged 10–15 inclusive are also under a duty to attend and a summons and/or warrant may be issued to secure their attendance. The parents (or guardian) of a youth aged 16 or 17 may attend.

Practice

Identification of the juvenile defendant

2.02.03   The clerk will usually identify the defendant by name, date of birth and address, for example:

> **"Are you** (*name of defendant*)**? When were you born? And where do you live?"**

After the defendant has been identified, he is then usually referred to by his first name only.

Identification of the parents (or guardian or other adult appearing with the juvenile)

The clerk will then usually identify the parent(s), for example: **2.02.04**

"(*To the juvenile*) **And do you appear here today with your parents/mother/father/social worker?"**

"(*To the parents*) **And are you** (*name of parents/mother/father/ social worker*)?"

"Do you understand why (*name of juvenile*) **is here today?"**

The charge or summons

The charge or summons is read to the juvenile by the clerk, who will **2.02.05** also usually explain to the parties the nature of the allegation in ordinary language.

There may be preliminary applications, see **1.06.10**. **2.02.06**

The clerk will then ask the juvenile: **2.02.07**

"Do you plead guilty or not guilty to the charge?"

If the juvenile pleads guilty to the charge or summons, see **2.02.08** **2.02.16–26**.

If the juvenile pleads not guilty to the charge or summons the prosecution will call evidence to prove the case.

Age of the child/young person

The age of the juvenile is important in a criminal trial in the youth **2.02.09** court because of the doctrine of *doli incapax* (incapable of crime).

(a) A child under the age of 10 years is presumed to be incapable of crime and (if charged) not guilty of any offence. The presumption is irrebuttable.
(b) A child between the ages of 10–13 years is presumed to be incapable of crime but the presumption can be rebutted by the prosecution on the proof, beyond reasonable doubt, that the defendant knew what he was doing was wrong. The prosecution should prove this as part of the case.

The presumption becomes weaker (and its rebuttal easier) as the defendant increases in age between 10–13 years.
(c) A young person aged between 14–18 years is presumed to be capable of crime.

2.02.10   The prosecution should pay particular attention to **2.02.09(b)**. If the prosecution fails to rebut the presumption of *doli incapax* the defence may make a submission of no case to answer.

Order of presentation

2.02.11   Follow the practice in **1.06** summary trial:
- Prosecution opening, see **1.06.15.**
- Prosecution evidence, see **1.06.16–29.**
- Submission of no case to answer, see **1.06.30–32.**
- Defence evidence, see **1.06.33–41.**
- Evidence in rebuttal, if appropriate, see **1.06.42.**
- Speeches, see **1.06.43–46.**

2.02.12   There are few set formulae of words in criminal proceedings in the youth court because the proceedings are conducted informally and in a conversational manner. The advocate should, however, remember that he is in court and not at a case conference.

Finding of guilt

2.02.13   After all the evidence has been called and any party entitled to address the court has addressed the court, the magistrates may retire to consider their decision.

2.02.14   When announcing the decision, the court may say:

> **"We find you guilty,** *or* **We find you not guilty."**

A finding of guilt to a lesser offence is not available in the youth court.

2.02.15   If the finding is not guilty, the youth is discharged. The defence may make an application for the defendant's costs, see **20.02.22(b)**.

Determining the order on a finding of guilt (Sentence)

2.02.16   The court (or the clerk) may will ask the juvenile whether there is anything that he wants to say (before the court hears information about the juvenile's background). The chairman may say:

> **"**(*To the advocate*) **Is there anything that** (*name*) **wishes to say at this stage?"**

The advocate is advised to consult briefly with the juvenile before answering (usually: **No**).

Previous findings of guilt

The court may hear information (usually from the prosecution) about   **2.02.17**
or receive any documents setting out, any previous findings of guilt
and/or police cautions recorded against the juvenile.

The information should be read to the juvenile and his parent(s)/
social worker so that they, or the juvenile's representative may explain,
admit or deny (as appropriate) any previous matter.

Reports

The court may consider reports from any suitably qualified person,   **2.02.18**
for example:

(a) Pre-sentence report.
(a) Social services' report.
(b) School report.
(c) Medical and/or psychiatric report.

The reports are not usually read aloud, but the substance of any
report material to a party should be disclosed to that party in order he
has the opportunity to comment on it.

The magistrates will usually retire to read the reports.

If any of the reports are not available and the court feels it needs   **2.02.19**
information on a particular matter before making an order, the court
may adjourn the case, for example:

> **"We feel we need to know more about** (*state matter*)**. We will
> remand this case for a** (*state nature of*) **report."**

The defence or the juvenile, his parent or guardian, may address the   **2.02.20**
court in mitigation, see **7.04.01–15**.

Decision

After consideration of the reports and hearing any mitigation or   **2.02.21**
representations, the magistrates will usually retire to make their
decision.

When the magistrates return to court, the chairman will tell the
parties how they are considering dealing with the case and invite
representations.

If this procedure is followed, the defence should not repeat the representations in **2.02.20**. The defence will usually only address the court if the proposed order has not been recommended in any report.

2.02.22   The court will then announce its decision. The court must explain the nature and effect of any order in ordinary language to the juvenile and his parents or guardians.

2.02.23   The range of sentences available to the youth court is similar to those available to the adult courts. However, different procedural rules apply which should be researched in the appropriate practice manuals.

The advocate should note that a youth court is no longer able to "sentence" a juvenile into care although the circumstances of the offence may cause the local authority to apply to the family proceedings court for a care or supervision order.

Costs

2.02.24   See **20.02.09–10**. The court may order costs to be paid by the parents of a juvenile.

Appeal

2.02.25   Appeal against a finding of guilt (where the juvenile pleaded not guilty to the charge) and/or order of the juvenile court is to the crown court, see **5.06**. It is a rehearing of the case.

The notice of appeal must be served within 21 days on:

(a) The prosecution.
(b) The clerk to the youth court.

2.02.26   A parent or guardian may also appeal where the youth court has ordered him to pay the fine, compensation or costs ordered against the juvenile.

CHAPTER 3

Family Proceedings Court

1. INTRODUCTION

Introduction

The family proceedings court is a specialist magistrates' court which **3.01.01** deals with matters of family law and the welfare of children ("family proceedings") including:

(a) Applications under the Children Act 1989.
(b) Applications under the Domestic Proceedings and Magistrates' Courts Act 1978 (for financial provision and protection from domestic violence).
(c) Adoption.

The jurisdiction of the family proceedings court overlaps with with **3.01.02** that of the county court and the High Court and, in private law proceedings, the parties are able to choose the court to hear the case (subject to certain limitations).

In practice, all care proceedings commence in the family proceedings court (although there are some exceptions).

The court

A family proceedings court is composed of not more than three **3.01.03** magistrates from the family proceedings panel, including, so far as practicable, both a man and a woman.

3.01.04   The proceedings are conducted in private (usually only the parties, their legal representatives and the welfare agencies attend).

3.01.05   Other persons may be present during the hearing, see **2.01.13** (except **(e)**).

Applications procedure

3.01.06   The applications procedure under the Children Act 1989 applies to fresh, variation and revocation applications:

3.01.07   Under section 4, Children Act 1989
  ● Parental responsibility orders.

3.01.08   Under section 8, Children Act 1989
  ● Residence orders.
  ● Contact orders.
  ● Prohibited steps orders.
  ● Specific issue orders.
Applicants who may apply as of right:
  (a) Parent or guardian
  (b) Contact orders, prohibited steps orders or specific issue orders only: Any person who has a residence order in relation to the child.

Applicants who may apply with leave, see **3.01.19:**

  (a) Anyone else including the child.
  (b) Residence orders and contact orders only: Foster parents with the leave of the local authority.

3.01.09   Under section 31, Children Act 1989
  ● Care orders and supervision orders.
Under sections 44-45, Children Act 1989
  ● Emergency protection orders.
Only the local authority or an "authorised person" (at present only the NSPCC) may apply for a care order or a supervision order.

3.01.10   Under Schedule 1, Children Act 1989
  ● Financial provision for a child.
A parent, guardian or person in whose favour a residence order is in force may apply.

3.01.11   Under Domestic Proceedings and Magistrates' Courts Act 1978
  ● Financial provision.
  ● Family protection orders and exclusion orders.
Either party to a marriage may apply.

Under the Adoption Act 1976   **3.01.12**
  • Adoption
Applicants and child must live together in the UK otherwise the
application is to the county court or the High Court.

This is not a full list of orders available, although the most common   **3.01.13**
are included, and where there are particular rules as to time limits,
residence etc. these have been omitted.

The parties should note that, in applications under section 8 and   **3.01.14**
some other cases, where an application is before the court, the court
may exercise any of its powers under the Children Act (even if not the
subject of the application).

Parental responsibility

Persons (usually the parents of a child) who have parental respons-   **3.01.15**
ibility are responsible for the child's care and upbringing. In certain
circumstances, a local authority can acquire parental responsibility for
the child in care proceedings, see **3.01.09**. This does not mean that the
parents lose parental responsibility but the local authority are very
much "in control".

The following person(s) have parental responsibility: **3.01.16**

(a) The married or adoptive parents of the child.
(b) A person who is granted a residence order.
(c) A person who is appointed guardian of the child.
(d) An unmarried father in favour of whom a parental responsibility
    order is made.

The principles

The following principles apply in applications for orders under the   **3.01.17**
Children Act. In order to avoid protracted hearings, generating animosity between the parties, it is important to bear these principles in mind
at each stage:

(A) The welfare of the child

When a court determines any question with respect to the upbring-
ing/property/income from property of a child, the child's welfare shall
be the court's paramount consideration.

(B) Welfare checklist

In an opposed application to make/vary/discharge a section 8 order or care or supervision order, the court shall have regard to:

(a) the ascertainable wishes and feeling of the child concerned (considered in the light of his age and understanding);

(b) his physical, emotional and educational needs;

(c) the likely effect on him of any change in his circumstances;

(d) his age, sex, background and any characteristics of his which the court considers relevant;

(e) any harm which he has suffered or is at risk of suffering;

(f) how capable each of his parents, and any other person in relation to whom the court considers the question to be relevant, is of meeting his needs;

(g) the range of powers available to the court under the Act in the proceedings in question.

(C) Without delay

Any delay in determining questions with respect to the upbringing of a child is likely to prejudice the welfare of the child, but:

(D) Making an order

The court may not make an order under the Act unless it considers that doing so would be better for the child than making no order at all.

Commencement of proceedings

Applications

3.01.18   Under the applications procedure, proceedings start by completing a standard application form and serving a copy of that form together with a notice of hearing of a directions appointment or of a hearing before the family proceedings court on each of the respondents.

In some circumstances the court may require that other potential respondents are given notice of the directions appointment or the hearing.

3.01.19   Where leave is required, the applicant must apply (on a standard form) to the court stating reasons why leave should be given. Leave may be granted by the clerk or a single justice without an oral hearing. If in doubt, the clerk's office should be consulted.

In most cases the respondent(s) must serve an answer, usually on a **3.01.20** standard form.

Complaint

The complaint procedure applies to some applications for the varia- **3.01.21** tion of pre-Children Act orders and to all enforcement applications of maintenance orders. The standard method of commencing proceedings is by the making of a complaint leading to the issue of a summons out of the court office.

The summons is in standard form and will require the person named **3.01.22** therein (the respondent) to appear before the court.

Except where personal service has been effected, if the respondent fails to appear, evidence (for example, a certificate of service) will be required to show that the summons has come to his knowledge before the complaint may be proved in his absence.

The hearing of a complaint for the enforcement of a maintenance **3.01.23** order is not considered here. The practice at the hearing is similar to but less formal than a summary trial in the magistrates' court, see **1.06**.

Service of evidence

After the application has been made, the rules provide for the service of **3.01.24** evidence (in rule 4.17 statement form) by one party on the other and on the court, in practice, in all cases.

This should be done as soon as practicable.

In section 8 applications, the statements and documents should not **3.01.25** be deposited with the court (but should be served on the other parties) until the clerk or the court directs, usually at a directions appointment. However, it may be local practice to encourage the depositing of the statements with the court before the directions appointment and the clerk should be consulted.

The following documents are likely to be served (not necessarily all at **3.01.26** the same time):

(a) Statements of evidence, signed and dated with the declaration that:

"(*Name of person making the statement*) **believes the statement to be true and understands that it may be placed before the court.**"

(b) Welfare reports.

(c) Guardian *ad litem* reports.

(d) Statements of means.

(e) Any other document that the party proposes to use at the hearing.

Welfare and guardian ad litem reports

3.01.27   A welfare report (private law proceedings) is likely to be requested where there is concern for the welfare of a child or there is a dispute about with whom the child should live or with whom the child should have contact.

In care proceedings (public law proceedings) a guardian *ad litem* will be appointed and he will prepare a report for the court.

Both welfare reports and the reports of guardians *ad litem* generally carry significant weight with the court.

2. DIRECTIONS APPOINTMENTS

Introduction

3.02.01   Where the clerk receives an application under the Children Act, he will consider (either of his own motion or at the request of either party) whether a directions appointment should be held in advance of the hearing.

In practice, at least one directions appointment is almost always held.

3.02.02   A directions appointment is usually held by the clerk, although it may also be held by a single justice.

The function of the clerk is similar to that of the district judge in the county court.

Conduct

3.02.03   The parties should attend, unless excused. The welfare officer or guardian *ad litem* (if appointed) will also usually be present. The emphasis is on the informal. For right of audience, see **1.01.02**, but not next friend. The advocates are not robed but will be suitably attired in business wear.

The directions appointment may be in the courtroom or in an office or in a room set aside for family cases. The parties are advised to ask the clerk, as a matter of courtesy, where he would like them to sit.

Practice

The clerk is addressed as **sir/madam** or simply **Mr/Mrs/Miss** (name). **3.02.04**
The parties are likely to be referred to as **Mr/Mrs/Miss** (name) and not **the applicant** or **the respondent**.

In practice, the clerk will discuss the case with the parties. He will **3.02.05** consider the welfare or guardian *ad litem*'s reports with the parties and will advise them that where the welfare officer or guardian *ad litem* is making a recommendation, it is likely that the magistrates will follow it unless there is a good reason in law for not doing so.

On any directions appointment, the parties may address the clerk on **3.02.06** matters of law. He is likely to provisionally consider the arguments between the parties over the interpretation of disputed points of law so that, if there is to be a contested hearing, it is likely to be on the facts only.

Specimen directions

Directions which may be given may include any of the following **3.02.07** matters:

(a) Timetable for the proceedings.
(b) Time limits for complying with the rules.
(c) Attendance of the child.
(d) Appointment of a guardian *ad litem* or solicitor.
(e) Service of documents.
(f) Submission of evidence (in statement form), including experts' reports (and, in a case where paternity is in dispute, blood tests and/or DNA fingerprinting) and statements of means.
(g) Preparation of welfare reports.
(h) Transfer of proceedings to another family proceedings court or (usually in a complex case) to a county court, where the district judge may then transfer it to the High Court.
(i) Consolidation with other proceedings (which may include transfer).

3.02.08   The list is not exhaustive and the emphasis is on "sorting out" as much as possible at the directions appointment(s). It is the focal point of the applications procedure and it is advisable that the advocate who is proposing to attend the full hearing also attends the directions appointment.

Negotiations at the directions appointment may lead to pre-hearing conciliation.

3.02.09   If a party has not seen the welfare officer or guardian *ad litem*, the clerk may take the oportunity of advising that party to do so and ordering a report. The clerk may then fix a further directions appointment.

3.02.10   If the case is going to be contested there may be a further directions appointment.

Appeal

3.02.11   Appeal from the decision of a clerk/single justice/court at a directions appointment is to the High Court Family Division, as of right.

3. PRACTICE AT THE HEARING

Introduction

3.03.01   In the applications procedure there are no hard and fast rules. The procedure has been deliberately designed to be flexible.

The rules provide for the magistrates to have read the written statements and reports prior to the hearing. They should be familiar with the case they are about to hear.

Conduct

3.03.02   For right of audience, see **1.01.02**, except next-friend. The advocates are not robed but will be suitably attired in business wear. The bench is addressed as **sir/madam** to the chairman.

Practice varies widely as to whether the advocate should stand or sit to address the court. If it is not possible to ascertain the practice of the court in advance, the advocate should stand, although he may later be invited by the court to sit.

Practice

Attendance of the parties

The parties should attend, unless excused. **3.03.03**

If the applicant appears, but one of the respondents is absent, the court may proceed with the case.

If one or more of the respondents appear, but the applicant does not, the court may refuse the application or, if sufficient evidence has already been received, carry on with the case.

Identification of the parties

The clerk will usually identify the parties by name and address. The **3.03.04**
clerk will also usually identify the advocates.

Opening remarks by the clerk

The clerk opens the case by "setting the scene". The clerk is likely to: **3.03.05**

(a) Give a general account to the court of the nature of the application.
(b) Summarise the history of the application.
(c) Refer the court to any order made on directions, for example:

"The following directions were given on (*date***) namely . . . "**
(d) Indicate the issues which are in dispute and those which are not in dispute.

Order of presentation of case

It is good practice in a case which is obviously going to be contested **3.03.06**
for the clerk to have given directions at a directions appointment for the hearing of the case, for example, the order of presentation of each party's case.

For example, in a case where an applicant is seeking an order for contact with a child in the care of the local authority, the clerk may say:

"Directions were also given:
Respondent number 1 (*the Local Authority***) proceeds first. He will be calling the following persons as live witnesses (***names***). The following evidence is in the form of Rule 17 statements (***names***). Applicant will proceed next. (***Repeat directions***). Followed by the 2nd respondent. (***Repeat directions***). Followed by the guardian ad litem, who will remain in court throughout."**

3.03.07   In a simple case (for example, an application for contact by a father) where directions may not have been given, the likely order of presentation is:

(a) Applicant.
(b) Any person with parental responsibility.
(c) Other respondents.
(d) The child.

3.03.08   In any case where the advocate is unsure of the order of presentation (or, of any other matter relevant to the presentation of his case, for example, what statements or reports have been seen by the magistrates), he should ask the clerk (ideally before the court sits). If the bench is sitting, the advocate may say:

> **"May I enquire of your learned clerk one or two points before you hear the evidence. Perhaps I could have a short adjournment."**

Presenting the case

3.03.09   The advocate presenting his case first need only say by way of opening:

> **"I understand that you have read** (*list documents*)**. This is the issue in dispute** (*state issue*)**. And I call** (*applicant/ respondent/ witness*) **on that point."**

3.03.10   The parties will then call witnesses in order of presentation on the issue(s) in dispute.
The evidence in the case may take the form of:

Witnesses

3.03.11   The advocate may only call a witness (without leave) whose statement has been served in accordance with the rules, see **3.02.07(f)**.
Witnesses should stand to take the oath but may later be invited by the court to sit to give evidence.

Written evidence

3.03.12   The written evidence will be in the form of reports and statements served in accordance with the rules. The evidence should not be read to the court (in the manner of a section 9 CJA statement in criminal proceedings) but it may be referred to in submissions after the conclusion of all the (live) evidence.

Admitted facts

A party need not call evidence in respect of stated facts which are **3.03.13** admitted and not in dispute but the facts may be referred to in submissions after the conclusion of all the (live) evidence.

Submissions

At the conclusion of all the evidence, the parties may address the bench **3.03.14** on the law and facts, see **22.01 & 22.03**.

Once again, there is no set practice but, as a matter of courtesy, the advocate should ask the permission of the magistrates before making any submissions (it is rarely refused) as follows:

"May I address you now on (*state point(s)*)**."**

The advocates may have been ordered on a directions application to **3.03.15** prepare and submit draft reasons/draft orders to which they may refer in closing submissions.

The magistrates will usually retire to reach their decision. **3.03.16**

Decision

Before the court announces its decision the justices' clerk must **3.03.17** record in writing the court's findings of fact and the reasons for the decision. The clerk draws up this document in consultation with the magistrates.

Costs

The court may order either party to pay costs. The court must give **3.03.18** reasons for its decision.

Appeal

Appeal of a final decision of the Family Proceedings Court is to the **3.03.19** Divisional Court of the Family Division, as of right.

CHAPTER 4

Bail Proceedings

Introduction

4.01.01 This section is intended for use in any court having the jurisdiction to consider or reconsider, (see **4.04.01–10**, bail).

In some courts (for example, a busy magistrates' court), the decision to withhold bail is announced as follows:

> **"Bail is refused. Schedule 1, paragraph 2(c) applies."**

For this reason, the paragraph numbers in the Bail Act, 1976, have been followed where possible.

4.01.02 The court must consider the question of bail at each hearing and may either grant bail or withhold bail without application by either party.

Exceptions to the right to bail

Imprisonable offences

4.01.03 A defendant appearing before the court should be granted bail except where the court is satisfied that there are substantial grounds for believing that, if released on bail, the defendant would (under Bail Act 1976, Schedule 1, Part I):

Paragraph 2(a) Fail to answer bail.

Paragraph 2(b) Commit an offence whilst on bail.

Paragraph 2(c) Interfere with witnesses or obstruct the course of justice.

Bail may also be refused in the particular circumstances listed in Bail Act 1976, Schedule 1, Part I:

Paragraph 3 For the defendant's protection.

Paragraph 4 Defendant serving a custodial sentence.

Paragraph 5 Insufficient information on defendant.

Paragraph 6 Defendant arrested for actual or probable breach of bail or conditions in current proceedings.

Paragraph 7 Bail impractical in order to prepare report on defendant.

Non-imprisonable offences

A defendant appearing before the court should be granted bail except   **4.01.04**
where the court is satisfied that (under Bail Act 1976, Schedule 1, Part II):

Paragraph 2 The defendant has previously failed to answer bail and would fail again.

Paragraph 3 The defendant needs protection.

Paragraph 4 The defendant is serving a custodial sentence.

Paragraph 5 The defendant has been arrested for actual or possible breach of bail or bail conditions in the current proceedings.

Reasons for finding exceptions to right to bail

When considering a bail application the court should have regard to   **4.01.05**
the following:

(a) The nature and seriousness of the offence (and the probable method of dealing with the defendant).

(b) The strength of the evidence against the defendant.

(c) The likelihood of further offences.

(d) The defendant's previous failure to comply with bail (or conditions).

(e) The defendant's lack of fixed address.

(f) The defendant's character and antecedents.

(g) The defendant's associations and community ties.

(h) The likelihood of the defendant:
   (i) Interfering with witnesses,
   (ii) Interfering with property,
   (iii) Assisting others not yet charged,
   (iv) Being injured by others.

(i) Bail enquiries incomplete due to lack of time.

(j) Any other matter which appears to be relevant.

Practice

4.02.01 The court will grant the application by either side for a remand or adjournment, for example:

> **"I/We will grant the application for a remand. What is the position as to bail?"**

In the magistrates' court, the court is likely to postpone consideration of a new date if the defendant is in custody and a bail application is to be made.

4.02.02 The prosecution may say:

> **"The prosecution object to bail on the grounds that** (*state exceptions to right to bail*) *or* **The prosecution ask for bail with conditions because** (*state exceptions to right to bail*)."

4.02.03 The prosecution will usually briefly describe the circumstances of the alleged offence and give reasons, see **4.01.05**, why the remand should be in custody and not on bail, see example in **4.02.10**.

4.02.04 The prosecution will usually give the objections to bail (exceptions to right to bail), although in some cases (for example, a serious offence where the bail application is being made at short notice) the officer in the case may be present at court and be called to give the objections to bail from the witness box (either on oath or otherwise). The defence may then cross-examine the officer.

Bail application

4.02.05 The defence may then address the court, giving reasons why the defendant should be released on bail, and may call evidence relevant to the proceedings.

There is no set formula for a bail application. The defence should consider each objection (exception to right to bail) and should address the court or call evidence to rebut any reason for finding exceptions to the right to bail.

4.02.06 When making a bail application, the defence may offer bail conditions (conditional bail).

The suggested bail conditions must be relevant to the reasons for finding exceptions to the right to bail.

Method

4.02.07 The defence should approach the application as follows:

(a) Why are the prosecution objecting to bail? see **4.01.05**.
(b) How can the objection(s) be answered?
(c) What bail conditions can be offered, see **4.02.08**, which are relevant to the defendant's circumstances, see **4.02.09**.

Bail conditions which may be offered

(a) The provision of a surety (imprisonable offences only). **4.02.08**
(b) The provision of a security (where the defendant is unlikely to remain in the U.K. only).
(c) A condition of residence.
(d) A condition to remain at a place of residence during certain times (curfew).
(e) A condition to report to a police station.
(f) A condition to surrender passport and/or not to apply for any travel documents.
(g) A condition not to go within a certain distance of a named location.
(h) A condition not to contact or approach any named individual (usually a prosecution witness) or co-defendant either directly or indirectly.
(i) A condition to co-operate in the preparation of medical/psychiatric/pre-sentence reports.
(j) Any other appropriate condition.

Other relevant considerations

When making a bail application, the defence may address the court **4.02.09**
and/or call call evidence of the defendant's:

(a) Residence (and proof thereof).
(b) Home circumstances.
(c) Financial circumstances (see legal aid application).
(d) Job (or job prospects).
(e) Previous convictions.
(f) Any other special circumstances, for example, medical condition.

Example

After briefly describing the circumstances of the offence, the pro- **4.02.10**
secution may say:

"The prosecution believe that the defendant would, if released on bail, fail to answer bail. The defendant has (–) previous convictions for absconding (*state dates and circumstances*). **It is also believed that the address he gave the police is temporary accommodation."**

4.02.11   What is the objection to bail and how can it be met?

(a) The prosecution are objecting to bail under Schedule 1, Part II, paragraph 2(a).

(b) The objection can be answered if the defence is able to offer bail conditions which make it unlikely that the defendant will fail to answer bail.

(c) The bail conditions which may be considered are: **4.02.08: (a) (c) (e)** and, perhaps, **(f)**.

4.02.12   It would not be a sufficient answer to the objections for the defence to ask the court, for example, to consider a condition that the defendant should not go within a certain distance of a named location, condition **(g)**.

The imposition of such a condition would not answer the objection that the defendant would fail to answer bail.

4.02.13   The defence may conclude:

"Unless I can assist the court further, there are no other matters upon which I would wish to address (*the court*)."

4.02.14   The court will then announce its decision:

"Bail is refused for the following reasons (*state reasons*). (*omit* **4.02.17–25**)"

or

"(*The court***) grants conditional/unconditional bail.** (*omit* **4.02.16–24**)"

or

"(*The court***) is considering bail with a surety of** (*state amount and/or conditions*)."

4.02.15   If the defendant is charged with murder or attempted murder, manslaughter, rape or attempted rape the court will give reasons for granting bail:

"The court is prepared to grant bail. The reasons for granting bail are (*state reasons*)."

70

If bail is refused and custody time limits apply, the defendant may not **4.02.16** be remanded in custody for longer than a specified time.

The prosecution should check whether a custody time limit applies and if necessary apply for an extension of time.

Sureties

If the court grants bail with a surety, the surety will usually be taken by **4.02.17** the court. The defence may make an application for the surety to be taken (later) at a police station, or by a court clerk.

If the surety is taken at a police station, the defendant will not be released until the court has been informed accordingly.

If the proposed surety is taken by the court he will be called by the **4.02.18** defence to the witness box, sworn and identified by name and address. The defence may say:

> **"(***Name***) do you agree to stand surety for the attendance of the defendant at this court (***or, name of court***) on (***date of adjourned hearing***) in the sum of (***state amount***)?"**

The following matters may be considered in examination of the **4.02.19** proposed surety:

(a) The relationship of the proposed surety to the defendant.
(b) The proximity of his home address.
(c) Whether the proposed surety regularly associates with the defendant.

The defence may then say: **4.02.20**

> **"Do you understand what is meant by standing as a surety: that if the defendant fails to attend court you could lose all or part of that sum and, if you do not have it, you could go to prison? How could you raise that sum?"**

The proposed surety will reply (usually giving evidence of money in a bank account, equity in a house, jewellery).

> **"The surety is acceptable to the prosecution. Is the court satisfied that (***name***) is a suitable surety for the attendance of the defendant at court?"**

The defence is advised to provide the full name, address and date of **4.02.21** birth of the proposed surety to the prosecution before the bail application in order that the prosecution can check those details and any previous convictions.

4.02.22   The court will then announce its decision.

4.02.23   If bail is granted with a surety and the surety is taken in court, the defence should ensure that the surety is made continuous until the disposal of the case (*i.e.* the surety does not have to attend court to be taken again).

4.02.24   If the deposit of a security is required, the defendant will not be released until the deposit (in cash or banker's draft) is with the court.

Pronouncement of bail

4.02.25   The court should explain bail and/or conditions of bail to the defendant:

> **"You are released on unconditional/conditional bail with the following conditions (*state conditions*). If you fail to attend court on (*date*) you will have committed an offence which is punishable by a fine and/or imprisonment. Do you understand?"**

Magistrates' court only

4.03.01 The defendant is permitted to make only two bail applications as of right. Subsequent bail applications cannot be made unless there has been a significant change of circumstance, except on committal to the Crown Court, although practice varies, see **1.05.38**.

4.03.02   If bail is refused the court should issue a "full argument certificate" under the Bail Act 1976 (s.5(4) & (5)).

The defence may ask for a full argument certificate in order to:

(a) Appeal the decision to the crown court, see **5.05**.
(b) Avoid repeated requests by the defendant (who may not appreciate the rule in **4.03.01**) for further bail applications.

Remand in absence of defendant

4.03.03   If the defendant is remanded in custody and the period of remand is longer than the defendant's right (in practice) to weekly production before the court, the court may say to the defence:

> **"Does the defendant object to being remanded in his absence until (*a date not more than 4 weeks away*)?"**

If it is anticipated that the defendant will be remanded in custody, the defence should have taken instructions on his remand in absence beforehand.

Variation of bail conditions

Bail conditions may be varied upon application to the court by either the prosecution or the defence where there is a change of circumstance, for example: **4.03.04**

> **"This case is listed at the request of** (*name of party*) **for an application to change bail conditions. The application is/is not opposed. The application is for** (*state bail conditions sought*).**"**

Appeal of refusal of bail

Appeal to the Crown Court

Appeal of refusal of bail from the magistrates' court is usually to the Crown Court, see **5.05**, or it may be to a judge in chambers of the High Court, see **4.04.04–09**. **4.04.01**

The usual practice is to apply for bail to the Crown Court and, if unsuccessful, then to apply to a judge in chambers of the High Court. **4.04.02**

If bail is refused by the Crown Court or by a judge in chambers, the defence may make a subsequent application to the magistrates' court if there has been a change of circumstance, although there is usually little chance of success. **4.04.03**

Appeal to a judge in chambers

The application is made on summons supported by affidavit (giving reasons for the application), copies of which must be served on the prosecution, in practice, 24 hours before the hearing. **4.04.04**
The application is heard in chambers in the judge's room. The advocates are not robed. They remain seated even when addressing the judge. The style of the application may be described as conversational.

The application is heard on affidavit evidence. For practice generally, see **9.02.29–37**. **4.04.05**

The defence introduce the parties. The defence may then open the case, for example: **4.04.06**

> **"This is an application for bail by** (*name*)**. I appear on behalf of** (*name*)**. (***Name***) appears on behalf of the prosecution. The defendant is charged with** (*offences*) **which are listed in paragraph (–) of the affidavit. He was arrested on . . .** (*and so on*)**."**

4.04.07   It is likely that the judge will take the initiative at the hearing. He may say, for example, that he has read the affidavit.

He may then ask the prosecution to briefly describe the circumstances of the alleged offence and give objections to bail.

He may then ask the defence if they have anything to add to the affidavit or whether there is any particular matter on which the defence wishes to address him.

4.04.08   In any other case, after introducing the parties and opening the case, the defence may invite the prosecution to give objections to bail. The defence may then refer the judge to any relevant paragraphs in the affidavit(s) (which should have been prepared with a view to answering the anticipated objections to bail).

4.04.09   The judge will then announce his decision, usually with a very short judgment.

Appeal to the Court of Appeal after conviction and sentence

4.04.10   Where the defendant has been convicted, the defence may apply to a single judge of the Court of Appeal for bail on service of the notice and grounds of appeal, see **11.01.11–12**.

CHAPTER 5

Crown Court

1. INTRODUCTION

Introduction

The hearing of any matter in the Crown Court takes place in open court **5.01.01**
unless otherwise stated. A hearing not in open court is in chambers. The
most common application in chambers is appeal of refusal of bail from
the magistrates' court, see **5.05**.

Right of audience

Barristers. **5.01.02**
Solicitors (in appeals, including appeal of refusal of bail and committals for sentence where they or, sometimes, a partner in the same firm
represented the defendant in the magistrates' court).
Defendant in person.

Dress

Barristers and solicitors are robed except in chambers. **5.01.03**
Defendants in person should be respectably dressed.

Mode of address

5.01.04

Court List	*Mode of Address*
Mr Justice (name)	**My Lord**
His Honour Judge (name), sitting as a Judge of the High Court	**My Lord**
All Judges sitting at the Central Criminal Court	**My Lord**
His Honour Judge (name)	**Your Honour**
His Honour Judge (name) sitting as a Deputy Circuit Judge	**Your Honour**
Mr Recorder (name)	**Your Honour**
Mr Assistant Recorder (name)	**Your Honour**

Seating in court

5.01.05　　In court, the defence will usually sit in the rows and/or seats closer to the jury.

Addressing the court

5.01.06　　Any party addressing the court should do so standing.

Order of presentation

5.01.07　　The order of presentation and speeches follows the title order of the case in the court list except in appeals where the respondent usually presents his case and makes his speech first.

Witnesses

5.01.08　　Witnesses should remain outside court until called to give evidence. The witness should then remain in court until the conclusion of the case or until he is given permission to leave by the court, except **5.09** Appeal in licensing proceedings.

2. PRE-TRIAL HEARINGS

Introduction

5.02.01　　A case which has been committed from the magistrates court to the Crown Court may (and a serious fraud case, which is transferred to the Crown Court must) be listed for a pre-trial hearing.

In practice, pre-trial hearings are the only interlocutory proceedings in criminal proceedings, compare **9.02**. The hearing is always *inter partes* except an application by the prosecution for a voluntary bill of indictment which is made on affidavit to a high court judge, see **1.05.08**.

A case may be listed for a pre-trial hearing on the court list as follows: **5.02.02**
For Mention
No Witnesses
For Plea(s) *or* **For Pleas: No Witnesses**
For Pre-Trial Review *or* **For Directions**
For Pleas and Pre-Trial Review *or* **Directions**
Preparatory Hearing

Practice

For mention

A case may be listed for mention by the prosecution, the defence or   **5.02.03**
the court. The purpose of mentioning a case is to bring the case to the attention of the court for a reason.

The party (or the court) having the case listed for mention should   **5.02.04**
bring to the attention of the other parties (and the court) the reason for doing so a reasonable time before the hearing.
A case may be listed for mention to enable either party (or the court) to seek an order which could otherwise be obtained at a pre-trial review, see **5.02.10(a)-(l)**. If reasonable notice is given the order may be agreed before the hearing. If not, the court may hear argument.
A case may be listed for mention where the prosecution is applying for the extension of a custody time limit or where either party or the court is applying to break a fixed date for hearing, see **5.02.15**.

No witnesses

A case is likely to be listed for no witnesses before the defendant has   **5.02.05**
entered pleas to the indictment in order that pleas can be taken. If the case is listed after pleas have been taken, the same procedure is likely to be adopted as in a case listed for mention.

For plea(s)

If a case is listed for pleas(s), the court will expect pleas to be entered   **5.02.06**
by the defendant. If the indictment is being drafted by the prosecution

rather than the court, it should be ready for any hearing listed for pleas(s).

The defence should have taken sufficient instructions to enable the defendant (on advice) to enter realistic pleas to each count on the indictment.

5.02.07   If the defendant (or defendants) plead guilty (or offer acceptable pleas), the prosecution will usually be expected to open the facts of the case and the court will proceed to sentencing. If the defendant (or defendants) plead not guilty, the case will usually be stood out for trial and the hearing may be treated as a hearing for pre-trial review or directions, see **5.02.09**.

5.02.08   In a case involving more than one defendant, if a co-defendant pleads not guilty, the case of the defendant pleading guilty will usually be stood out for sentence to the conclusion of the trial of the other defendant.

For pre-trial review or directions

5.02.09   At a hearing for pre-trial review or directions the court may consider the following matters listed in the Practice Rules. The same paragraph lettering has been adopted because the judge will often conduct a pre-trial review in "shorthand", for example:

> **"What directions do you want me to make? Under (a) . . . ? Under (b) . . . ?"**

5.02.10   (a) Pleas (and/or alternative pleas) to be tendered on trial (if not entered at the pre-trial hearing).

(b) Which prosecution witnesses are required by the defence at the trial. In particular, whether any witness can be made conditionally bound or dispensed with altogether.

The judge may say:

> **"Witness orders?** *or* **Under (b) . . . ?"**

The defence may say:

> **"I have provided** (*the prosecution*) **with a list.** *or* **May I have (7/ 14/21/28) days?** (*depending on the complexity of the case*)."

(c) Whether the prosecution is likely to serve any notice(s) of additional evidence before the trial. The defence will usually ask for a time limit on any notice(s) of additional evidence, as follows:

> **"I would ask for an order that any notice(s) of additional evidence be served within** (*for example*) **28 days."**

(d) Admissions by either party which can be agreed and put in writing under section 10, Criminal Justice Act 1967.

(e) Realistic estimate of length of trial.

(f) Exhibits and schedules which can be admitted.

(g) Medical condition of the defendant, if appropriate, and any relevant reports where the medical condition may affect the disposal of the case.

(h) Points of law which can be agreed and, if not agreed, a list of authorities and/or written submissions (a skeleton argument, see **22.01.03**). Questions of admissibility (including the agreed editing of witness statements and documentary exhibits).

(i) Disclosure of any unused material by the prosecution and/or the names and addresses of witnesses who have made statements. The defence will usually ask for a time limit on the disclosure of any unused material, as follows:

"I would ask that any unused material be disclosed within (*for example*) **28 days."**

(j) Alibi evidence and, in particular, whether an alibi notice should be served. If the prosecution are of the opinion that the defence may later apply to call alibi evidence (see **5.04.76**), the prosecution will usually ask for a time limit on the service of a notice of alibi.

(k) Order and page numbering of bundle(s) of prosecution statements and documentary exhibits and, if possible, order of calling prosecution witnesses (although this is usually considered as part of (l)).

(l) Any other matter (for example, provision by the prosecution of an opening note and/or case summary, disclosure by the defence of any expert's report upon whom the defence is intending to rely, provision of screens/video link in sex cases).

Preparatory hearing

A preparatory hearing takes place in serious fraud cases. The purpose of the preparatory hearing is to: **5.02.11**

(a) Identify the issues which are likely to be material to the verdict of the jury.

(b) Assist the jury's comprehension of those issues.

(c) Expedite the proceedings before the jury.

(d) Assist the judge's management of the trial.

The procedure is complex. The practice in **5.02.10 (a)-(l)** may be followed as a useful guide except the court has power to order the service of both prosecution and defence case statements. **5.02.12**

Practice

5.02.13   Practice on any pre-trial hearing varies greatly. The parties are advised to state, in correspondence before the hearing (in a complex case) or to discuss at court (in a less complex case), the pleas and directions required in order that the required directions in **5.02.10(a)-(l)** can be outlined to the judge (usually by the prosecution).

The date of the trial

5.02.14   If the defendant enters a plea of not guilty a date may be fixed for trial or the case may be stood out to be listed in the usual way.

5.02.15   When the required directions are being outlined to the judge, either party may apply for a date to be fixed for the trial after **5.02.10(a)** (where, in the experience of the parties, the court is likely to agree to a fixed date) or after **5.02.10(e)** (where it is not known whether the court is likely to agree to a fixed date), as follows:

> **"Could this trial be fixed for** (*state date, if a provisional date has been indicated by the list office*)**?** *or* **Could this trial be fixed by agreement with the list office?"**

> **"The witness dates to avoid are** (*state dates when witnesses are not available*)**.** *or* **The prosecution will undertake to inform the list office of the dates to avoid within (7/14/21/28) days."**

Bail

5.02.16   At the conclusion of a pre-trial hearing the defence may apply for bail, see **Chapter 4**, Bail Applications. If pleas are entered at the pre-trial hearing, the court should not (by reason of the pleas entered alone) alter the bail position.

3. SEEING THE JUDGE

Introduction

5.03.01   An informal discussion called "seeing the judge" may take place between counsel and the judge. If it takes place, it will usually only take place before the actual trial or sentencing judge on the day of the case (which may be listed, see **5.02**, For trial or For plea(s)).

The practice is disapproved of by the court of appeal. For this reason it is very much the exception and not the rule for counsel to ask to see the judge.

"Seeing the judge" may be arranged as follows: **5.03.02**

(a) The party wishing to see the judge should indicate informally to the other party or parties that he wishes to see the judge.
(b) The party or parties should then ask the clerk if the judge will see them and state briefly the reasons for the request.

It is a matter for the discretion of the judge whether he will see **5.03.03** counsel. If the judge agrees to see counsel:

(a) The judge will not usually see a party in the absence of the other party or parties.
(b) The judge will usually ask for a (shorthand) note to be taken.

Different judges take different views as to whether they are prepared to see counsel privately. The clerk will usually be able to let counsel know whether the judge will see them.

Although almost all judges are prepared to see counsel in relation to **5.03.04** matters of confidential mitigation, see **5.03.14**, and some in relation to the personal problems of counsel, see **5.03.15**, some judges are often not prepared to see counsel privately in relation to the ultimate disposal of the case ("an indication"). The reason for this is that the practice of seeing the judge for "an indication" has been abused by counsel and, if the practice is to continue at all, counsel should scupulously follow the following guidelines.

Counsel should exercise discretion: **5.03.05**

(a) When making the initial approach through the clerk.
(b) When addressing the judge in his room.
(c) When advising the defendant about what was said in the judge's room. Counsel should not present a part-indication, see **5.01.13**, to the defendant as a promise by the judge.

Dress

Counsel will usually remain robed in the judge's room. The judge **5.03.06** may invite counsel to remove wigs.

Mode of address

In the judge's room, the judge is addressed as **Judge**. A recorder or **5.03.07** assistant recorder is usually addressed as **Judge** although it has been known for a recorder to insist on the technically correct (but not so grand) mode of address of **Sir**.

Conduct

5.03.08   Counsel should not sit down unless invited to do so by the judge. Counsel must be careful not to embarrass the judge or compromise the hearing of the case in open court.

Practice

Introduction of the parties

5.03.09   Counsel who has asked to see the judge will usually introduce the other counsel:

> **"Thank you for seeing us, judge. I represent** (*name of party*). **(***Name***) represents** (*name of party*). **It is my request to see you. Are you familiar with the papers in this case? The reason that I have asked to see you is** (*state reason*)**."**

Reasons for seeing the judge

Pleas

5.03.10   Counsel should *not* plea bargain. A potential plea may be introduced as follows:

> **"Would you take the view that if the defendant were to plead to count (–) that would meet the justice of the case. Perhaps, if I told you the reasons** (*state reasons*). **It would avoid the need for a trial and** (*state time saved*)**."**

Points of law

5.03.11   **"It would assist me in advising the defendant on his plea if you could indicate your view of the law on** (*state count and nature of evidence*)**."**

Sentence (an "indication")

Counsel should *not* ask the judge to indicate the actual sentence **5.03.12** which he is minded to impose. A potential disposal of the case may be introduced as follows:

> **"If the defendant were to plead to count (–), he is obviously anxious about the possible sentence.** (*State features of the offence which make it less serious, for example:*) **It is not the most serious offence of its kind. The defendant would be entitled to credit for a plea of guilty and** (*state very briefly best feature(s) of mitigation*). **Perhaps, you could indicate your view?"**

The judge may either give a definite indication or he may give no **5.03.13** indication or he may simply say:

> **"This is/is not a serious case and I would sentence accordingly."**

In this example, it is unlikely that the judge will give any better indication and counsel should not press the judge to do so.

Confidential mitigation

> **"The defendant will be pleading to** (*state pleas*). **There are** **5.03.14** **certain matters that I do not wish to raise in mitigation in open court** (*state matters*) **because** (*state reasons, for example,*) **the defendant is an informer.** (*If the defendant is an informer, counsel must be in the position to produce evidence to this effect, usually in the form of a letter from the police*)."

Personal problems of counsel

For example: listing problems, illness in the family. **5.03.15**

Any other matter

Counsel may raise any other matter which they feel should be raised **5.03.16** privately and not in open court, for example, where it is suspected that there has been an improper communication between the defendant and/or the jury and/or prosecution witnesses.

Leaving the judge's room

At the conclusion, counsel who made the request to see the judge **5.03.17** will usually say:

"Thank you for seeing us, judge."

4. TRIAL ON INDICTMENT

Introduction

Attendance of the defendant

5.04.01 The defendant must attend his trial. If the defendant fails to attend, a bench warrant (with or without bail) may be issued or bail may be enlarged, see **1.02.02–06**.

The defendant will usually be warned by his solicitors of the likely date of his trial when his case comes into the warned list (if it has not been fixed). It is the defendant's duty to keep in contact with his solicitors.

Surrender to custody

5.04.02 The defendant surrenders to custody when he enters the dock. The defendant then remains in custody (even if he attended court on bail) until he is granted bail by the court.

In order to avoid the procedure of surrender to custody and subsequent re-consideration of bail, some formal matters which are likely to be the subject of agreement may be dealt with without the defendant surrendering to custody, for example, standing a (floating) case out (of the list) when there is insufficient time to hear it, see **5.04.06**.

The waiting jury ("in" or "out")

5.04.03 The clerk (or usher) may informally ask the parties (usually the defence) when the case is called but before the judge enters court:

"Do we need a jury? (*i.e. Is the defendant pleading not guilty?*)"

"Do you want the (waiting) jury in court? (*i.e. Are there any preliminary applications that you do not want the jury to hear?*)"

5.04.04 The waiting jury is usually kept out of court where the indictment contains more than one count and the defendant is pleading guilty to one or more of the counts or, where the indictment charges more than one defendant and one of them is pleading guilty.

Identification of the defendant

When the case is called, the clerk will usually identify the defendant **5.04.05**
(whether or not he has surrendered to custody) by name, for example:

"Are you (*full name of defendant*)**?"**

- OMIT paragraphs **5.04.06–10**, if considered at a pre-trial hearing.

Preliminary applications after identification where the defendant does not surrender

The most common application at this stage is for the case to be stood **5.04.06**
out, although any other matter listed in **5.02.10** (including indication of
plea, but not the plea itself, see **5.04.08–09**) may also be dealt with at
this stage, usually by agreement.

Preliminary applications after surrender but before the indictment is put to the defendant.

The following applications must be made at this stage: **5.04.07**

(a) For the indictment to be signed (out of time).
(b) To amend the indictment.
(c) To quash the indictment.
(d) To the jurisdiction of the court.

The following applications may be made at this stage:

(e) For joinder of counts and/or defendants.
(f) For severance of counts and/or defendants.

Any other matter listed in **5.02.10** (including indication of plea) may
also be dealt with at this stage, usually by agreement.

Pleas

The indictment is then put to the defendant by the clerk, for example: **5.04.08**

**"(Name of defendant) you are charged on an indictment con-
taining** (*number*) **counts.**
　　On the first count you are charged that (*the statement and
particulars of the offence are then read to the defendant*).
　　To that count do you plead guilty or not guilty?"

The defendant pleads either guilty or not guilty (or, exceptionally, **5.04.09**
makes an alternative plea, for example, *autrefois acquit*).

Preliminary applications after the indictment is put to the defendant

5.04.10 The following applications (if not made at **5.04.07**) must be made at this stage:

(a) For severance of counts (usually where **5.04.04** applies).
(b) For severance of defendants (usually where **5.04.04** applies).
(c) For joinder of counts and/or defendants.
(d) For an order in relation to the reporting of the proceedings, see **5.04.11**.

Any other matter listed in **5.02.10** may also be dealt with at this stage, usually where there is to be argument.

Reporting restrictions

5.04.11 The judge may raise the question of reporting restrictions or either party may apply for an order imposing such restrictions, for example: Juveniles:

> **"One of the defendants is a juvenile/a number of the witnesses in this case are juveniles. Would you make an order under the Children and Young Persons Act that the defendant/witnesses not be identified."**

Second Trial:

> **"The defendant is to be tried on a second indictment following on from this indictment. Would you make an order under the Contempt of Court Act that this matter not be reported until the conclusion of the second trial."**

The defence should not attempt to make an application to impose reporting restrictions for the personal convenience of the defendant.

Attendance of prosecution witnesses

5.04.12 If any prosecution witness(es) fail to attend court the prosecution may apply for the case to be stood out or adjourned.

5.04.13 The defence may oppose the application, for example:

> **"This case has been fixed for (–) months/This is the (–) time the prosecution have applied to stand out/adjourn this case. The defendant has been in custody since (*date*)."**

5.04.14 If the application is refused, the prosecution must decide whether to proceed on the evidence available or to offer no evidence. If the prosecution offer no evidence, the defence may say:

"I would invite you to enter a formal verdict of not guilty and for the defendant to be discharged."

The defence may apply for costs, see **5.04.98**.

Conduct of the trial

At the conclusion of any preliminary applications, the court may consider any matter in relation to the conduct (in particular, the time-tabling) of the trial.   **5.04.15**

Questions of admissibility: a "preliminary view"

After the defendant has pleaded to the indictment, but before the jury are sworn, either party may invite the judge to determine a question of admissibility where the prosecution would have no evidence to put before the jury if that evidence were excluded (although this practice is generally thought to be wrong and the practice in **5.04.28** is usually followed).   **5.04.16**

Alternatively, either party may ask the judge to take a preliminary view as a way of "forcing the issues", for example, where, on the face of the papers, the evidence is so weak that the case is unlikely to get past half time, see **5.04.57**. The issue may be raised as follows: **5.04.17**

"Before the jury is sworn, there are certain matters upon which the prosecution/the defence/we would seek your guidance."

Bail during the trial

If the waiting jury has been excluded, the defence may address the judge on the question of bail during the trial. The usual form of words is: **5.04.18**

"The defendant has been on unconditional/conditional bail to date. Would you grant bail on the same terms, during the course of the trial/until further order?"

If the jury has not been excluded, the defence may address the judge on the question of bail immediately before the next adjournment of the court. The usual form of words is: **5.04.19**

"I have an application which does not concern the jury."

The judge will either exclude the jury and hear argument or the prosecution will indicate that bail is not opposed by saying, for example: **There is no objection.**

Swearing the jury

5.04.20   At the conclusion of applications the judge may say:

"Can we have the jury in now? (*i.e. Can we start?*)**"**

5.04.21   The prospective jurors are identified by name and called to the jury box by the clerk. All jurors must take the oath in the presence of each other.

5.04.22   The prosecution may "stand by" any prospective juror, for example, if it appears that the juror is incompetent or unwilling to try the case. The prosecution should not use the right to stand by jurors to obtain a pro-prosecution looking jury.

Before the juror is sworn, the prosecution may call out:

"Stand by for the Crown."

5.04.23   Challenges by the defence can only be made "for cause", namely that the juror is not a proper person to try the case. The cause must be personal to the juror.

Before the juror is sworn, the defence may call out:

"Challenge for cause."

Challenging for cause

5.04.24   The practice on challenging for cause is not clear. The following is intended as a guide:

(a) The cause should not be stated in the presence of the juror and/or jury except where the juror is known to the defendant or the defence, in which case the defence may challenge the juror as follows:

"This juror is known to the defendant/me."

(b) The jury should be excluded and the matter argued before the judge.

(c) If necessary, evidence should be called to establish the cause.

5.04.25   When all the jurors have been sworn the clerk will read the (amended, see **5.04.10(a)&(b)**) indictment to the jury and may conclude:

"To this indictment the defendant has pleaded not guilty and it is your charge to say, having heard the evidence, whether he is guilty or not."

Conduct in the presence of the jury

The parties should remember that any contact between themselves **5.04.26** and the jury should always be made through the judge. This has the effect of requiring the parties to put any question to the jury into the third person, for example:

> *"(To the jury:)* **Are the jury able to see** (*for example, a place marked on a plan*)?"

As a matter of courtesy, any documents or exhibits should only be given to the jury with the leave of the Judge.

Introductory remarks by the judge

The judge may (either at this stage or immediately before any **5.04.27** adjournment of the court):

(a) Direct the jury not to discuss the case outside court.
(b) Direct the jury that they are the judges of the facts and that when matters of law arise, they may be asked to leave court, see **5.04.40**.
(c) Direct the jury on any matter relating to time/practice.

Questions of admissibility before the prosecution opening

The judge may determine a question of admissibility before the **5.04.28** prosecution opening:

(a) Where the prosecution would have no evidence to put before the jury if that evidence were excluded, for example: where the only evidence is admissions which it is proposed to challenge in a trial within a trial, see **5.04.42–43**.
(b) Where the inclusion or exclusion of any evidence would materially affect the prosecution opening.
(c) Where it is convenient to all the parties to do so.

The usual form of words is:

> **"Before the prosecution open the case, there is a matter of law on which the prosecution/the defence/we would seek your ruling."**

For the procedure on objecting to the admissibility of evidence, see **5.04.29** **5.04.41–43**.

The case for the prosecution

5.04.30 The judge will usually indicate when he is ready for the prosecution to open the case.

Introduction of the parties to the jury

5.04.31 The prosecution will usually introduce the parties to the court, as follows:

> **"May it please** (*your honour*)**, members of the jury, I appear on behalf of the prosecution. My learned friend** (*name*) **appears on behalf of the** (*first*) **defendant who sits** (*on the left*) **in the dock** (*and so on*)**."**

The prosecution then opens the case.

Prosecution opening

5.04.32 The prosecution opening to the jury should contain:

(a) A brief introduction of the case describing the circumstances of the case in words the jury will understand.
(b) An explanation of the nature of the charge(s). Copies of the indictment may be handed to the jury (with the leave of the judge).
(c) An outline of the evidence upon which the prosecution intends to rely.
(d) An explanation of the burden and standard of proof.

5.04.33 The purpose of opening is to assist the jury (and, in a complex case, the judge and the defence) to understand the case, see **Chapter 22**, Speeches.

If the prosecution have prepared an opening note, see **5.02.10(l)**, it should have been made available to the defence and the judge before the trial. The prosecution do not provide a copy to the jury.

5.04.34 The prosecution should not open matters to the jury which are likely to be the subject of argument over admissibility, see **5.04.41–43**.

5.04.35 The prosecution may conclude the opening by saying:

> **"I have nothing further to say by way of opening the case and I now propose to call the evidence. The first witness is** (*name of witness*)**."**

The following phrase is sometimes used: "**And with your honour's leave, I now propose to call** (the first witness)." It is a elegant phrase but, strictly speaking, it is unnecessary because the leave of the judge is not required to call witnesses (except **5.04.43(vi)**).

Prosecution evidence

Witnesses subject to full witness orders

The prosecution must ensure the attendance at court of all fully bound witnesses (the old fashioned phrase "witnesses on the back of the indictment" is sometimes used) and any witness whose statement is served as a notice of additional evidence (unless dispensed with), whether or not the prosecution intend to rely on the evidence of that witness.   **5.04.36**

The witness is called and identified by the prosecution as follows: **5.04.37**

> "**Are you** (*name*)? **What is your address?** (*and, if relevant*) **What is your occupation?**"

The usual rules as to the examination, cross-examination and re-examination of witnesses apply, see **Chapter 21**, Examination of witnesses.   **5.04.38**

Objecting to evidence

A witness may be giving or about to give evidence to which the defence objects. The defence may interrupt the prosecution and/or witness as follows: **5.04.39**

> "**I object to this evidence.**"

If the evidence is clearly inadmissible (for example, hearsay), the judge may direct the prosecution, in the presence of the jury, to omit that evidence.

In any other situation and/or where there is likely to be an argument over the admissibility of the evidence the jury should be excluded.

In order to exclude the jury, either party may say: **5.04.40**

> "**There is a matter of law on which I wish to address you in the absence of the jury.**"

The judge may then explain to the jury the reason why they are being excluded from court, see **5.04.27(b)**.

Submissions on questions of admissibility

5.04.41 All matters of law (which include questions of admissibility of evidence) are decided in the absence of the jury. Where there is an argument over a question of admissibility, the order of submissions is usually as follows:

(a) Either party (usually the defence) identifies the evidence to which an objection is taken.
   (i) If the objection is on a point of law (for example, whether the evidence is hearsay) the argument can be made on the statements/depositions and no evidence need be called.
   (ii) If the objection is on mixed fact and law (for example, the circumstances in which an alleged admission was made are disputed) evidence may need to be called in a trial within a trial, see **5.04.43**.
(b) The defence gives reasons for the objection and refers to any relevant law.
(c) Reply by the prosecution.
(d) Response by the defence dealing with any new points raised by the prosecution or the judge but not repeating the submission(s) in (b).
(e) Decision by the judge.
(f) Jury recalled.

Trial within a trial (voire dire)

5.04.42 A trial within a trial takes place in the absence of the jury. It is usually held where there is argument over the admissibility of a confession or other admission by the defendant and evidence is to be called. It is usually held immediately before that evidence is called (or before the prosecution open the case to the jury, see **5.04.28**).

5.04.43 Between **5.04.41(a)(ii) and (b)** the court will usually hear evidence, as follows:

(iii) The prosecution call witness(es) to prove that an alleged confession or other admission was made by the defendant, and that it was made in circumstances that make it admissible (for example, that it was made voluntarily).
(iv) The defence will cross-examine.
(v) The prosecution may re-examine.
(vi) The defence may, with the leave of the judge (which, in practice, is never refused), call the defendant to prove that the alleged confession or other admission was not made in circumstances that make it admissible. The usual form of words is:

"With your leave, I will call the defendant."

(vii) The prosecution will cross-examine the defendant.

(viii) The defence may, with the leave of the judge (which, in practice, is never refused), call witnesses (for example a doctor who gives evidence of recent injury to the defendant on release from police custody).

5.04.41(b)–(f) should then be followed.

Witnesses subject to conditional witness orders

Conditionally bound witnesses are witnesses upon whose evidence the prosecution rely and whose evidence is not disputed by the defence.   **5.04.44**

The evidence of a conditionally bound witness is usually introduced by the prosecution as follows: **5.04.45**

"The next witness is (*name of witness*) **who is conditionally bound and whose evidence will be read."**

The judge may then say to the jury: **5.04.46**

"What this means is that the defence do not dispute the evidence of (*name of witness*)**. There is no point in him coming to court and, therefore, his statement will be read to you. But you must treat his evidence in exactly the same way as if he had come to Court and given evidence from the witness box."**

The prosecution usually reads the statement of the witness. The statement should be edited to delete any inadmissible material. The prosecution usually introduce the statement, as follows: **5.04.47**

This is the statement of (*name*) **of** (*address*) **who makes the following declaration:**

This statement consisting of (*number*) **pages, each signed by me, is true to the best of my knowledge and belief and I make it knowing that, if it is tendered in evidence, I shall be liable to prosecution if I have wilfully stated in it anything which I know to be false or do not believe to be true.**

The statement is dated (*date*)**. It is signed by** (*name of witness*) **and the signature is witnessed.**

He states: (*the statement is then read*)**.**

The evidence of subsequent conditionally bound witnesses is usually introduced by the prosecution as follows: **5.04.48**

> **"The next witness is (*name*) whose evidence will be read. The witness' address is (*address*). He makes the usual declaration (*that the statement is true*). The statement is dated (*date*).**
> **He states: (*the statement is then read*)."**

Evidence under the Criminal Justice Act 1988

5.04.49   In certain circumstances, the prosecution may read the statement of a witness even though the evidence of that witness is disputed and, by reason of it being read, that witness cannot be cross-examined by the defence.

5.04.50   The circumstances in which this can be done are briefly:

(a) The witness is dead or (very) unfit to attend.
(b) The witness is outside the UK and it is not reasonably practicable to secure his attendance.
(c) The witness cannot be found despite diligent search.

5.04.51   The prosecution do not have to give formal notice to read the statement but must apply for leave to do so at the trial. The defence may object, see **5.04.41**.

Oral admissions

5.04.52   An admission need not be in writing in the Crown Court. The prosecution may be asked to make a simple oral admission, for example, that the defendant is of good character:

> **"I am asked to make an admission that the defendant is of good character, and I do so."**

Written admissions

5.04.53   Admissions in writing are introduced by the prosecution in the following way:

> **"(*Name of defence*) and I have agreed a formal admission. It is in writing/it is typed. I hand the original, which is signed (*by both counsel*), to the court. There are copies available for the jury (*in the case of a complex or important admission*)."**

The judge will then explain the nature of an admission to the jury. The admission is then usually read to the jury by the prosecution.

Other formal evidence

Schedules, maps, plans, photographs, computer print outs, etc. may **5.04.54** be agreed and admitted in the same way, although computer print outs must be proved to have been produced on a computer that was operating properly.

A view of the locus in quo

An application for a view of the *locus in quo* may be made by either **5.04.55** party. A view attended by the judge and jury is rare.

A view means exactly what it says. It is not a discussion of the evidence at the *locus in quo*.

Close of prosecution case

When the prosecution has called and/or read all the evidence and **5.04.56** any admissions have been made, the case is said to be closed.

The usual form of words is:

> **"That is the case for the prosecution** *or, more simply,* **That is the case."**

Submission of no case to answer

A submission of no case to answer is a matter of law and is made in the **5.04.57** absence of the jury, see **5.04.40**.

The law on this subject is complex. The following is a brief guide:

In practice, the order of submissions is as follows: **5.04.58**

(a) The defence may begin:

> **"I submit that there is no case to answer** (*on count (–) of the indictment*):
> **(i) on the ground that the prosecution has failed to establish** (*an essential ingredient of the offence*)
> *and/or*
> **(ii) on the ground that the evidence is so weak that no reasonable jury, properly directed, could convict on it."**

(b) The defence should identify the evidence to which he refers and direct the judge to any relevant law.

(c) Reply by the prosecution.

(d) Response by the defence dealing with any new points raised by the prosecution or the judge but not repeating the submissions in (b).

(e) Decision by the court.

(f) Jury recalled.

5.04.59   If a submission of no case to answer is upheld in relation to one or more, but not all the counts on the indictment, the judge will usually direct the jury to find the defendant not guilty of those counts when the jury are recalled.

If the submission is upheld in respect of all the counts on the indictment, the judge will direct the jury to find the defendant not guilty of all the counts on the indictment when the jury are recalled.

The defendant is then discharged. The defence may apply for costs, see **5.04.98**.

The case for the defence

Introduction

5.04.60   In a case where there is more than one defendant, the order of presentation and speeches follows the title order in the indictment.

If a defendant is giving evidence and calling witnesses, the witnesses are called after the defendant has given evidence and before the case of the next defendant in title order in the indictment.

5.04.61   The order of cross-examination of a defendant or defence witness follows the title order in the indictment except that the prosecution cross-examine last, for example:

The third defendant (or a witness on behalf of the third defendant) has given evidence in chief. The order of cross-examination is: first defendant, second defendant, fourth defendant, prosecution. The third defendant may re-examine.

When can the defence open?

5.04.62   In practice the defence do not usually make an opening speech unless:

(a) The defence consider the jury might have difficulty understanding the defence case.

(b) The defence consider that emphasis should be given to the defence evidence (or any part of it).

5.04.63   The defence is permitted to make an opening speech where:

(a) The defendant is giving evidence and the defence are proposing to call other evidence on the facts.
(b) The defendant is not giving evidence but the defence are proposing to call other evidence on the facts.

The defence is not permitted to make an opening speech where: **5.04.64**

(a) No evidence is being called on behalf of the defendant.
(b) The defendant only is giving evidence and the defence are not proposing to call other evidence on the facts.
(c) The defence is calling character evidence only.

Defence opening speech

The defence opening may contain the following: **5.04.65**

(a) An outline of the evidence upon which the defence intends to rely (including evidence of alibi). The defence should not open the evidence in the same detail as the prosecution.
(b) A criticism of the prosecution evidence.
(c) An explanation of the burden and standard of proof.

The defence may conclude the opening by saying: **5.04.66**

"I have nothing further to say by way of opening the case and I now propose to call the defendant. (*Name*) could you come into the witness box."

Defence evidence

Evidence of the defendant

The defendant must always be called first where the defence are   **5.04.67**
calling other evidence (including evidence of character).

As a matter of practice, special care should be taken to allow the defendant to "tell his own story".

The usual rules as to the examination, cross-examination and re-   **5.04.68**
examination of witnesses apply, except see **5.04.69**.

Evidence of the defendant's character

The defendant may not be cross-examined as to credit, namely   **5.04.69**
whether he is likley, by reason of his bad character, to be untruthful. The law on this subject is complex. The following is intended as a brief guide.

5.04.70   If the defendant is of good character:

(a) The defence will usually prove the defendant's good character in cross-examination of an appropriate prosecution witness, for example:

"Is it correct that the defendant is of good character/that there are no convictions recorded against the defendant?"

(b) The defence may call the defendant to give evidence of his good character.

(c) The defence may call witnesses of the defendant's good character whether or not the defendant himself gives evidence. In practice, the prosecution do not cross-examine character witnesses but may do so.

5.04.71   If the defendant is of bad character:

(a) The defence may make imputations on the character of a prosecution witness in cross-examination but the defendant may be at risk of being cross-examined about his bad character if he gives evidence.

The prosecution may only cross-examine the defendant on his bad character with the leave of the judge.

(b) The defence may choose not to call the defendant in which case the prosecution cannot introduce evidence of his bad character.

(c) The defence may not call witnesses of the defendant's good character if, where (a) applies, the defendant does not give evidence.

(d) The defence may call evidence of the defendant's good character if, as a general rule, evidence of the defendant's bad character is also adduced: (the rule is said to be "part in, all in").

5.04.72   Where there is more than one defendant and one defendant gives evidence against a co-defendant in the same proceedings (for example, a "cut throat defence"), the co-defendant may cross-examine that defendant on his bad character.

In a case where there is likely to be an argument as to whether one defendant has given evidence against a co-defendant, the co-defendant should seek the leave of the judge (in the absence of the jury) before cross-examining that defendant on his bad character.

Defence evidence

5.04.73   The evidence on behalf of the defence is subject to the same rules and is presented in the same way as the evidence on behalf of the prosecution, see **5.04.36–54**.

Alibi evidence

Alibi witnesses are called, in the usual way, after the defendant has given evidence. **5.04.74**

Evidence of alibi may not be called unless an alibi notice has been served by the defence on the prosecution. The notice should be served within 7 days after the end of committal proceedings, see **1.05.36**. **5.04.75**

In practice, evidence of alibi may be called if the notice is served a reasonable time before the trial, see also **5.02.10(j)**, but the leave of the judge (to serve the alibi notice out of time) will be required. **5.04.76**

Close of defence case

The usual form of words is: **5.04.77**

> **"That is the case for the defence** *or, more simply,* **That is the case."**

Evidence in rebuttal and other evidence

The prosecution must apply for leave to call evidence in rebuttal. This will usually only be given where the relevance of the evidence could not possibly have been foreseen earlier. **5.04.78**

It is more likely that either party will make an application for leave to recall a witness where: **5.04.79**

(a) Either party examined that witness inadequately, for example:

> **"There is an important matter which I omitted to put to** (*name of witness*) **namely** (*state matter*). **I understand that the witness is at court/has been made available. And I would seek your leave to ask the witness about that matter."**

(b) The defence failed to examine a prosecution witness on a relevant matter. The prosecution may say:

> **"In his evidence the defendant said** (*state evidence*). **That matter was not put to** (*name of witness*). **The witness is at court/has been made available. And I would seek your leave to recall that witness in order that** (*name of defence*) **should properly challenge his evidence."**

Speeches

Legal argument before speeches

5.04.80   After the close of all the evidence, either party or the judge may:

(a) Seek clarification of relevant matters of law (usually, in order to be able to properly address the issues in speeches or summing up).

Or, the defence may, in rare circumstances:

(b) Renew a submission of no case to answer.
(c) Seek the leave of the judge for special verdict(s).

Prosecution closing speech

5.04.81   The prosecution closing speech may contain:

(a) A summary of the main points of the evidence (including the evidence of the defendant and any defence witnesses) tending to show that the defendant is guilty of the offence charged.
(b) An explanation of the burden and standard of proof.

5.04.82   ·   The prosecution should not, without good reason, make a closing speech where:

(a) The defence called no evidence.
(b) The defence called evidence but the case lasted only a short time.

The prosecution may say, for example:

> **"Members of the jury, although I am entitled to address you in closing, there is little I can add to what I said in opening/this has been a short case, and I do not propose to address you again."**

Defence closing speech

5.04.83   The defence may make a closing speech even if the defendant has not given evidence.

The defence closing speech may contain:

(a) A summary of the defence case,
(b) A summary of the weaknesses in the prosecution case,
(c) A summary of the allegations made in cross-examination of the prosecution witnesses, where each tends to show that the defendant is not guilty of the offence charged.

(d) An explanation of the burden and standard of proof.

The defence closing speech should not contain: **5.04.84**

(a) Any reference to the likely sentence if the defendant is convicted.
(b) Any reference to the defendant's instructions which are not in evidence.
(c) Any attack on the prosecution's witnesses which was not made in cross-examination.
(d) A politically motivated attack on the (prosecuting) authorities.

Summing up

Checklist

The judge's summing up should contain: **5.04.85**

(a) Functions of the judge and jury.
(b) Burden and standard of proof.
(c) The ingredients of the offence(s) charged.
(d) Separate consideration of defendants and/or counts.
(e) The effect of good or bad character.
(f) Other directions as appropriate to the case (for example: identification, corroboration, accomplice).
(g) A summary of the evidence for the prosecution.
(h) A summary of the evidence for the defence.

The defence should make a note of the judge's summing up for the purpose of advising on appeal.

The judge will usually conclude his summing up with a direction to **5.04.86** the jury to reach a unanimous verdict.

The judge will then indicate to the jury bailiff that he is ready for the jury to retire.

Correcting errors in the judge's summing up

A party should exercise care before correcting an error in the judge's **5.04.87** summing up. If necessary, it should be done before the jury bailiff takes the jury oath.

As a rough guide, the jury should be excluded where the correction is on a matter of law or mixed law and fact. The prosecution or the defence may say:

> **"Before the jury bailiff is sworn, there is a matter on which I would wish to address you in in the absence of the jury."**

5.04.88   Despite the authorities to the contrary, a correction may be made by either party. It should only be made where the judge has made an important error either in law or in fact, for example:

> **"You omitted to summarise to the jury the evidence of the defendant. Perhaps that is a matter which you would wish to consider."**

Retirement of the jury

5.04.89   After the jury bailiff has taken the jury oath, the jury will retire to consider their verdicts.

The jury may take with them:

(a) Any exhibits (or copy exhibits)
(b) Any documents or copy documents produced during the trial.
(c) Any notes made during the trial.

Questions from the jury

5.04.90   A question from the jury is usually written down and handed (via the jury bailiff) to the judge who will hand it to the parties for consideration. The judge will usually canvass the parties in open court (in the absence of the jury) for an agreed answer.

When the jury return to court, the judge will answer the question but the jury may not:

(a) Hear further evidence.
(b) Hear submissions from either party.

Majority direction

5.04.91   The judge may give a majority direction after at least 2 hours 10 minutes. The judge will usually ask both parties (in the absence of the jury):

> **"I propose to give a majority direction. Do either of you have anything to say about that?"**

5.04.92   The majority varies according to the size of the jury:

Number of jurors	Size of the majority
12	11–1 or 10–2
11	10–1
10	9–1
9	(Majority verdict not permitted)

Verdicts

The jury must return verdicts (of guilty or not guilty) on each count and in respect of each defendant unless the judge has discharged them from giving a verdict, see **5.04.59**, (or where there are alternative counts on the indictment).   **5.04.93**

If the majority direction has been given, the jury will be required to state the size of the majority only where the defendant is found guilty.   **5.04.94**

A special verdict may be returned where, by agreement between the parties and the judge after legal argument, see **5.04.80(c)**, the jury have been asked to consider it.   **5.04.95**

If the verdict is guilty, see **Chapter 7**, Sentencing.   **5.04.96**

If the verdict is not guilty, the defence will usually say: **5.04.97**

"Could the defendant be discharged?"

Costs

The defence may make an application for the defendant's costs, see **20.02.20–27**, for example: **5.04.98**

"Would you make a defendant's costs order?"

The effect of the order is that costs reasonably incurred by the defendant are paid out of central funds. There is no power to reimburse the defendant for loss of income during the trial.

Appeal

Appeal against conviction and/or sentence is to the Court of Appeal, see **Chapter 11**, Court of Appeal (Criminal Division).   **5.04.99**
The notice of application for leave to appeal either conviction or sentence and the grounds of appeal must be served on the Crown Court within 28 days.

If sentence is delayed, it may be necessary to serve the notice and grounds of appeal against conviction before the final disposal of the case.

5. APPEAL OF REFUSAL OF BAIL

Introduction

5.05.01 Where a magistrates' court has refused bail, the defence may appeal to the Crown Court.

5.05.02 The application is made on notice on a standard form which must be accompanied by the full argument certificate (from the magistrates' court, see **4.03.02**), to the Crown Court and to the prosecution at least 24 hours before the hearing.

5.04.03 The court may also require the defence to complete a form stating the reasons for the bail application, the address at which the defendant proposes to live, the names of any potential sureties, etc.

Practice

5.05.04 The application is a rehearing of the bail application before the magistrates' court.

5.05.05 The application is heard in chambers (usually in court although it may be in the judge's room). The defendant is usually not produced for the hearing.

It is a more informal hearing than the original application to the magistrates' court, in part, because the defendant is not present. The defence should avoid open court style of advocacy.

5.05.06 For right of audience, see **5.01.02**.

5.05.07 If the application is in the judge's room, the parties are not robed. The judge is addressed as **judge**.

If the application is heard in chambers in court, the parties are not robed. However, the advocate should beware that in some courts (and the Central Criminal Court) the parties are robed. For mode of address, see **5.01.03**.

Conduct

If the hearing is in chambers in court, any person addressing the court   **5.05.08**
should do so standing. If the hearing is in the judge's room, the parties
will usually remain seated.

Practice

Follow the practice in **4.02.02–14**. If bail is granted with sureties,   **5.05.09**
these are usually taken by a court clerk after the hearing.

6: APPEAL TO THE CROWN COURT AGAINST CONVICTION

Introduction

An appeal to the Crown Court against conviction is heard by a judge   **5.06.01**
and usually two magistrates.

An appeal against conviction can only be made where the appellant   **5.06.02**
pleaded not guilty at the magistrates'/youth court. If the appellant
pleaded guilty at the magistrates'/youth court (for example, as a result of
misunderstanding the nature of the charge) he must apply to the Crown
Court for leave to appeal.

The appeal is a rehearing of the case before the magistrates'/youth   **5.06.03**
court. This means that either party may call witnesses who were not
called (or not call witnesses who were called) at the magistrates'/youth
court.

Practice

Attendance of the appellant

The appellant must attend. If he fails to do so, his appeal will usually   **5.06.04**
be dismissed unless he has been involuntarily detained. If the appellant
was sentenced to imprisonment or detention his solicitors must inform
the prison or young offender institution to arrange for his production.
Note: It is the appellant's application and therefore there is no power
to issue a warrant to secure his attendance.

5.06.05 **Identification of the appellant**

The clerk may say:

"This is an appeal against conviction by (*name*)**. Are you** (*name*)**?"**

If the appellant is produced from prison or young offender institution he will sit in the dock. In any other case, the court will usually arrange for the appellant to sit near his legal representatives.

Introduction of the parties

5.06.06 The respondent opens the case:

"I appear on behalf of the respondent in this case. (*Name*) **appears on behalf of the appellant."**

Respondent's opening

5.06.07 The respondent may then say:

"The appellant was convicted before the (*name*) **magistrates'/ youth court on** (*date*) **of** (*state briefly the nature of the offence*)**.**
    He now appeals against that conviction/finding of guilt by a notice of appeal dated (*date*) **on the ground(s) that** (*state briefly the nature of the ground(s), or*) **he is not guilty of the offence."**

5.06.08 Although the Crown Court will have a copy of the notice of appeal, the judge and magistrates will not usually know the sentence or order imposed by the magistrates'/youth court.

It is not considered good practice to state, in opening, the sentence or order imposed.

Practice

5.06.09 Repeat the practice in: **1.06** Summary trial or **2.02** Criminal trial in the youth court.

Decision

5.06.10 At the conclusion of the hearing, the judge announces the decision of the court (either with or without a short judgment):

"This appeal is allowed *or* **This appeal is dismissed."**

Care should be taken to ensure that the appellant understands the decision. It often happens that an appellant, hearing the word "dismissed", believes that the charge against him has been dismissed whereas, in fact, he has lost the appeal.

Reviewing the sentence

If the appeal is dismissed, sentence is said to be "at large" even if the sentence has not been appealed. This means that the sentence can be reviewed and, in some cases, increased provided that any sentence imposed by the Crown Court could have been imposed by the magistrates'/youth court.

5.06.11

Guidelines

The judge may say to the respondent:

5.06.12

"Could you tell us what sentence was passed by the magistrates'/ youth court?"

After having heard the details of any sentence or order, the judge may say to the appellant:

"Do you want to address us on sentence?"

If sentence was appealed, the appellant may address the court in mitigation, see **7.04.01–15**.

5.06.13

If sentence was not appealed or the appellant no longer wishes to appeal against sentence, the appellant may say:

5.06.14

"Sentence was not appealed *or* The appellant does not wish to appeal against sentence."

The judge may say:

5.06.15

"But sentence is at large *or* We may want to reconsider the sentence/order. Do you want to address us on sentence?"

This may mean that the court is considering reviewing the sentence (and may indicate to the appellant any proposed sentence). A short plea in mitigation may be made or the appellant may say:

"There's nothing I wish to say."

Or, the judge may say:

5.06.17

"But this court has power to increase the sentence."

This may mean that the court is considering increasing the sentence and a full plea in mitigation may be made.

Sentence

5.06.18   The court will then proceed to sentence.

Costs

5.06.19   (a) If the appeal is allowed, the court may make a defendants' costs order, see **20.02.22(b).**
        (b) If the appeal is dismissed, the court may order the appellant to pay the respondent's costs, see **20.02.09(c).**

Appeal

5.06.20   In practice, there is no appeal from the decision of the Crown Court except (in very rare circumstances) an appeal by way of case stated to the Divisional Court of the QBD on a point of law only, see **13.04** Appeals to the Divisional Court.

7. APPEAL TO THE CROWN COURT AGAINST SENTENCE

Introduction

5.07.01   An appeal to the Crown Court against sentence is heard by a judge and usually two magistrates.

5.07.02   The appeal is a rehearing of sentencing before the magistrates'/youth court. The sentence is "at large", see **5.06.11**.

Practice

5.07.03   For attendance and identification of the appellant and introduction of the parties, see **5.06.04–06.**

Respondent's opening

The respondent may then say: **5.07.04**

"The appellant was convicted/pleaded guilty before the (*name*)
magistrates'/youth court on (*date*) **of** (*state briefly the nature of
the offence*) **and received a sentence of** (*state sentence*). **He now
appeals against that sentence."**

The respondent may then continue: **5.07.05**

"The facts of the case are:"

Repeat the practice in **Chapter 7**, Sentencing.   **5.07.06**

Sentence

At the conclusion of the hearing, the judge announces the decision of **5.07.07**
the court (either with or without a short judgment):

**"This court will allow the appeal and substitute the following
sentence:** (*The appellant is re-sentenced*). **or This appeal is
dismissed."**

Costs

(a) If the appeal is allowed, the court may make a defendant's costs **5.07.08**
    order, see **20.02.22(b).**
(b) If the appeal is dismissed, the court may order the appellant to
    pay the respondent's costs, see **20.02.09(c)).**

Appeal

In practice, there is no appeal from the decision of the Crown Court **5.07.09**
except (in very rare circumstances) where the sentence is wrong in law
(when an appeal may be made by way of case stated to the Divisional
Court of the QBD, see **13.04** Appeals to the Divisional Court).

It sometimes happens that because the Crown Court is considering **5.07.10**
magistrates/youth court penalties, see **5.06.11**, that the court imposes a
sentence which is wrong in law. Where this happens, rather than
appeal, the appellant may invite the court office to re-list the case

before the same judge so that the sentence can be corrected under the "slip rule".

8. COMMITTAL FOR SENTENCE

Introduction

5.08.01 A committal to the Crown Court for sentence is heard by a judge and usually two magistrates.

5.08.02 If the magistrates' court is of the opinion that: "a longer custodial sentence should be inflicted [on the defendant] than it has power to impose having regard to the seriousness of the offence (or in the case of a sexual or violent offence) is necessary to protect the public from serious harm from [the defendant]", see **1.04.17**, in rare circumstances it may commit the defendant to the Crown Court for sentence. The defendant is usually committed in custody.

5.08.03 The magistrates' court may also commit the defendant to the Crown Court for sentence where the defendant already has outstanding matters before the Crown Court and it is proper that the defendant is sentenced for all matters at the same time.

Practice

Attendance of the defendant

5.08.04 If the defendant is not committed in custody, he must attend. If he does not attend, a warrant may be issued to secure his attendance, see **1.02.03**.

Identification of the defendant

5.08.05 The clerk may say:

> **"Are you** (*name*)**? On** (*date*) **were you convicted/did you plead guilty, before the** (*name*) **magistrates' court of** (*state offence*)**? And were you committed from that court to this for sentence?"**

5.08.06 The practice in **Chapter 7**, Sentencing is then followed.

9. APPEAL TO THE CROWN COURT IN LICENSING PROCEEDINGS

Introduction

An appeal in licensing proceedings is heard by a judge and usually 4 **5.09.01** magistrates, 2 of whom must be magistrates in the petty sessional area in which the case originated.

The appeal is a rehearing of the proceedings before the magistrates' **5.09.02** court. The appeal is heard in open court.

The applicant or the objector or an aggrieved party may appeal to the **5.09.03** Crown Court although an objector to the grant of a licence who did not object to the application at the magistrates court may not appeal to the Crown Court.

The parties may include a barrister appearing on behalf of the licensing justices.

Either party may call witnesses who were not called (or not call **5.09.04** witnesses who were called) at the magistrates' court.

Practice

Attendance of the parties

If the appellant does not attend, the appeal will usually be dismissed. **5.09.05** If the respondent does not attend, the appeal may be heard in his absence.

Identification of the parties

If the appeal is in relation to a public house, it may be listed in the **5.09.06** court list under the name of the public house, rather than the name of the appellant. The clerk (or the applicant/respondent) may say:

> **"This is an appeal of a refusal/grant/revocation of a** (*state type of*) **licence in respect of** (*title and address of premises*) **by** (*state name of appellant*)."

Practice

The practice in **1.08.03–30** is then followed except service/display/ **5.09.07** advertisement of the notice of application need not be proved, see **1.08.14–15**.

Costs

5.09.08   The Crown Court has power to award costs to the successful party. The parties should be ready to state their costs to the court in the event of a successful appeal.

CHAPTER 6

Court Martial

1. INTRODUCTION

Court martial

A court martial is a court which is convened to try any person subject **6.01.01**
to service (Army, Air Force or Royal Navy) law (including civilians).

Army, Royal Air Force and Royal Navy court martials

This chapter explains the practice principally in an army court **6.01.02**
martial with some guidance on the different practices in courts martial
in the other services.

There are three types of court martial: **6.01.03**

(a) A General Court Martial (in which the total sentence is open).
(b) A District Court Martial (not RN) (in which the the total sentence
    available to the court should not exceed 2 years imprisonment).
(c) A Field General Court Martial (which is convened only during
    times of war or states of emergency), not described in this section.

General Court Martial (GCM)

In an army General Court Martial, the court will consist of a president **6.01.04**
who is usually a brigadier or a full colonel. The other members are
usually either lieutenant colonels, majors or captains.

In the RAF the president is a group captain. The other members are
usually the Permanent President of Courts Martial (PPCM) who is a wing
commander, a squadron leader and two flight lieutenants.

In the navy the president is a captain. The other members are usually commanders, lieutenant commanders or lieutenants. Where a Royal Marine is charged, a Royal Marine will usually be a member.

A judge advocate must sit with a General Court Martial.

District Court Martial (DCM)

6.01.05   In an army District Court Martial, the court will consist of a president who is usually a major. The other members are usually captains or lieutenants.

In the RAF the president is the usually the PPCM or sometimes another wing commander. The other members are a squadron leader and a flight lieutenant. The Royal Navy does not have the equivalent of a DCM.

A judge advocate may sit with a District Court Martial depending on the complexity of the case.

An officer may not be tried by a District Court Martial.

The Judge Advocate (JA)

6.01.06   The role of the judge advocate is very similar to that of a Crown Court judge. He will decide all matters of law and will sum up the evidence at the end of the case.

His advice on the law must be followed by the board. He may be asked to deal with certain matters such as the admissibility of evidence in the absence of the board, see **5.04.41**.

The judge advocate takes no part in reaching a decision on the facts.

The advocate

6.01.07   An advocate wishing to appear before a court martial on legal aid should apply to the MOD to have his name enrolled on the Army, RAF or Royal Naval courts martial lists.

6.01.08   Whether an advocate is instructed to appear before a court martial will depend largely upon the nature of the offence(s) and likely plea(s).

2. PRACTICE BEFORE THE HEARING

Investigation of the offence

6.02.01   Where a soldier/airman/rating is suspected of having committed a (military or civil) offence, the matter will be investigated by the service police.

During the investigation, the soldier may be held either in open or close arrest or (usually) not at all. There is no provision as to bail.

A private soldier in close arrest, or an NCO in any form of arrest, **6.02.02** hands over his duties, does not attend parades and merely keeps himself clean. A private soldier in open arrest may be ordered to perform all duties and attend parades.

Once the investigation has been concluded, the statements, records **6.02.03** of interview and any documentary exhibits are fowarded to the local office of the Army Legal Corps (ALC) or (in the RAF) the Directorate of Legal Services (DLS) who will advise the convening authority on the appropriate charges. There are different procedures in the RN, see **6.02.11**. The convening authority is (in the army) a Division or (in the RAF) a Group or Command or (in the RN) a ship (which includes establishments ashore).

The convening authority then decides what charges go ahead for trial.

Summary dealing

The commanding officer may deal summarily with certain less **6.02.04** serious charges and hear the evidence himself or he may order an abstract or a summary of evidence.

The commanding officer must give the accused the choice of being tried by court martial where the punishment is other than a severe reprimand, reprimand, admonishment, any other minor punishment or a (usually small) forfeiture of pay. The offence may be, for example, failing to attend for duty or common assault.

If the accused is dealt with summarily, the practice is similar to a summary trial in the magistrates' court before the commanding officer.

If the accused accepts the commanding officer's jurisdiction, he is **6.02.05** also agreeing to accept his award (sentence) (if found guilty). The commanding officer may say:

"Will you accept my award or do you wish to be tried by court martial?"

Election for trial by court martial

If the commanding officer has no jurisdiction to try the offences or the **6.02.06** accused elects to be tried by court martial, the commanding officer must order an abstract or a summary of evidence.

Abstracts of evidence and summaries of evidence

6.02.07   An abstract of evidence is usually prepared by an officer of the ALC or, in the RAF, by the "P1" (personnel one) officer of the unit assisted by an officer of the DLS.

He may assemble all the statements and other documents into an abstract of evidence.

6.02.08   A summary of evidence is usually prepared by an officer of the ALC or, in the RAF, by an officer appointed by the commanding officer with advice from an officer from the DLS. The officer holding the summary will examine the witnesses.

Witnesses give their evidence on oath and are subject to cross-examination by the accused or his defending officer. The accused may be represented by an officer of another legal branch or by counsel or solicitor at his own expense. Legal aid is not available until after he has been remanded for trial by court martial.

6.02.09   The summary of evidence is similar to an old style committal, see **1.05.22–25**, except that no submissions are made.

6.02.10   The evidence, once completed in either abstract or summary form, is then submitted together with the charge sheet to the commanding officer who will then remand the accused for trial by court martial.

6.02.11   There is no separate process of producing abstracts or summaries of evidence in the Royal Navy.

In the Royal Navy, where a serious offence has been committed, the commanding officer will submit a report called a circumstantial letter to the office of the Commander in Chief (CINC) Fleet or to the office of his Area Flag Officer, together with all documentary evidence and statements. The Fleet legal adviser to the CINC Fleet or the staff legal adviser to the Area Flag Office will examine the charges and the supporting evidence and advise his Admiral whether or not to proceed to court martial. The Admiral may then authorise a court martial.

Documents

6.02.12   The accused should be given:

(a) A copy of the charge sheet.
(b) A copy of the abstract or summary of evidence.
(c) The names of any witnesses upon whom the prosecution does not intend to rely (unused material).
(d) Notice of any additional evidence.
(e) The names of the president and members of the court martial (which will be on a copy of the convening order).

The right to legal advice

Once the accused has been remanded by his commanding officer for trial by court martial, he has the right to seek legal advice from an officer of the ALC (army or, sometimes, RAF) or (RAF and RN) directly from a civilian solicitor or barrister usually on legal aid or (RN only) from a naval barrister. **6.02.13**

The interview will be arranged by the accused's unit/squadron/ship. The accused will attend together with his defending officer (an officer, acceptable to the accused, appointed by the commanding officer). **6.02.14**

The purpose of the interview is: **6.02.15**

(a) To provide the accused with some general advice about the charges and the evidence against him.
(b) To make a preliminary assessment as to the likely plea(s).
(c) (Army only). To ascertain whether the accused requires representation by a barrister or solicitor and, if so, whether the accused wishes to apply for legal aid.

Representation

The accused may be represented by: **6.02.16**

(a) A civilian barrister or solicitor (nominated by the accused or appointed by the Ministry of Defence, see **6.01.08**), either under the legal aid scheme or at his own expense (where legal aid is refused).
(b) An officer of the ALC or a legal officer from another service.
(c) The accused's defending officer (usually where the offence is not serious and the plea is guilty).

Application for legal aid

(Army only, for the RAF and RN see **6.02.13**). If an accused decides to apply for legal aid, the application is submitted by the interviewing ALC officer to the Ministry of Defence. **6.02.17**

Appointment of counsel/solicitor advocate

If the accused is unable to nominate a barrister or solicitor, the MOD will appoint one on his behalf, see **6.01.07**. **6.02.18**

(Army only). The ALC officer who conducted the interview will usually prepare and foward to the MOD for the attention of counsel: **6.02.19** (a)–(e) See **6.02.12(a)–(e).**

(f) A note to assist counsel.

(g) Any other relevant information.

6.02.20   The MOD will prepare the brief and formally instruct counsel.

6.02.21   If counsel requires further evidence (including the evidence of any witness for the defence) or any other assistance he should contact the accused's defending officer.

In more serious cases (and RAF and RN, usually), counsel may approach the MOD if he requires a conference with the accused. In practice, counsel will usually prepare the case on the papers and will have a conference with the accused on the day before the court martial.

3. PRACTICE AT THE HEARING

Introduction

Right of audience

6.03.01   Barristers, solicitors, serving officers, accused in person.

Dress

6.03.   Barristers and solicitor advocates are robed.

Serving officers and soldiers taking part in the proceedings will be in full number 2 (RAF, number 1; and RN, number 4, or number 1 for ratings and WRNS) uniform (RN, with sword).

Military personnel, other than the accused, wear head-dress until the court has been convened. It is then removed and not worn again during the proceedings, usually until verdict.

If ordered, officers (except the accused) will also wear a sword.

Mode of address

6.03.03 Judge advocate:	**Sir**
Any officer of the court:	**Sir**
The advocate may also say:	**(Sir), Mr President and gentlemen of the court**

Conduct

6.03.04   The conduct of the hearing is highly formal. A court martial is, in fact, a parade. It is much more ceremonial than civilian court proceedings.

The president is likely to proceed on the basis that everyone involved has been fully briefed on the procedure.

Seating

At a district court martial, the 3 members of the court (and in some cases, the judge advocate), and at a general court martial, the 5 members of the court and the judge advocate, will sit at a table facing the court room. They are called the board. **6.03.05**

The prosecuting officer will sit at a table on the left hand side of the court room facing the board. **6.03.06**
Witnesses will sit beside the table, facing the court, to give evidence (unless a witness box is provided).

The defending officer and/or advocate will sit at a table on the right hand side of the court room facing the board. **6.03.07**
The accused and his escort will sit beside the table, facing the board.

Officers under instruction will sit either side of the board between them and the prosecuting officer and/or defence advocate (sometimes resembling a jury, although they take no part in the proceedings). **6.03.08**

Addressing the court

Any party addressing the court or examining or cross-examining a witness should do so standing. **6.03.09**

Burden and standard of proof

A court martial is a criminal court. The burden of proof is on the prosecution. The standard of proof is "beyond reasonable doubt". **6.03.10**

Order of presentation

The order of presentation and speeches follows the title order of the case. **6.03.11**

Witnesses

Witnesses should remain outside court until called to give evidence, but see **6.03.19**. After giving evidence, a witness may be released or required to remain outside the court. **6.03.12**

The civilian advocate at the court martial

6.03.13   If the court martial is taking place outside the United Kingdom, the advocate will usually be accommodated by the accused's regiment/squadron. In the RN, the accused is almost always brought back to the UK for trial.

6.03.14   On the day of the court martial, the defence advocate will be conveyed to the court martial centre or the room in which the court martial is being held by the defending officer.

The defending officer will usually remain in attendance throughout the proceedings to assist the defence advocate.

6.03.15   At the court martial centre or room, the defence advocate will be provided with robing accommodation and a room in which to interview the accused.

The accused at the court martial

6.03.16   The accused will have a medical examination on the morning of the first day of the trial.

During the proceedings, the accused will be in close arrest and in the custody of an escort (although not handcuffed). The convening officer may direct that he be in open arrest while the court is not actually sitting.

Practice

Opening the proceedings

6.03.17   At the appointed time, the board will be seated in the court martial room. The door is likely to be closed. The defence advocate should not enter the court martial room until invited to do so.

The president will then order the court orderly to bring in the parties. The parties should be ready. The officers will be wearing head-dress.

Entering the court martial room

6.03.18   When the court martial room door opens, the prosecuting officer walks smartly to the centre of the room and salutes the board.

The defence advocate walks in either behind or with the prosecuting officer. He will be followed by his defending officer. The advocate stands next to the prosecuting officer and bows. The advocate then goes to his table and stands behind his chair until invited to sit.

The prosecuting officer then goes to his table and stands behind his chair until invited to sit.

Attendance of witnesses and the public

The president will then order the court orderly to bring in the **6.03.19** witnesses to hear the convening order read. The court orderly will then march the service witnesses into the court martial room. The civilian witnesses will walk in. The president will then invite members of the public into the court martial room.

Attendance of the accused

The president will then order the court orderly to march in the **6.03.20** accused.

The accused will be marched in together with his escort. The accused will not be wearing head-dress. The escort will be wearing head-dress. He will carry the accused's headress under his left arm. (RN) The accused officer surrenders his sword and it rests "athwart-ships" on the table in front of the president.

The accused will be halted in front of the board.

Identification of the accused

The judge advocate or the president will identify the accused, for **6.03.21** example:

> **"Are you** (*number, rank, name*)**?"**

At this point, or before the prosecuting officer goes to his table, see **6.03.22** **6.03.18**, the prosecuting officer usually hands to the president a medical certificate showing that the accused is fit to be tried. He is also likely to hand to him a certificate signed by the accused acknowledging his right to be medically examined at any stage.

Convening the court

The judge advocate or the president will then usually tell the accused **6.03.23** that he is going to read the convening order and that, if he does not understand either the convening order or any of the proceedings, he is free to consult with his advocate at any stage.

He will then read the convening order which includes the names of the officers appointed to form the board. The accused will be asked if he objects to any of them. Whenever possible the defending officer should inform the convening authority of any objections in advance.

If there is an objection, the waiting member will then come foward. If there is more than one objection, the court will adjourn to find another officer(s).

6.03.24   The court is then sworn. The judge advocate will usually administer the oath to the president and members.

Where there is no judge advocate, the president will usually administer the oath to the members and the senior member will administer the oath to the president.

All military personnel remove their head-dress.

6.03.25   The witnesses are then marched out of (or invited to leave) court. If there are officers under instruction, the judge advocate or the president may explain that they play no part in the proceedings.

Preliminary applications

6.03.26   Either party may make any preliminary application(s) to the court, for example, an application for a (short) adjournment or a plea to the jurisdiction, before the accused is arraigned (see **5.04.07–10**). The party may say:

> **"Before the accused is arraigned, there is a preliminary matter upon which I would seek to address the court."**

The arraignment

6.03.27   The judge advocate or the president will then read the charge to the accused.

The accused should plead guilty or not guilty.

6.03.28   If the accused pleads not guilty, the court will proceed to trial, see **6.03.30**.

6.03.29   If the accused pleads guilty and the board is satisfied that the accused understands the nature and consequences of his plea the board will formally find him guilty, subject to confirmation.

The advocate should note, when advising the accused on his plea, that the judge advocate or the president is obliged to question the accused as to whether:

(a) He understands the legal ingredients of the charge.
(b) He understands the consequences of a plea of guilty, including an explanation of what would happen if his plea were not guilty.
(c) He is still content to plead guilty, after considering (a) and (b).

The court will then proceed to sentence, see **6.03.37–42**.

Conduct of the trial

The conduct of the trial is identical to a trial on indictment in the **6.03.30** Crown Court. A submission of no case to answer may be made.

The practice in **5.04.30–84** should be followed.

If the case is not concluded on the first day, the court adjourns in the usual way.

Summing up

At the conclusion of the case, the judge advocate will sum up the **6.03.31** case, see **5.04.85**.

The judge advocate then withdraws from the court martial room and the court will be closed, or the board will retire in order to consider its verdict.

Where there is no judge advocate, the board will consider its verdict without a summing up.

The verdict

After considering its verdict the board will return to the court martial **6.03.32** room. The door is likely to be closed. The president will then order the court orderly to bring in the parties.

The parties assemble as in **6.03.18.** The accused is marched in last. All parties except the accused should be wearing head-dress.

There are some very rough indications as to the likely verdict. If the **6.03.33** board is not wearing head-dress, the verdict is likely to be guilty because head-dress is only worn again at the conclusion of the case (avoiding putting it on and then taking it off again). (Navy only) If the accused's sword on the table is pointing to the accused, the verdict is guilty.

The president then announces the verdict. **6.03.34**

If the verdict is not guilty, the accused is discharged. The verdict is **6.03.35** not subject to confirmation. The accused may apply to the MOD for a refund of defence costs.

If the verdict is guilty, the court will then proceed to sentence. **6.03.36**

Sentence

Prosecution opening (plea of guilty)

The prosecution will open the facts from the abstract or summary of **6.03.37** evidence in as much detail as is thought necessary. The prosecution will read or summarise any statement made by the accused.

123

The prosecution may then offer to read any other matter from the abstract or summary of evidence requested by the defence, see **7.01.03–04**.

Plea in mitigation by defending officer after plea of guilty

6.03.38   Where the accused has pleaded guilty and he is represented by a defending officer, the defending officer will mitigate (usually in writing) before **6.03.39–40**.

The reason for this is that, if the defending officer (who is not legally qualified) pleads in mitigation matters which are inconsistent with a plea of guilty, the court will not be prejudiced in then hearing the case because it will not have heard, at that stage, the matters in **6.03.39–40**.

The defending advocate may mitigate at this stage or, more usually, at **6.03.42**.

Evidence of service record and antecedent history

6.03.39   The prosecution will call an officer to give evidence of the accused's service record and to produce his conduct sheets.

The prosecution will then read or call evidence of any previous civil convictions not recorded against the accused on his conduct sheets.

6.03.40   The prosecution will then call an officer (usually the adjutant of the accused's unit) to tender to the court a statement of evidence under RP71(3) which includes all the accused's details, his family background and any relevant reasons which point to his commission of the offence. The statement may conclude with the words:

> **"His commanding officer does/does not wish to retain him in the unit/squadron. (*RN*) (*Name*) is/is not an asset to the service."**

6.03.41   The defence advocate may cross-examine any officer called by the prosecution.

Plea in mitigation after verdict of guilty or by defence advocate after plea of guilty

6.03.42   The advocate may make a plea in mitigation, see **7.04.02–15**.

In a court martial, the contents of the plea may be taken down by the judge advocate or the president. The advocate should be prepared to take the plea in mitigation slowly.

Sentence

6.03.43   At the conclusion of the plea in mitigation, the board may retire or the court may be closed to consider sentence. If a judge advocate is present, he will usually remain with the board to advise them on tariff and ensure that the sentence is not wrong in law or in principle. When the court is ready to sentence the accused the parties will re-assemble as in **6.03.18**.

The accused is then sentenced.

Confirmation of sentence

Every finding of guilt and sentence by a court martial is subject to confirmation by the confirming officer. This may take some weeks especially if the proceedings need to be transcribed. **6.03.44**

Petition to confirming officer

An accused may petition the confirming officer against a finding of guilt and/or sentence. **6.03.45**

The form of the petition is similar to the draft grounds of appeal, see **11.01.08**.

Appeal

If the finding of guilt and/or sentence is confirmed, the accused may petition the Army/RAF/Admiralty Board. **6.03.46**

If the appeal is against conviction and an appeal to the Army/RAF/Admiralty Board has been unsuccessful, the accused has the right to appeal to the Court Martial Appeal Court.

A civilian convicted by a court martial may appeal to the Court Martial Appeal Court against sentence.

Appeal from the Court Martial Appeal Court is, with leave, to the House of Lords. **6.03.47**

CHAPTER 7

Sentencing

Introduction

7.01.01 This section is intended for use in any court having the jurisdiction to consider and/or review sentence.
It will follow on from:

(a) A plea or summary trial in the magistrates' court.
(b) A plea or trial in the youth court.
(c) A plea, trial, appeal against conviction/sentence or committal for sentence in the Crown Court.
(d) A plea or trial in a court martial.
(e) An appeal against sentence in the Court of Appeal.

This section is designed to illustrate the practice in these courts. It is impossible to describe here the powers of the courts, which should be researched in the appropriate practice manuals.

Practice

Introduction of the parties

7.02.01 If this has not already been done, the prosecution will usually introduce the parties.

Adjournment for pre-sentence reports before opening

If a pre-sentence report has not been prepared, the defence should **7.02.02** inform the court at this stage in order that the court may adjourn the case for the preparation of a pre-sentence report before the prosecution open the facts (or, after **7.04.01**, if the same judge/bench will be sentencing the defendant at the adjourned hearing).

Presenting the facts of the case

The prosecution should open the facts of the case in as much detail as is **7.02.03** thought necessary depending upon the court and/or the nature of the offence.

The prosecution do not usually open the facts where the defendant is sentenced by the same court which convicted him after a trial except where the defendant has pleaded guilty to other offences and the facts of those offences have not been opened.

The prosecution opening should contain: **7.02.04**

(a) An outline of the facts of the offence. Where the facts are disputed, see **7.02.05−10**.
(b) Particulars of any injury or loss (as appropriate).
(c) Reference to any aggravating or mitigating feature of the offence.
(d) A summary of any explanation made by the defendant.

The prosecution should open the facts of the case fairly and not emotively.

Calling evidence of the facts: A "Newton hearing"

A defendant is entitled to be sentenced only for the admitted facts of **7.02.05** the offence to which he has pleaded guilty. If the defendant pleaded not guilty and has been found guilty after a trial, he will be sentenced on the version of the facts proved against him.

A significant dispute by the defence of the facts of the case will **7.02.06** usually only become relevant where there is likely to be a substantial difference in sentencing, depending on which version of the facts is accepted by the court, for example, the defendant accepts an assault by punching the victim but denies using a weapon.

The prosecution may call evidence in a "Newton hearing" to prove **7.02.07** the version of the facts put foward by the prosecution if the dispute

127

cannot be resolved by agreement (although courts are becoming increasingly reluctant to hold a "Newton hearing").

The prosecution or the defence may introduce a possible "Newton hearing" as follows:

> **"The prosecution allege that** (*state briefly the case against the defendant*). **The defendant contends that** (*state main point(s) of dispute between the parties*). **Perhaps** (*the court*) **could indicate whether it will be necessary to hold a "Newton hearing"."**

The court will then indicate whether it will sentence the defendant on his version of the facts or whether the prosecution should call evidence of the facts.

7.02.08 In a "Newton hearing" the usual standard of proof in criminal proceedings applies. If the court is left in some doubt as to whether the prosecution's version of the facts is correct, the defendant should be sentenced only for the admitted facts of the offence.

7.02.09 The practice in a "Newton hearing" is usually as follows:

(a) The prosecution will usually open the main points of dispute between the parties to assist the court in understanding the issues.

(b) The prosecution will call witness(es) to give evidence on the issues in dispute.

(c) The defence will usually cross-examine.

(d) The defence may call the defendant and/or witness(es) on his behalf to give evidence (except where the prosecution case has been discredited by cross-examination).

(e) The prosecution may cross-examine the defendant, and/or witnesses, if called.

(f) The defence may address the court on the facts.

(g) Decision by the court.

7.02.10 The court should express its view on the facts before hearing mitigation, for example:

> **"**(*The court*) **is minded to sentence on the basis that** (*state basis, for example*: **We accept the evidence of the victim).**"

- OMIT (magistrates' court only) **7.03.01–7.04.05** if unit fines apply.

- OMIT **7.03.01–03** if there are no offences to be taken into consideration. Continue at **7.03.04**.

Offences to be taken into consideration

After opening the facts of the case, or after **7.03.11**, the prosecution   **7.03.01**
may refer the court to any (usually similar) offences which the defendant is asking to be taken into consideration. The prosecution may say:

> **"The defendant is asking for** (*state number*) **offences, namely**
> (*state offences, if necessary*) **to be taken into consideration.**
> **There is a form signed by the defendant.**
>   (*To the court*) **Could those matters be put to the defendant?"**

The clerk (although sometimes the court) may say: **7.03.02**

> **"**(*Name of defendant*)**, have you read and signed this form? Does**
> **it contain details of** (*state number*) **offences committed by you?**
> **Do you wish the court to take these offences into consideration**
> **when dealing with you for the offence to which you have**
> **pleaded guilty/the offence of which you have been convicted?"**

The prosecution may then give details of the offences to be taken into   **7.03.03**
consideration, as required by the court. This may include the brief facts
and/or any application for compensation or forfeiture.

Presenting the defendant's previous convictions/breaches

The prosecution will usually give details of any previous convictions   **7.03.04**
and breaches of court orders/sentences, see **7.03.10–11**. In the Crown
Court the prosecution may call an officer in the case or a liason/
antecedents officer to give these details. The prosecution should check
the practice of the court.

The prosecution may say: **7.03.05**

> **"**(*To the court*) **Do you have** (*a list of previous convictions*)
> **relating to the defendant** (*name*)**?"**

The list may be variously titled depending on the court and the police
force involved.

> **"The defendant was born on** (*date*) **and is now aged** (*age*)**."**   **7.03.06**

> **"There are** (*state number*) **previous convictions recorded against**   **7.03.07**
> **him."**

In a case where there are a substantial number of previous convic-   **7.03.08**
tions the prosecution will usually ask the court:

"Where do you wish me to start?"

7.03.09   The prosecution will then usually read the details of the defendant's previous convictions and the sentences passed on him, for example:

> **"On** (*date*) **the defendant was convicted of** (*offence*) **for which he was** (*fined/sentenced to* (–) *months' imprisonment*)**."**

The prosecution should be ready to provide the court with the details of the most recent and/or similar offences.

- OMIT **7.03.10–11** if there is no breach of any court order. Continue at **7.03.12.**

Breach of court order/sentence

7.03.10   If the defendant is in breach of any court order or sentence (conditional discharge, suspended prison sentence), or the court intends to revoke any community order and re-sentence, it may be dealt with at this stage. The prosecution may say:

> **"On** (*date*) **the defendant was convicted of** (*offence*) **for which he was** (*for example*) **conditionally discharged for** (–) **years/months. He is therefore in breach.**
> (*To the court*) **Could that be put?"**

7.03.11   The clerk (or the court) may say:

> **"**(*Name of defendant*)**. Is it correct that on** (*date*) **at** (*state name of*) **court for an offence of** (*specify*)**, you were** (*for example*) **conditionally discharged for** (–) **years/months ?** (*Defendant:* **Yes**)
> **And do you accept that, by reason of your conviction/plea, you are in breach of that order?** (*Defendant:* **Yes**)**. And that this court can now deal with you for that offence?** (*Defendant:* **Yes**)**."**

- OMIT **7.03.12–14** if the defendant is not liable for endorsement or disqualification. Continue at **7.03.15**.

Endorsement and disqualification

7.03.12   In (road traffic) cases which carry endorsement or disqualification, the prosecution should be ready to assist the court as follows:

(a) The number of penalty points which may/must be awarded for the offence(s) for which the defendant is to be sentenced, and
(b) Whether he therefore becomes liable for a penalty points disqualification ("totting").

The prosecution may say: **7.03.13**

> **"The current offence carries (–) penalty points (*or*, between (–) and (–) penalty points)."**

and/or

> **"The defendant is liable to disqualification. He has not previously been disqualified/He has been disqualified (*once/twice*) in the last 3 years. And is therefore liable to (*6 months/1 year/2 years*) disqualification."**

The court may ask the defence whether he accepts the summary given by the prosecution.

For the provisions allowing a defendant to avoid endorsement or   **7.03.14**
disqualification ("special reasons" and "exceptional hardship"), see **1.07.04–28**.

Presenting the defendant's antecedents

The prosecution may then give details of the defendant's antecedent   **7.03.15**
history to the court (which may include the defendant's accommodation, job, education, financial circumstances and any other relevant matter).

- OMIT **7.03.16–17** if compensation is not claimed. Continue at **7.03.18.**

Compensation

The details of an application for compensation will usually be given by   **7.03.16**
the prosecution, for example:

> **"Compensation is sought by (*name*) in the sum of (*amount*) on** (*state the charge or count*)**. The claim is made up as follows** (*state how the amount is calculated*)**."**

Evidence may be called to substantiate the claim for compensation where there is a dispute between the parties although this is rare.

7.03.17   In a case where it is unlikely that the defendant will be able to pay compensation (for example where the compensation sought is substantial and/or imprisonment is likely) it is often sufficient for the prosecution to say:

"There is an application for compensation of (*amount*)**."**

- OMIT **7.03.18–24** if there is no claim for forfeiture, disposal or destruction or other similar order. Continue at **7.03.25**.

Forfeiture, disposal or destruction or other similar order

7.03.18   The prosecution may then say:

"There is an application for the forfeiture/disposal/ destruction of (*state nature of goods*)**."**

7.03.19   The prosecution may then mention any other matters relevant to the sentencing of the defendant and/or further disposal of the case at this stage (for example, an order for confiscation under the Criminal Justice Act 1988 or the Drug Trafficking Offences Act 1986).

Confiscation proceedings under the Drug Trafficking Offences Act 1986

7.03.20   (Crown Court only) The court may confiscate the defendant's assumed proceeds (see DTOA) of drug trafficking. The court must give consideration to a confiscation order before sentence.

7.03.21   The prosecution will usually serve on the defence, a reasonable time before the hearing, a section 3 (DTOA) statement to prove (a) that the defendant has benefited from drug trafficking, (b) his assumed proceeds (which are not the same as profit) from drug trafficking and (c) his realisable assets (not necessarily from drug trafficking).

The statement is likely to have been prepared by a police officer deputed to deal with applications under the DTOA.

If the defence accept the statement, continue at **7.03.24**.

7.03.22   In a case where there is a dispute, the prosecution will usually call the officer to be cross-examined on his statement (although this is not strictly necessary).

The defence may serve on the prosecution, a reasonable time before the hearing, a section 3 statement answering the prosecutions' statement (but rarely do so), or the defence may call the defendant and/or other evidence.

The practice in a contested DTOA hearing is usually as follows: 7.03.23

(a) The prosecution will usually open the hearing briefly on the section 3 statement(s).
(b) The prosecution will call the officer and any other witness(es).
(c) The defence will usually cross-examine.
(d) The defence may call the defendant and/or witness(es) on his behalf to give evidence.
(e) The prosecution may cross-examine the defendant, and/or witnesses, if called.
(f) The defence may address the court.

The court will then announce its decision, for example: 7.03.24

"(*The court*) **finds that the defendant has/has not benefited from drug trafficking. The value of the defendant's proceeds is £(–). The amount that may be realised is £(–).** (*The court*) **will therefore order confiscation in that sum."**

Costs

The prosecution may say: 7.03.25

"There is an application for costs of (*amount, and, where an explanation is called for:*) **made up as follows** (*state how the amount is calculated*)." *See* **20.02.09–15.**

Or (in a case where it is unlikely that the court will make an order for costs):

"Would you/the court consider an application for costs?"

Conclusion

The prosecution will usually conclude by saying: 7.03.26

"That is the case (for the prosecution)."

(Crown Court only) Where the court hears the case for the prosecution before ordering pre-sentence reports, the prosecution may say:

"Do you require the prosecution on the next occasion? (*If the court answers:* **No). Could the prosecution be released?"**

The case for the defence: plea in mitigation

Pre-sentence reports

7.04.01   In practice, a pre-sentence report must be obtained except (in the Crown Court) where the offence is indictable only, when it is discretionary.

The seriousness of the offence: general principles

7.04.02   There is no set formula for a plea in mitigation. The defence will usually address the court first on the seriousness of the offence namely, whether the offence or offences are so serious (see Criminal Justice Act 1991) as to consider (in order):

(a) a discharge,
(b) a financial penalty,
(c) a community sentence (which includes probation),
(d) a custodial sentence.

In the case of a violent or sexual offence, the defence may address the court in relation to (d) whether such a sentence is necessary "to protect the public from serious harm from [the defendant]".

7.04.03
The defendant's previous convictions (usually for similar offences) and, where appropriate, his response to previous sentences may be considered at this stage. However, the principal test is whether the seriousness of the offence moves the sentencing options either up or down (or within) the sentencing bands described in **7.04.02**.
The defence should consider guideline sentencing cases.

7.04.04   The defence may say:

> **"In my submission the offence is not so serious as to merit a custodial/community sentence/financial penalty. The proper sentence in this case is** (*state sentencing band*)**."**

7.04.05   If the defence has failed to consider any relevant aggravating (or mitigating) features of the offence, the court may direct the defence to those features which, in the opinion of the court, affect the seriousness of the offence.

• OMIT **7.04.06–09** (except where a fine is being considered). Continue at **7.04.10**.

The seriousness of the offence: fines

After hearing the circumstances of the offence and any mitigation **7.04.06** arising out of the offence, in a case where a financial penalty only is prescribed (or where the court indicates that a financial penalty is appropriate), the defence is likely to address the court in relation to **7.04.12(b)&(c)** only.

The court will then determine the appropriate level of the fine.

Unit fines: Magistrates' court only

In a case where a magistrates' court is considering a financial **7.04.07** penalty, the defendant may be required to (and must) complete a means enquiry form before the hearing. The form is then handed to the clerk.

Where a local unit fine system is in operation, a magistrates' court **7.04.08** may determine the amount of the fine in units (within the prescribed level for the offence).

The value of a unit is then determined according to 2 factors:

(a) actual weekly income, minus
(b) a figure representing an appropriate level of expenditure for the defendant (subject, in some courts, to a variation for actual weekly expenditure, which the defence should check).

The court will then multiply the number of units by the value of the unit to the particular defendant to determine the amount of the fine.

In this case, the proper sentence is determined by a formula (with **7.04.09** adjustments) and, in practice, other mitigation, see **7.04.10–14**, is irrelevant.

The defence is likely to address the court only in relation to the seriousness of the offence namely, the number of units to be awarded.

The proper sentence for the offender

After considering the proper sentence for the offence, the defence **7.04.10** may then address the court on the proper sentence for the offender (within the likely sentencing band or bands).

The defence may address the court in relation to the following **7.04.11** matters:

(a) Other mitigating factors arising out of the offence.
(b) Plea of guilty (if appropriate).
(c) Co-operation with police.
(d) Contrition and/or voluntary restitution.
(e) Alternative sentences (within the likely sentencing band) available to the court.

135

7.04.12   The defence may also address the court in relation to any mitigating factors arising out of the defendant's:

(a) Previous convictions, if appropriate.
(b) Employment.
(c) Financial circumstances.
(d) Education.
(e) Medical or psychiatric condition.

Character evidence

7.04.13   The defence may call character evidence. Character evidence is more persuasive to the court than an address by the defence based on his client's instructions.

Documents

7.04.14   The defence may produce any relevant documents, for example:

(a) Character references.
(b) Job references.
(c) Offers of employment.
(d) Offers of accommodation.

7.04.15   The defence may conclude:

> **"Unless I can assist the court further, there are no other matters upon which I would wish to address the court."**

Sentence

7.05.01   A bench (in the magistrates' court) or board (in a court martial) and some Crown Court judges (especially where the judge is sitting with magistrates) may retire to consider sentence.

The court will then proceed to sentence, including the announcement of any endorsement or disqualification or final order in confiscation (DTOA) proceedings which may already have been indicated and the announcement of any order for costs.

Appeal

7.05.02   After sentence, the defence should advise the defendant of any right of appeal, see also **11.01.06**, and likely outcome. The defence should be realistic in his advice.

CHAPTER 8

County Court

1. INTRODUCTION

Introduction

Relationship to practice in the High Court

The practice in the county court will usually follow the practice in the High Court.   **8.01.01**

Where no special procedure is laid down by the County Courts Act or the County Courts Rules, the Rules of the Supreme Court will apply, see generally **Chapter 9**, High Court.

Right of audience

Barrister   **8.01.02**
Solicitor
A Fellow of the Institute of Legal Executives or an articled clerk (usually in uncontested or procedural matters)
An authorised local authority employee (usually in landlord and tenant actions where the local authority has brought the action)
Party in person
A lay representative (in small claims before the district judge only)
Any person with the leave of the court

Dress

8.01.03 *In open court*:

Barristers:	Robed
Solicitors:	Robed
Party in person:	Respectably dressed
(or any other person)	

In chambers:

Barristers:	Respectably dressed
Solicitors:	Respectably dressed
Party in person:	Respectably dressed
(or any other person)	

Mode of Address

8.01.04

His Honour Judge (name)	**Your Honour**
Deputy Judge (name)	**Your Honour**
Judge (name)	**Your Honour**
Mr Recorder (name)	**Your Honour**
(Mr/Mrs) District Judge (name)	**Sir/Madam**
(Mr/Mrs) Assistant District Judge (name)	**Sir/Madam**
(Mr/Mrs) Deputy District Judge	**Sir/Madam**

8.01.05 A judge or district judge may sit in:

(a) Open court
(b) Chambers (in the court room)
(c) Chambers (in the judge's or district judge's room)

(a) & (b) Open court and in chambers (in the court room)

Seating

8.01.06 The advocates will sit in the rows and/or benches facing the judge.
The plaintiff will usually sit in the rows and/or seats on the left hand side of the court facing the bench.

8.01.07 Conduct

In open court, any person addressing the court should do so standing.

In chambers (in the court room), as a matter of courtesy the advocate and/or party should address the court standing. The court may invite the advocate and/or party to sit.

(c) Chambers (in the judge's or district judge's room)

Seating and conduct

If a hearing in chambers takes place in the judge's or district judge's **8.01.08** room, the advocates and/or parties will usually remain seated to address the judge or district judge. The parties will usually be seated at a table.

The hearing is less formal than in open court.

Admission of the public

When the court is sitting in open court, members of the public are **8.01.09** usually admitted.

When the court is sitting in chambers (in the court room), members of the public are almost always excluded. If a party wishes to have other persons in court with him, for example, family or friends, that party should seek the leave of the judge or district judge.

When the court is sitting in chambers (in the judge's or district judge's room), members of the public are always excluded.

Order of presentation

The party having the burden of proof will usually address the court **8.01.10** first.

In any other case the parties will usually address the court in title order of the case.

Witnesses

If the court is sitting in open court, witnesses will usually be present in **8.01.11** court throughout the proceedings and/or the day, or part of the day, on which the witness gives evidence. Witnesses may be excluded from court until they come to give evidence, either by agreement or by order of the court.

If the court is sitting in chambers (in the court room) practice varies **8.01.12** although witnesses will not usually be present in the court room.

If the court is sitting in chambers (in the judge's or district judge's **8.01.13** room), witnesses will very rarely be present in the room (except in small claims arbitrations, see **8.08.10**).

Proceedings generally

8.01.14   Proceedings may be commenced by:
(a) Summons.
(b) Originating application.
(c) Petition.

8.01.15   The action must be commenced either in the court for the district in which the defendant resides (or carries on business) or in which the cause of action arose, save for default actions (usually where only a specific sum of money is being claimed) in which case the plaintiff can start in any county court.

Service of proceedings

8.01.16   As a general rule, proceedings in the county court are usually served by the court by post although there are exceptions where personal service is required.

2. INTERLOCUTORY APPLICATIONS (METHOD)

Introduction

Interlocutory applications

8.02.01   An interlocutory application is any application made between the issue of proceedings and the final determination of the action, or part of the action, at trial.
Interlocutory applications may be made *ex parte* or on notice.

8.02.02   Practice is more straightfoward in the county court than in the High Court.
The practice in: **9.02.01–52** Interlocutory Applications (Method) should be read in conjunction with this section

Ex parte applications

8.02.03   An *ex parte* application is made by a party without giving notice to the other party or parties to the action.
The following applications are usually made *ex parte*:

(a) An application for leave to serve out of the jurisdiction (to a district judge).
(b) An application for an order restraining a party to a marriage from disposing of matrimonial assets (usually to a district judge, but sometimes to a judge).
(c) An application for the protection of a party to or child of a relationship, see **10.03**, (to a judge).
(d) An urgent application relating to the liberty or safety of the individual or the preservation of property.

Applications on notice

An application on notice is made by a party issuing and serving a notice of application, see **8.02.05**, on the other party or parties to an action. Interlocutory applications in the county court are usually on notice. **8.02.04**

The following applications are made on notice:

(a) Summary judgment, see **8.03.01–10**.
(b) Pre-trial review, see **8.03.11–14**.
(c) Directions generally.
(d) Applications for injunctions (except in urgent cases).

Notice of application

The notice of application is usually set out on a standard form available from the county court. **8.02.05**

The notice of application must set out:

(a) The order sought.
(b) The reason(s) for the application.

Affidavits

An affidavit in support of the application must be prepared and served with the notice of application (except in the most simple cases), see **9.02.04–07**. **8.02.06**

The respondent may serve an affidavit in reply, see **9.02.08**.

Applications to the district judge or judge

An interlocutory application may be made to the district judge, see **8.02.08–19**, or the judge, see **8.02.20–25**. **8.02.07**

Applications to the district judge

Introduction

8.02.08   Most interlocutory applications are made to the district judge except where an injunction is sought, (**8.02.03(b)** is the only exception).
The application is in chambers.

8.02.09   For right of audience, dress, mode of address and conduct generally, see **8.01.02–08**.

Attendance of the parties

8.02.10   As a general rule, if a party is represented at the hearing the party need not attend.

If the party is seeking to rely on an affidavit, the district judge may not allow its use if the maker is not present to be cross-examined, see **21.06**. The application may be dismissed.

If the respondent does not attend, the application may be granted in his absence.

8.02.11   A party may consent to the application by letter, see for example, **9.04.12**.

In a case where it would usually be expected for that party to attend, the party may apologise in the letter, as a matter of courtesy, for his non-attendance.

A party should never fail to attend on a directions hearing unless the other party consents and there is an agreed order because the district judge can enter judgment against the party failing to attend.

Preparation

8.02.12 The notice of application and affidavit must be served:
In most applications: 2 clear days before the hearing.
In applications for
summary judgment, see
8.03.05–10:   7 clear days before the hearing.

8.02.13   In an *ex parte* application, the advocate should hand the affidavit (and notice of application) to the usher for him to give to the district judge.

In an application on notice, the parties may hand any additional documentation to the district judge during the hearing if either party has not had the time to file the documentation in advance of the hearing.

The parties should attempt to file and serve all documents in advance. Late service of documents may lead to an adjournment of the application. **8.02.14**

Practice

The appointment

District judge's appointments are usually listed in blocks with time markings at, for example, 10.00, 10.30, 11.00, 11.30 and so on. **8.02.15**
If a case is likely to last longer than half an hour, the court should be notified and an appropriate listing will be arranged.

On arrival at court, the party should give his name to the usher. The party will then wait to be called in to see the district judge. **8.02.16**

The hearing

The practice at the hearing varies greatly. Some district judges will allow the parties to conduct the application as they see fit, others will take over completely. **8.02.17**

The parties are advised to follow the practice (with amendment) in: **9.02.18–21** for *ex parte* applications, and **9.02.29–37** for applications on notice. **8.02.18**

Appeal

Appeal against a decision of the district judge in interlocutory applications is to the judge, see **8.04.05–12**. **8.02.19**

Applications to the judge

Introduction

The application is usually in chambers (usually, in the court room). **8.02.20**

For right of audience, dress, mode of address and conduct generally, see **8.01.02–07**. **8.02.21**

For attendance of the parties, see **8.02.10–11**. **8.02.22**

For preparation, see **8.02.12–14**. **8.02.23**

The hearing

8.02.24   The parties are advised to follow the practice (with amendment) in: **9.02.18–21** for *ex parte* applications and **9.02.29–37** for applications on notice.

The parties should note that, unlike the High Court, the court will already have most of the documentation except where it has yet to be handed to the judge, see **8.02.13**.

Appeal

8.02.25   Appeal is to the Court of Appeal Civil Division, see **12.01.04**.

3. PRE-TRIAL PROCEDURE

Judgment in default and summary judgment

8.03.01   The practice in **9.03** Summary judgment, should be used as a guide.

8.03.02   Proceedings may be commenced by:

(a) Summons (with particulars of claim).
(b) Originating application.
(c) Petition.

8.03.03   The defendant/respondent will be served with a document setting out the requirements for acknowledging service and lodging a defence (or other response).

The period of compliance is usually 14 days.

Judgment in default

8.03.04   If the defendant fails to return the acknowledgement of service, the plaintiff may apply for judgment in default (of acknowledgement of service), see **9.03.05–11**.

Summary judgment

8.03.05   If the defendant returns the acknowledgement of service but fails to file a defence or files a defence and the plaintiff considers that there is no real defence to the claim, the plaintiff may apply for summary judgment, see **9.03.12–14**.

An application for summary judgment is known as an Order 9, rule 14 application.

Summary judgment may be obtained in any action except one where **8.03.06** possession of land is claimed or, where the case has been referred to small claims arbitration or, where the case involes a claim for defamation, malicious prosecution or false imprisonment.

An application for summary judgment is made by issuing an applica- **8.03.07** tion returnable before the district judge.

For preparation for the hearing, see **9.03.15–24**. **8.03.08**

Practice

The hearing is usually in the district judge's room. The parties will **8.03.09** usually be seated at a table.

In all other respects the practice in **9.03.25–41** should be followed except the parties should note that all documents apart from affidavits not yet filed are likely to be on the court file.

Appeal is to the judge. The time limit for the service of the notice of **8.03.10** appeal is 5 days.

Pre-trial review

A pre-trial review is the equivalent of a summons for directions in the **8.03.11** High Court. The practice in **9.04.11–16** should be used as a guide.

Directions as to the conduct of the action can be given at any time **8.03.12** during the course of the pre-trial procedure, see **9.04.17**.

For Directions generally, see **9.04.10**. **8.03.13**

Non-compliance

As a general rule, non-compliance will not be dealt with as severely **8.03.14** in the county court as in the High Court especially where the parties are not represented (unless obvious gross default is proved).

Discovery

The principles of discovery are identical in both the county court and **8.03.15** the High Court. The practice in **9.05** Discovery should be used as a guide.

One of the problems in the county court is that cases are often badly **8.03.16** prepared by people who are unqualified and do not understand the principles involved.

8.03.17   The court will usually permit a party in person to refer to a document which is produced at court on the day of the hearing if it is relevant to the issues even if it has not been disclosed.

However, an adjournment (with costs thrown away, see **20.03.12–13**) may be granted if a represented party produces a document on the day of the hearing.

8.03.18   If there is some evidence to show that a document has been wilfully concealed until the last moment (as opposed to overlooked) it is very unlikely that the court will permit its introduction and use at the hearing.

4. APPEALS FROM THE DISTRICT JUDGE TO THE JUDGE

Introduction

8.04.01   An appeal may be made from an order of the district judge to a county court judge.

The time limit for the service of the notice appealing an interlocutory application is 5 days.

The time limit for the service of the notice of appeal of a judgment or final order is 14 days.

8.04.02   The hearing is usually in chambers either in court or in the judge's room although it may sometimes be in open court, see **8.04.04**.

8.01.03   For right of audience, mode of address and conduct generally, see **8.01.02–13**.

Dress

8.04.04   The advocate is not usually robed. However, some judges may hear the appeal in open court when the advocate should be robed (except in family matters). The practice in **8.08.03** does not apply.

Appeal in an interlocutory matter

8.04.05   The appeal is a re-hearing of the case before the judge.

The party appealing the order opens the case (whether he was the plaintiff/applicant or defendant/respondent before the district judge).

The appellant's case

The party appealing the order may say: **8.04.06**

> **"I appear on behalf of the plaintiff/defendant, who appeals the order of** (*name of district judge*) **made at this court on** (*date*)**. The order was made on the plaintiff's/defendant's application for** (*state nature of application*)**. The order made was** (*state order appealed*)**. The plaintiff/defendant appeals against that order (or part of that order)."**

The party appealing the order may then read any affidavit(s) used at **8.04.07**
the hearing before the district judge.
    The party may also read and/or call any new evidence with the leave
of the judge.

The party appealing the order may then say: **8.04.08**

> **"It is the appellant's/plaintiff's/defendant's contention that the appropriate order is** (*state order sought*) **for the following reasons** (*refer to any relevant law*)**."**

The respondent's case

The respondent may then read any affidavit(s) used at the hearing **8.04.09**
before the district judge.
    The respondent may also read and/or call any new evidence with the
leave of the judge.

Submissions to the judge

The parties will usually be invited by the judge to address him (or the **8.04.10**
judge may give judgment without hearing either party).

If any of the parties have made a note of the judgment of the district **8.04.11**
judge it may be sent to him for his agreement or comment. At the appeal
the parties may refer to the agreed note of the judgment although the
judge is entitled to ignore it if he so wishes.

Costs

Costs will usually be awarded to the successful party, although it is **8.04.12**
not unusual for costs to be in the cause or reserved to the trial judge, see
20.03.08–09 & 14–15.

Appeal from judgments or final orders

8.04.13 An appeal from a judgment or final order of the district judge to the judge may be made on a matter of law only. In this case, the appellate jurisdiction of the county court judge is comparable to that of the Court of Appeal.

8.04.14 The judge may only interfere with the order of the district judge if the district judge has erred in law or the district judge has acted unreasonably in the exercise of his discretion.

8.04.15 If any of the parties have made a note of the judgment of the district judge it should be sent to him for his agreement or comment prior to the appeal. This is particularly important where the note is not agreed. The party appealing should make a copy of the note available to the judge.

At the appeal the parties may refer to the note of the judgment.

8.04.16 If no note is available, the district judge should be asked to state in writing his findings of fact and/or rulings on the law.

8.04.17 The practice is similar to the practice in appeals in interlocutory matters, see **8.04.05–11**, except that the judge is bound by the district judge's findings of fact (hence the need for an agreed note of judgment or authenticated transcript).

8.04.18 The party appealing the order may say:

> **"I appear on behalf of the plaintiff/defendant who appeals the order of** (*name of district judge*) **made at this court on** (*date*)**. The order was made on the plaintiff's/defendant's application for** (*state nature of application and order sought*)**. The order was** (*state order appealed*)**.**
>
> **There is an agreed note/authenticated transcript of the judgment.**
>
> **The** (*party*) **appeals against the whole of the order/part of the order** (*set out part of order appealed*)**. It is the appellant's contention that** (*name of district judge*) **was wrong in law for the following reasons** (*refer to any relevant law*)**."**

8.04.19 The practice in **12.02.02–18** is then followed.

Costs

8.04.20 Costs will usually be awarded to the successful party, although it is not unusual for costs to be in the cause or reserved to the trial judge (where as a result of the appeal, there is to be a trial of the action), see **20.03.08–09 & 14–15**.

Appeal from the district judge in a small claims arbitration

There is no appeal from the district judge to the judge. An appeal may be made on a point of law only to the Divisional Court of the QBD, see **13.03**. **8.04.21**

5. SEEING THE JUDGE

Introduction

An informal discussion called "seeing the judge" may take place between the advocates and the judge. For a discussion of the practice generally, see **5.03** Seeing the judge. **8.05.01**

Although it is a matter for the discretion of the judge, it is extremely unusual for the judge to see the advocate(s) privately in his room. **8.05.02**

If it takes place, it will usually only take place before the actual judge on the day of the hearing. The judge will not see non-qualified persons in this way.

If the judge agrees to see the parties he will not usually see a party in the absence of the other party or parties. **8.05.03**

The parties must be careful not to embarrass the judge or compromise the hearing of the case in open court.

For dress, mode of address and conduct generally, see **5.03.01–08**. **8.05.04**

Practice

Introduction of the parties

The party asking to see the judge will usually introduce the parties: **8.05.05**

> **"Thank you for seeing us, judge. I represent** (*name of party*). (*Name*) **represents** (*name of party*). **It is my request to see you."**

Reasons for seeing the judge

Once again, it must be emphasised that it is extremely unusual for the judge to see parties privately in his room. If it takes place at all, the following are some examples of the practice: **8.05.06**

Matters which a party may not wish to raise in open court

8.05.07 There may be sensitive matters which a party does not wish to raise in open court (for example, for fear of aggravating problems that exist between the parties). In a case where an agreement has been reached, a party may say:

> **"The proposed agreement may seem unusual. As a matter of courtesy we thought it would be best to explain the background without airing it in front of the parties as the situation is volatile."**

The party may then explain the background to the agreement and (as required by the judge) how the agreement is likely to assist the situation.

Order on breach in committal proceedings

8.05.08 The party should not ask the judge to indicate the actual order, although he may ask the judge to indicate the type of order which he is minded to make on breach of an order in committal proceedings, but even this must be approached with discretion.

 This may may be introduced as follows:

> **"If the respondent were to admit breach of the order** (*state breaches admitted*)**, he is obviously anxious about the order you would make. He would be entitled to credit for his candour and** (*state briefly best mitigating factor(s) or extenuating circumstance(s)*)**. Perhaps you could indicate your view?"**

8.05.09 The judge may either give a definite indication or he may give no indication or he may simply say:

> **"This is/is not a serious breach. I would make an order accordingly."**

In this example, it is unlikely that the judge will give any better indication and counsel should not press the judge to do so.

Personal problems of the advocates

8.05.10 For example, listing problems, illness in the family.

Any other matter

8.05.11 The parties may raise any other matter which either party feels should be raised privately and not in open court.

For example, where it is suspected that there has been an improper communication between a party and a witness.

Leaving the judge's room

At the conclusion, the party making the request to see the judge will usually say:　**8.05.12**

"Thank you for seeing us, judge."

6. TRIAL

Introduction

The practice in **9.06** Trial in the High Court should be used as a guide.　**8.06.01**

The trial of an action in the county court represents, in practice, the final decision of the issues between the parties which commenced with the issue of proceedings by:　**8.06.02**

(a) Summons.
(b) Originating application.
(c) Petition.

Interlocutory applications

There are likely to have been interlocutory applications between the issue of proceedings and the trial, see **9.02 & 8.02**.　**8.06.03**

Directions

The conduct of the trial will have been determined by the giving of directions, see **9.04** Directions and **8.03.11–14** Pre-trial review, made on the application of any party or by the court of its own motion.　**8.06.04**

It is now common practice for directions to be given for the exchange of witnesses' statements/proofs of evidence. A party preparing the case for trial is likely to be in possession of both his own and any other party's witnesses' statements/proofs of evidence.　**8.06.05**

In addition, all relevant documents should have been disclosed on discovery, see **9.05** and **8.03.15–18**.　**8.06.06**

Preparation

8.06.07   A party presenting a case should give consideration to the following:

    (a) Formal documents (usually in the possession of the court), for example, pleadings and orders of the court, see **9.06.07–11**.

    (b) Evidential documents (not usually in the possession of the court), for example, correspondence between the parties, which tend to prove the facts alleged in the pleadings, see **9.06.12–16**.

    (c) Law, see **9.06.22–24**.

8.06.08   For the presentation of documents in a bundle, see **9.06.17–21**.

Order of presentation of case

8.06.09   The plaintiff will usually present his case to the court first, except see **9.06.38–39**.

8.06.10   In the absence of any ruling by the court and/or agreement between the parties, the order of presentation and speeches is as follows:

8.06.11   Where the plaintiff and the defendant both call evidence:
Plaintiff opens
Plaintiff's evidence
Defendant opens, but see note (**A**) below.
Defendant's evidence
Defendant closes
Plaintiff closes
Defendant's response (if permitted).

8.06.12   Where the plaintiff calls evidence and the defendant calls no evidence:
Plaintiff opens
Plaintiff's evidence
Plaintiff closes, but see note (**B**) below.
Defendant closes
Plaintiff's response (if permitted).

8.06.13   Where there are two or more defendants and/or other parties:
The plaintiff calls evidence and the defendants and/or other parties call no evidence:
Plaintiff opens
Plaintiff's evidence
Plaintiff closes, but see note (**B**) below.
Defendants and/or parties close in order of title

Plaintiff's response (if permitted).

Where there are two or more defendants and/or other parties: **8.06.14**
The plaintiff and the defendants and/or other parties all call evidence:

Plaintiff opens
Plaintiff's evidence
First defendant opens, but see note (**A**) below.
First defendant's evidence
    Continue in order of title
Defendant and/or other parties close in order of title
Plaintiff closes
Defendant's and/or other parties' responses (if permitted, in such
    order as determined by the court).

Where there are two or more defendants and/or other parties: **8.06.15**
The plaintiff calls evidence and one or more but not all of the defendants and/or other parties call evidence:

Plaintiff opens
Plaintiff's evidence
First defendant opens, if calling evidence, but see note (**A**) below.
First defendant calls evidence
    Continue in order of title
Defendant and/or parties calling evidence close in the order that
    they presented their cases
Plaintiff closes, but see note (**B**) below.
Defendant and/or other parties not calling evidence close in order
    of title
Defendant's and/or other parties' response (if permitted, in such
    order as determined by the court).

Note (A)

It is important to note that in the county court the defendant does not **8.06.16**
normally open, as of right. Different judges have different views on the
matter and some are quite flexible.

The rule is said to be that the defendant has the right to one speech
only and, therefore, if the defendant opens he does not close. Some
judges will actually stop the defendant opening if he tries. Others, if
asked, especially in complex cases, will permit both opening and
closing speeches.

If in doubt, the judge's practice should be checked in advance, for **8.06.17**
example:

"I am unaware of the practice in this court. If I were to open the case (*for example*, on the defence bundle) would you permit me to address you in closing after all the evidence has been heard."

Note (B)

8.06.18   Where a defendant and/or party calls no evidence, practice sometimes varies as to whether:

(a) The plaintiff gets a second speech.
(b) The defendant closes after the plaintiff if the plaintiff is permitted to close.

If in doubt, the judge's practice should be checked in advance.

8.06.19   For speeches generally, see **9.06.46–49** and **Chapter 22**, Speeches.

Practice

Introduction

8.06.20   For right of audience, dress, mode of address and conduct generally, see **8.01.02–07**.

Conduct of the trial

8.06.21   The trial of an action is held in open court before a judge or district judge.

If the public are excluded and the court is sitting *in camera*, the conduct of the trial and mode of address are the same as in open court. The advocates are usually robed.

For jury trials, see **9.06.26** (except defamation actions).

Calling the case

8.06.22   The clerk of the court will read out the name of the case. If the parties are already in court, the parties should go to their seats.

If the parties are not in court, the usher will usually call the parties into court. The clerk of the court will then read out the name of the case.

Presence of parties and/or witnesses in court

8.06.23   The parties and/or witnesses will normally be present in court throughout the proceedings or on the day or part of the day on which the party and/or witness gives evidence.

A party may make application to exclude a witness where, for example, there is an allegation of misconduct by that witness.

Introduction of the parties

The plaintiff usually introduces the parties to the court: **8.06.24**

> **"In this action I appear for the plaintiff. My learned friend,** (*name of counsel*) (*or*) **My friend,** (*name of solicitor*) **appears for the** (*name of defendant/party*)**."**

or

> **"The defendant,** (*name*) **appears in person."**

Where a party appears in person, the judge may ask if the unrepresented party is present and is content not to be represented.

Presentation of the case

After the introduction of the parties, the trial proceeds in the same way **8.06.25** as in the High Court, see:
- Attendance of the parties **9.06.30–35**
- Preliminary applications **9.06.36–39**
- The plaintiff's case **9.06.46–69**
- Submission of no case to answer **9.06.70–75**
- The defendant's and/or other parties' case **9.06.76–82**
- Speeches **9.06.83–86**
- Judgment **9.06.87–89**
- Judgment order **9.06.90–91**
- Interest and costs **9.06.92–96**

Taking a note

In the county court there is no court shorthand writer. Apart from the **8.06.26** judge's judgment which is usually tape recorded (particularly in a contested case) there is no tape recording of the proceedings. It is therefore important to try to obtain as accurate note as possible in order that the judge's (a) findings of fact, (b) rulings on the law and, (c) method of applying the law are recorded for later consideration.

The lack of a good note may hamper the chances of a successful **8.06.27** appeal.

Appeal

8.06.28   Appeal is to the Court of Appeal Civil Division.

The notice of appeal should be served within 4 weeks from the date on which the judgment or order was made (not drawn up), see **Chapter 12**, Court of Appeal Civil Division.

7. POSSESSION ACTIONS

Introduction

8.07.01   Possession actions are usually commenced by summons and particulars of claim, or may be commenced by originating application.

The date of the first hearing is usually given at issue and served on the defendant together with the summons or originating application.

8.07.02   Summary judgment is not available in possession proceedings in the county court. It is therefore quite common, particularly in residential tenancy cases, that there will be no defence filed by the first hearing.

First hearing

8.07.03   At the first hearing the landlord should be in a position to prove the case by calling evidence.

The landlord must be able to prove:

(a) Title to the property.
(b) A tenancy (or the lack of one).
(c) Service of notice of the proceedings.
(d) A ground for possession.
(e) That he is entitled to the order sought, namely, that it is reasonable to make an order for possession.

Adjournment

8.07.04   If the landlord does not have the evidence available and/or is not able to prove the case, and/or the tenant asks for an adjournment at the first hearing, the district judge will usually grant the adjournment and give directions, see **8.03.11–14**, for the filing of a defence, discovery, see **8.03.15–18**, and setting down for trial (except where an adjournment is sought in order to deliberately delay the case).

Order for possession or suspended possession

If the parties attend and the tenant admits the allegations a posses-　**8.07.05**
sion, or a suspended possession (usually in a case of non-payment of
rent), order may be made.

The plaintiff opens:

> **"In this action I appear for the plaintiff who is the landlord of**
> (*address*)**. The defendant is** (*name*) **who is the tenant of that**
> **property.**
>
> **I have had the opportunity of discussing the case with him and**
> **he admits the alleged arrears of rent which amount to £(–) up to**
> **the last rent date/today/end of the week. He offers to pay the**
> **current rent together with £(–) per week off the arrears which**
> **the plaintiff would be happy to accept on the basis of a sus-**
> **pended possession order."**

The district judge will usually ask the tenant if he agrees with the　**8.07.06**
summary made by the plaintiff and understands the nature of a suspended possession order.

The plaintiff may then ask for an order, as follows:　**8.07.07**

> **"I therefore ask for an order for possession and judgment in the**
> **sum of £(–), judgment to be suspended on payment of the**
> **current rent together with £(–) per week as of the next rent**
> **date."**

If the tenant admits the alleged arrears and, either makes no propo-　**8.07.08**
sals for the payment of the arrears and/or, offers to vacate the property,
the plaintiff may say:

> **"I therefore ask for an order for possession and judgment in the**
> **sum of £(–)."**

Full trial

If the action is adjourned, at the full trial of a possession action, the　**8.07.09**
practice in **8.06** Trial in the county court and **9.06** Trial in the High
Court should be used as a guide.

Costs

The successful party is entitled to costs. In a simple case the court may　**8.07.10**
award an assessed fixed sum, see **20.01.05**.

8. SMALL CLAIMS ARBITRATIONS

Introduction

8.08.01   An arbitration is usually heard by a district judge. It is a less formal hearing than a trial in the county court before a judge.

    The district judge is entitled to adopt any procedure he may consider to be convenient and therefore practice will vary according to the methods of each district judge.

8.08.02   As the hearing is less formal the strict rules of evidence are not usually applied.

    The parties are often not represented at an arbitration. A party may have an unqualified representative in a small claims arbitration as long as the party is also in attendance.

8.08.03   The advocates are not robed, although, if a judge has taken part or all of a district judge's list in his court, he may expect the advocates to be robed.

    An advocate who has not taken his robes to court may address the judge as follows:

> **"I apologise that I am not robed as this matter was listed as an arbitration before the district judge. Perhaps you would nevertheless allow me to be heard on behalf of** (*name of party*)**."**

8.08.04   Arbitrations are held where there is a small claim (the advocate should check the current financial limits) or where the parties agree.

Formal documents: pleadings and orders

8.08.05   The claim is usually made on summons with particulars of claim. The particulars of claim should set out the basis of the claim and specify the amount claimed with interest (if appropriate).

8.08.06   A party contesting the claim should file a defence and/or counterclaim.

    There may also be a defence to the counterclaim.

8.08.07   Directions, see **8.03.11–14**, are made by the court of its own motion or on notice by either party. The parties will have the orders made on directions and/or any other interlocutory order.

Evidential documents

Copies of all documents on which a party intends to rely to prove his **8.08.08** case are usually prepared by both parties and should be served on the court a reasonable time in advance of the hearing, see also **9.06.12–15**.

Practice

The hearing

The hearing is usually in the district judge's room. The parties and **8.08.09** their advocates usually remain seated when addressing the district judge.

If the hearing is in a courtroom, the parties and their advocates may be required to stand when addressing the district judge. If an advocate has not had the opportunity of checking the practice of the district judge before the case, the advocate should stand to address the district judge until invited to sit.

Witnesses

The witnesses will usually be present in court throughout the pro- **8.08.10** ceedings, although if the hearing is in the district judge's room witnesses may be required to wait outside until called.

Some district judges do not require evidence to be given on oath. If **8.08.11** an advocate has not had the opportunity of checking the practice of the district judge before the case, the advocate may say:

"I am unfamiliar with the practice in this court. Is it your practice to require witnesses to be sworn?"

A party and/or witness taking the oath should always do so standing.

Conduct of the hearing

If both parties are represented the district judge may permit the **8.08.12** advocates to conduct the hearing as a trial, see **8.06** Trial in the county court.

If no party, or only one party, is represented, the district judge may conduct the hearing as a type of impartial inquisition or he may assist the parties to conduct the hearing as a trial.

8.08.13   If an advocate has not had the opportunity of checking the practice of the district judge before the case, the advocate should treat the hearing as a trial until the district judge indicates with what informality he may treat the usual rules of the court.

8.08.14   The advocate should always remember to treat matters briefly and to note with care any indications from the district judge to shorten the case.

Evidence

8.08.15   Strict rules of evidence do not usually apply although the advocate should present his case on the basis that strict rules of evidence will be applied. Some district judges will accept bills, estimates, engineers' reports without the maker of the document being present at the arbitration.

Costs

8.08.16   Costs are only awarded for:

(a) The costs of the summons (issue fee)
(b) Witness expenses
(c) Unreasonable conduct (usually dishonesty) of a party.

Appeal

8.08.17   There is no appeal on the facts from the finding of the district judge on a small claims arbitration.

8.08.18   The decision may be set aside by the Divisional Court, see **13.02**, on a matter of law only where it can be shown that either:

(a) There was an error of law, or
(b) The district judge's behaviour was such as to be considered misconduct.

8.08.19   If the finding and award are set aside there may be a rehearing.

CHAPTER 9

High Court

1. INTRODUCTION

Introduction

Divisions of the High Court

There are three divisions of the High Court. The distribution of the work between the three divisions is complex. The following is intended as a brief guide: **9.01.01**

Queen's Bench Division	Contract
	Tort
	Defamation
	The Divisional Court of the Queen's Bench Division exercises supervisory jurisdiction over courts of lower jurisdiction and tribunals.
Chancery Division	Trusts
	Companies
	Land
	Administration of estates
	Insolvency
	Intellectual property
	Contentious probate
Family Division	All family matters

9.01.02   The work of the divisions overlaps and the commencement of proceedings in the wrong division is rarely fatal to the claim.

9.01.03   The essential purpose of the divisions is to enable some specialisation as to subject matter.

As a general rule, the differences in practice between the divisions are mainly procedural. The differences are noted (where appropriate) in the following sections.

9.01.04   The High Court sits at the Royal Courts of Justice (RCJ) in London and at District Registries in other major towns in England and Wales.

9.01.05   Each division operates on two levels:
Masters/district judges
Judges

Masters and district judges

9.01.06   In practice, a master or district judge exercises all such powers as may be exercised by a judge in chambers, subject to certain specified exceptions.

Mode of address

9.01.07   Master   **Master** (both sexes)
District judge   **Sir/madam**

Right of audience

9.01.08   Barristers, solicitors, experienced solicitors' clerks, party in person.

Dress

9.01.09   Barristers and solicitors are not robed. All parties should be respectably dressed.

Seating

9.01.10   The parties usually stand before a QBD master for all hearings in chambers. At the invitation of the master, the parties are usually seated on private room appointments, see **9.02.30**. The parties usually sit before a chancery master.

In private room appointments, solicitors (or their clerks) attending counsel should sit beside counsel in order to:

(a) Take a note.
(b) Produce any necessary papers.
(c) Give instructions.

Conduct

The hearing is usually less formal than in open court. The parties are **9.01.11** encouraged to be brief and not to exceed the duration of the appointment.

The advocate who prepares his case in advance, who has his papers in order and available and presents his case clearly will build up for himself and his future clients a fund of goodwill with the masters who, next time round, will give him credit and assistance.

Admission of the public

Members of the public are almost always excluded except when the **9.01.12** hearing is in open court (for example, for assessment of damages, trials of interpleaders and trials by consent of the parties).

Judges

A judge will hear the trial of the action and some interlocutory **9.01.13** applications.

Mode of address

Description of Judge	Status of Judge	9.01.14
The Honourable		
Mr Justice (name)	High Court Judge	
His Honour Judge (name)	Circuit Judge sitting as a High Court Judge or Official Referee	
Mr Recorder (name)	Recorder sitting as a Deputy High Court Judge	

In practice, all judges sitting in the High Court are referred to as **My Lord/Lady** (except Official Referees who are referred to as **Your Honour**).

Right of audience

Barristers, solicitors (in some uncontested applications), parties in **9.01.15** person.

Dress

9.01.16 Open court   Barristers and solicitors are robed.
Chambers   All parties should be respectably
                                       dressed.

Seating

9.01.17   The advocates will sit in the rows and/or benches facing the judge.
Queen's Counsel sit "within the bar of the court" (which is a small
gate in most courts in the RCJ), junior counsel sit outside it. Solicitors
attending Queen's Counsel sit at a table in front of the Queen's
Counsel, but sit behind junior counsel when only a junior is instructed.
The plaintiff will usually sit in the rows and/or seats on the left hand
side of the court facing the bench.

Conduct

9.01.18   In open court and in chambers (in the court room), any person
addressing the judge should do so standing.
In chambers (in the judge's room), any person addressing the judge
will usually do so seated.

Admission of the public

9.01.19   When the judge is sitting in open court, members of the public are
usually admitted.

9.01.20   When the judge is sitting in chambers (in the court room), members
of the public are almost always excluded. If a party wishes to have other
persons in court with him, for example, family or friends, that party
should seek the leave of the judge.

9.01.21   When the judge is sitting in chambers (in the judge's room), members
of the public are always excluded.

General practice

Witnesses

9.01.22   If the judge is sitting in open court, witnesses will usually be present
in court throughout the proceedings and/or the day, or part of the day,

on which the witness gives evidence. Witnesses may be excluded from court until they give evidence either by agreement, or by order of the court.

If the judge is sitting in chambers (in the court room), practice varies although witnesses will not usually be present in the court room.

If the judge is sitting in chambers (in the judge's room), witnesses will very rarely be present in the room.

A witness should always take the oath standing. The solicitor should always check beforehand in what manner the witness wishes to be sworn (and inform the usher accordingly). **9.01.23**

Relationship to practice in the county court

As a general rule a plaintiff in an action in contract or tort, will be able to choose whether to bring proceedings in the High Court or the county court if the value of the claim is below the current financial limit(s). To issue certain proceedings in the High Court, the plaintiff must certify that damages are likely to exceed £50,000. **9.01.24**

An action in the High Court is likely to be more expensive than an action in the county court.

The High Court is more appropriate where complex questions of law are involved. **9.01.25**

The county court is more appropriate where the plaintiff requires a speedy resolution of the proceedings. **9.01.26**

However, many London and some provincial solicitors use the High Court for claims where the county court limits would otherwise apply due to:

(a) The greater experience of masters in resolving interlocutory applications.
(b) The more effective methods of execution available.
(c) The ease of process, for example, a party can issue and serve a writ the same day out of the central office, whereas in the county court they must rely on the court staff to do so.

Service of proceedings

As a general rule, proceedings in the High Court are served by one party on the other and are not served by the court. **9.01.27**

2. INTERLOCUTORY APPLICATIONS (METHOD)

INTRODUCTION

Interlocutory applications

9.02.01   An interlocutory application is any application made between the issue of proceedings and the final determination of the action, or part of the action, at trial.

Interlocutory applications may be made *ex parte* or by summons or motion on notice.

Ex parte applications

9.02.02   An *ex parte* application is made by a party without giving notice to the other party or parties to the action.

The following applications are usually made *ex parte*:

(a) An application of an administrative nature which does not directly affect the existing parties, for example, leave to issue a third party notice, service of writ of possession of vacant premises.

(b) An application in relation to any matter before the service of the originating process, for example, service out of jurisdiction.

(c) An urgent application where proper notice is not possible, for example, an urgent injunction application, habeas corpus.

(d) An application where proper notice is not desirable, for example, for a Mareva order.

(e) Certain applications to enforce judgments, for example, garnishee orders nisi or charging orders nisi.

Applications by summons or motion on notice

9.02.03   An application by summons or motion is made by a party on notice to the other party or parties to an action.

The following applications are usually made on notice:

(a) Interlocutory injunctions.

(b) Summary judgment (Order 14).

(c) Directions.

Affidavit

An interlocutory application is almost always made on affidavit. **9.02.04**
The affidavit may be made by the applicant or any authorised person, for example, the solicitor having the day to day conduct of the action.

The affidavit should contain: **9.02.05**

(a) The name, address and status of the deponent.
(b) The purpose of the affidavit, for example:

"I make this affidavit in support of my/the plaintiff's/the defendant's application for (*state relief sought*)**."**

(c) The matters upon which the applicant relies in support of the application.

As a general rule the affidavit should contain only matters which are within the deponent's own knowledge and belief, although an affidavit may also contain hearsay.
Where information is derived from hearsay (usually apart from information derived from a party's own solicitor) its source should be stated, for example:

"I am informed by (*name*) **and verily believe that** (*state grounds and sources of any belief*)**."**

A party should: **9.02.06**

(a) Note, in the top right hand corner of the first page of the affidavit, the name of the party on whose behalf the affidavit is filed, the name of the deponent, the number of the affidavit and the date, for example:
Pl. A.Smith. 2nd. 4.1.93.
(b) Initial all alterations.
(c) State the full address at which the affidavit was sworn.
(d) Paginate exhibits containing correspondence.

A party should not: **9.02.07**

(a) Bind exhibits into the body of the affidavit.
(b) Place the jurat (stating where and before whom the affidavit was sworn) on a separate page to the body of the affidavit.

Affidavit in reply

In an application by summons or motion on notice, where the party **9.02.08** responding to the application wishes to rely on an affidavit in reply, the affidavit should be served a reasonable time before the hearing.

Where the affidavit is served either immediately before or at the hearing and the applicant has no opportunity to answer it, the applicant may apply for an adjournment with costs against the other party.

QUEEN'S BENCH DIVISION

Introduction

9.02.09   In the Queen's Bench Division, all interlocutory applications are heard by the master, although any application may be heard by a judge in chambers if the leave of a master has first been obtained.

9.02.10   As a general rule, applications of an administrative nature are made to the master.

Certain applications, such as for a Mareva, have to be made to the judge as they carry a penalty involving the liberty of the individual.

Right of audience

9.02.11   Barristers although:

  (a) A certificate for counsel is unlikely to be granted in *ex parte* applications and applications by summons on notice in the solicitors' (10.30, 11.00 and 11.30) list.
  (b) A hearing may be adjourned with costs if a party instructs counsel without notifying the other party or parties in advance.

Solicitors.
Experienced solicitors' clerks.
Parties in person.

Dress

9.02.12   Barristers and solicitors are not robed. All parties should be respectably dressed.

Mode of address

9.02.13 Master   **Master** (both sexes)
            Judge   **My Lord/My Lady**

Conduct

On an *ex parte* application or a short application in solicitors' or **9.02.14**
counsel's list the master will be seated. The parties will remain standing
to address him.

Practice on an interlocutory application varies greatly. As a general
rule, the application will be dealt with briefly. The advocate should
take care to draw to the attention of the master the most important
points of the application.

The party making the application should always ensure that his **9.02.15**
opponent has an equal share of the time allotted for the hearing.

Masters of the Queen's Bench Division

Ex parte applications

Preparation

An *ex parte* application is usually made by lodging the affidavit in **9.02.16**
support of the application with the masters' secretary's department.

An *ex parte* application (usually in an urgent matter) can also be
made to the practice master of the day at the RCJ. The practice master is
listed in the cause list and a board appears on his door.

Some matters can be dealt with by post but, as this takes longer, a **9.02.17**
party will usually attend in person.

Practice

The party should attend at the master's room. **9.02.18**

If there are any other persons waiting, the party should join the
queue. If there are no other persons waiting, the party should knock on
the door and enter the room. If the master is busy the party should leave
the room and wait.

If the master is ready, the party should go to the master's desk. The **9.02.19**
party may then say:

"Master, this is my application for (*state nature of application*)**."**

The party should hand to the master: **9.02.20**

    (a) The original of the writ and any appropriate pleading (or draft pleading), if required by the master. (The party should always have these documents ready).

    (b) Any affidavit in support of the application (if not already filed). If filed at an earlier hearing, the party must bespeak (apply for) the affidavit from the registry.

    (c) The draft order.

9.02.21   The party may then refer the master to any relevant pleading (or draft pleading) and the affidavit (in such detail as required).

The master may indicate that he wishes to read the documents. He may then ask some questions to clarify matters.

The master will hear the party (and any other party, if present) before making the order, see **9.02.38**.

Appeal

9.02.22   Appeal of an order of the master lies to a judge in chambers.

The notice of appeal must be issued usually within 5 days of the order appealed against.

Applications by summons on notice

9.02.23   An application by summons on notice is made by issuing the summons out of the masters' secretary's department. The clerk will allocate an "assigned master" and all subsequent summonses must be issued before the same master unless he releases it.

The party should always use the original summons and not a copy.

Notice required

9.02.24   The length of the notice required varies according to the nature of the application.

An application will usually require at least 3 clear working days notice. The following are common examples:

Summary judgment (Order 14)   10 days
Summons for directions   14 days

Types of hearing

9.02.25   There are 3 types of hearing:

Solicitor's List (for applications not exceeding 10 minutes): Summonses in the QBD are usually listed in the solicitors' list (usually at 10.30 11.00 and 11.30). Note: **9.02.11(a).**

Counsel's List (for applications not exceeding 20 minutes): If a party taking out a summons intends to instruct counsel at the hearing, this should be stated on the summons. The summons will be listed in counsel's list (usually at 12.00).

Private room appointments: If it is anticipated that the hearing will take longer than 20 minutes, the parties should apply to the master's secretary, on a standard form, for the application to be taken out of the list and heard as a private room appointment.

Practice in solicitors' or counsel's list

The parties should report to the usher for the appropriate room. The party whose summons it is should give the original summons to the usher. **9.02.26**

If the case is listed in the solicitor's list, the usher will allow all the parties in a particular list to go and sit at the back of the room. The parties should not talk.

If the case is listed in counsel's list the parties will wait outside the master's room until the case is called.

When the master calls the case on, the parties should stand at the master's desk. The party making the application should hand to the master: **9.02.27**

(a) Any pleadings (if appropriate).
(b) The affidavit(s).

The practice in **9.02.32–37** is then followed except that the parties should always remember to be brief.

When the master has made his order, he will keep the affidavits but will hand back the summons on which he will have written his minute of order, see **9.02.38**. **9.02.28**

Practice in a master's private room

It is prudent for the parties to attend the masters' corridor early as much can be negotiated before going before the master. **9.02.29**

The parties enter the room and sit down. The party making the application should then hand to the master: **9.02.30**

(a) The original summons (the master may refuse to accept a photocopy).

(b) Any affidavit in support of the application (if not already filed), see **9.02.20**.

The party should have available any exhibits and copy correspondence (if appropriate) for the master.

9.02.31   The party making the application should give the master a note of the names of counsel. The party making the application will usually introduce the parties:

> **"Master, I appear on behalf of** (*name of party*)**. My name is** (*name*)**. My (learned) friend, Mr** (*name*)**, appears on behalf of** (*name of party*)**.**
>
> **This is my application for** (*state nature of application*)**.**
>
> **This is an agreed application/The application is opposed."**

9.02.32   The party making the application will then:

(a) Outline the nature of the application.

(b) Explain the facts giving rise to the application.

(c) Direct the master to any relevant pleading (or draft pleading) and/or document.

(d) Direct the master to any affidavit or part thereof.

(e) Direct the master to any relevant law. (A list of authorities should be provided to the masters' messengers room before 10.00 am on the day of the hearing).

(f) (If appropriate) state the power of the master to give the order.

Agreed application

9.02.33   On an agreed application, the party making the application may omit **9.02.32(b)–(f)**.

The party may briefly outline the application (with reference to the affidavit) and conclude by asking for the order "by consent".

Opposed application

9.02.34   On an opposed application, the party may address the master in relation to **9.02.30(a)–(f)** (with reference to the affidavit) in such detail as required.

The case for the party opposing the application

9.02.35   The party opposing the application may then present his case in the same way, see **9.02.32 & 34**.

If the party is relying on an affidavit in reply, see **9.02.08.**

The party opposing the application may: **9.02.36**

(a) Outline the reasons for opposing the application.
(b) Direct the master to any relevant pleading (or draft pleading) and/ or document. In an application for summary judgment the defendant may have a draft defence.
(c) Direct the master to any affidavit or any part thereof.
(d) Direct the master to any relevant law.

The master may invite either party to address him for a second time   **9.02.37**
on the merits of the application although practice varies.

The order

The master may grant or refuse the application and/or give further   **9.02.38**
directions, see **9.04** Directions.
    The master will endorse a minute of his order on the summons, affidavit or draft order.
    The master's minute of order will be written in shorthand which the solicitor will have to interpret when he draws the full order, for example:

J	Judgment
O2	Unconditional leave to defend
O3/O4	Conditional leave to defend
Pl	Plaintiff
Df	Defendant
Pl c	Plaintiff's costs
S/c	Scale costs
ciae	Costs in any event
cic	Costs in cause
CON/A	Charging order nisi/absolute
GON/A	Garnishee order nisi/absolute
on a/s	On affidavit of service
TTRIA	Time to run in August

Counsel should always remember to ask for a certificate for counsel,   **9.02.39**
see **20.03.22–27.**

Appeal

Appeal from the refusal of a master to make an order lies to a judge in   **9.02.40**
chambers. If the master's order would dispose of the action whichever order he made, appeal is to the Court of Appeal.

The notice of appeal must be issued usually within 5 days of the order appealed against.

Judge in chambers in the Queen's Bench Division

Ex parte applications

Documents

9.02.41   A party making an *ex parte* application to a judge in chambers should have the following documents:

(a) Writ.
(b) Any pleading (or draft pleading).
(c) Affidavit in support, see **9.02.04–07.**
(d) Draft minute of order.

The documents should be in proper form, although in urgent cases an unsworn affidavit may be accepted.

Listing an ex parte application

9.02.42   An *ex parte* application may be listed for hearing before a judge in chambers at 10.00 am on any weekday by a party delivering the relevant documents to the chief clerk to the judge in chambers by 3.00 pm on the preceding day.

Urgent applications

9.02.43   An appointment in an application of exceptional urgency may be made by telephoning the clerk to the judge in chambers.

9.02.44   An application may also be made by a party attending with the relevant documents at Room 98, RCJ, (off the waiting area known as the Bear Garden).

The party should attend before 9.50 am for an appointment in the judge in chambers' 10.00 am list, and before 1.50 pm for an appointment in the 2.00 pm list.

9.02.45   The party should wait outside Room 98. The usher will come out and ask if there are any *ex parte* applications. The usher will ask the party to complete a form and to hand him the completed form and any documentation.

Practice

Follow the practice before the master, see **9.02.18–21.**   **9.02.46**

Appeal

Appeal is (usually with leave) to the Court of Appeal, see **12.01.04.**   **9.02.47**

Applications by summons (on notice)

An application by summons on notice is made by issuing the summons   **9.02.48**
out of the central office.

A fixed date may be given or the application may be listed to go into the warned list at a future date.

A date will usually be given for a Room 98 appointment which can either be used or vacated by agreement between the parties.

Documents

A party making an application by summons on notice should prepare   **9.02.49**
a bundle containing the following documents:

(a) The notice of application or appeal.
(b) The pleadings (as appropriate), see **9.02.41.**
(c) The originals of any affidavits which, if filed at an earlier hearing should be bespoken from the registry (see **9.02.20(b)**), (together with any exhibits) on which the party is intending to rely.
(d) Any relevant order made in the action.

The bundle

The bundle should be agreed and copies made available to the other   **9.02.50**
party or parties to the application.

On a fixed date appointment the bundle should be filed at least 5 days before the hearing.

In any other application, the bundle should be filed at least 48 hours after the case has entered the warned list or notification has been given of the date of the hearing.

Practice

9.02.51 Follow the practice in the master's private room, see **9.02.29–37.**

Appeal

9.02.52   Appeal is (usually with leave) to the Court of Appeal, see **12.01.04.**

CHANCERY DIVISION

Introduction

9.02.53 In the Chancery Division, interlocutory applications are usually heard by the master in chambers.
   Most of the matters dealt with by a judge in chambers in the other divisions are dealt with in court on motion.

9.02.54   Apart from some statutory exceptions (and any application which is referred to the judge by the master), an interlocutory application is usually only made to a judge where the order sought is for:

(a) A Mareva injunction.
(b) An Anton Piller order.
(c) An injunction restraining a threatened wrong or to preserve the status quo until trial.
(d) A declaration of right.

Masters in the Chancery Division

Introduction

9.02.55   For right of audience, dress, mode of address and conduct generally, see **9.02.11–15.**

Ex parte applications

9.02.56 Chancery masters are available at 2.15 each day to hear short *ex parte* applications without appointment.

An *ex parte* application is usually made on affidavit without a summons by attending before the master. The court file should be bespoken, see **9.02.20(b)**, before noon on the day of the application.

Certain applications may be made simply by leaving the affidavit with the master's clerk, for example: **9.02.57**

(a) Application for leave to serve process outside the jurisdiction.
(b) Application for substituted service.
(c) Application for charging or garnishee order.

Practice

Follow the practice before the master, see **5.02.18–21.** **9.02.58**

Appeal

See **9.02.40** **9.02.59**

Applications by summons (on notice)

Preparation

The summons is issued out of Chancery Chambers in London (or out of the District Registry). The length of notice required varies according to the nature of the application. **9.02.60**

The summons will bear a date and time. If the summons gives a time estimate for the application which the respondent considers is unrealistic, an application should be made for another appointment.

Practice

Follow the practice in the master's private room, see **9.02.29–37.** **9.02.61**

The court file will be before the master at the hearing and should contain all filed documents. The party should have copies of the documents available in case documents lodged recently for filing have not actually been placed upon the court file. **9.02.62**

Appeal

9.02.63   See **9.02.40.**

Judges in the Chancery Division

Right of audience

9.02.64   Barristers, party in person.

Dress

9.02.65   Barristers are robed, a party in person should be respectably dressed.

Mode of address

9.02.66   Judge: **My Lord/My Lady.**

Conduct

9.02.67   The hearing is in open court. A party addressing the court should do so standing. The party should be brief and to the point.

Introduction

9.02.68   As a general rule, interlocutory applications to a judge of the Chancery Division are made by motion.

A court is set aside each day for the hearing of motions (although other judges may assist).

9.02.69   *Ex parte* applications on motion may be heard at any time on application to the judge's clerk. Applications on motion on notice are listed before the judge. Both are heard in open court in the absence of any special reason to the contrary.

The court

9.02.70   The court sits at 10.30 am each day. The clerk will usually be present in court before 10.30 am and should be given any additional documents or affidavits.

A party should inform the clerk before the hearing starts if he has an urgent application (if this has not been done beforehand).

Practice

It is up to the advocate to make sure he is in court at the right time. The 9.02.71
ushers do not usually call the parties into court.

If a party is not ready, a motion is likely to be struck out.

Ex parte motions and applications by motion on notice

The usual practice is to distinguish between effective and ineffective 9.02.72
motions.

An effective motion is one which is either *ex parte* (so that the
evidence has to be read) or *inter partes* and opposed.

The list is called first time round and a party is expected to tell the 9.02.73
judge simply whether the case is effective or ineffective, and, if
effective, to give a time estimate.

The party making the application may say:

> **"This is my application for** (*state nature of application*)**. The**
> (*name of party*) **is represented by** (*name*)**. The application is**
> **ineffective."**

or

> **"The application is effective. I would say** (*state time estimate, for*
> *example,* **half an hour to an hour)."**

Ineffective applications

The judge will usually take all ineffective applications before dealing 9.02.74
with an effective application unless the application is exceptionally
urgent.

The judge may say:

> **"I will take all ineffective matters first."**

The party making the application may say: 9.02.75

> **"We are agreed that the case is ineffective** (*state reason*)**. And**
> **would therefore ask that the case be stood out for (–) days."**

Effective applications

The court will not entertain an opposed application on a motion day 9.02.76
if it is likely to last for more than 2 hours. When the evidence is
complete, the party making the application may say:

> **"Would you stand over the motion to come on as a motion by order on a day to be fixed (not before the (–) day of (–)) with a time estimate of** (*state time estimate*)**."**

9.02.77　　This may be done before the evidence is complete when the words **"not before the (–) day of (–)"** will be included in order to enable it to be completed.

Directions may be given at this stage, see **9.04.**

Applications in camera

9.02.78　　It is usual on an application for an Anton Piller order and, sometimes, on a Mareva to ask the court to sit *in camera.*

The party making the application may say:

> **"This is an application for** (*state nature of application*)**. If the public are admitted, irreparable damage may be caused. I therefore ask that the court sit in camera."**

Agreements

9.02.79　　On an *ex parte* application or on an application which is *inter partes* and the parties are agreed on the order, the parties are advised to provide the judge with a draft of the order he is being asked to make (which may be signed by the parties). This will save time. The agreement is then handed to the judge.

The parties should take care to use correct English usage as Chancery judges often pick up poor grammar and/or syntax.

Hearing a motion

9.02.80　　A motion is heard on affidavit evidence. It is usual to read all affidavits aloud and in full unless the judge indicates that he has already read them. It is unusual for the court to hear oral evidence.

The party moving opens the case

The practice in **9.02.29–37** is then followed save that the parties stand to address the court.

Appeal

9.02.81　　Appeal is (usually with leave) to the Court of Appeal, see **12.01.04.**

FAMILY DIVISION

Introduction

The family division deals primarily with matters relating to: **9.02.82**

(a) Divorce or judicial separation, see **10.02.**
(b) Applications for ancillary relief, see **10.05.**
(c) Applications in relation to children, see **10.06.**
(d) Applications in relation to family property (under the Matrimonial Homes Act and Married Womens Property Act and some applications under the Inheritance Act and section 30 Law of Property Act.

In London most family matters are dealt with in the divorce registry **9.02.83** which is comprised within the principal registry and has the equivalent status to the county court.

Outside London, most matters are dealt with by the county court.

There is concurrent jurisdiction between the High Court, county **9.02.84** court and the magistrates' court (family proceedings court) in proceedings under the Children Act.

Almost all applications in the Family Division are in chambers, see **9.02.85** **10.01.06.** Some exceptions are committals for breach of an order or undertaking (see **10.04**), defended petitions, Children Act appeals, judicial review and declarations as to status.

Judgments are sometimes delivered in open court.

The district judge

In the Family Division the business undertaken by a master in the **9.02.86** QBD and Chancery Division is undertaken by the district judge.

For right of audience and dress, see **9.02.11 & 12.** **9.02.87**

Mode of address

District judge: **Sir/madam** **9.02.88**

Conduct

A district judge will usually adopt a less formal and more flexible **9.02.89** approach than a master of the QBD because of the nature of the business of the Family Division.

Ex parte applications

9.02.90 An *ex parte* application to the district judge may be made, for example, to restrain a party from disposing of or dealing with matrimonial assets or, to dispense with service of a petition on a respondent.

Preparation

9.02.91 An *ex parte* application may be made by attending before the district judge of the day at the divorce registry or at a county court having family jurisdiction.

It is usually possible to arrange an appointment at short notice by telephone, see **10.03.19–20.**

Documentation

9.02.92 The applicant should have:

(a) An affidavit (or draft affidavit) in support of the application.
And, where time permits:
(b) The notice of application.
(c) A draft order for signing.

Practice

9.02.93 Follow the practice before the master, see **9.02.18–21**, except the order is drawn up by the court.

Applications on notice

9.02.94 The following applications are on notice:

(a) Applications for ancillary (financial) relief, see **10.05.**
(b) Applications in relation to children, see **10.06.**
(c) Directions.

Appeal

9.02.95 Appeal of an order of the district judge lies to a judge in chambers.

Judge in chambers in the Family Division

Ex parte applications

The most common *ex parte* applications are in relation to children and the personal safety of any party or any children. **9.02.96**

Preparation

An *ex parte* application may be made by attending before a judge at the RCJ with the jurisdiction to hear both High Court and county court matters. **9.02.97**

It is possible to arrange an appointment at short notice by telephone.

Documents

The applicant should have: **9.02.98**

(a) An affidavit (or draft affidavit) in support of the application.
And, where time permits:
(b) The petition.
(c) The summons (or draft) summons.
(d) A draft note of order.

Where proceedings have not been commenced, the party should be ready and willing to undertake to commence proceedings (or to swear and/or file any documents required).

Practice

Follow the practice before the master, see **9.02.18–21.** **9.02.99**

If the hearing is in the court room, the parties will stand to address the judge.

Applications by summons (on notice)

See **Chapter 10**, Family Proceedings. **9.02.100**

Appeal

Appeal is (usually with leave) to the Court of Appeal within 28 days, see **12.01.04.** **9.02.101**

3. JUDGMENT IN DEFAULT AND SUMMARY JUDGMENT (ORDER 14)

Introduction

9.03.01   Proceedings may be commenced by:

(a) Writ
(b) Originating summons
(c) Originating motion
(d) Petition.

9.03.02   In an action commenced by writ the defendant will be served with a form of acknowledgement of service.

9.03.03   The defendant must return the acknowledgement of service within 14 days to the court office where the writ was issued.

9.03.04   If the defendant fails to return the acknowledgement of service or returns the acknowledgement of service but fails to serve a defence, the plaintiff may apply for judgment to be given against the defendant in default.

Judgment in default

9.03.05   The plaintiff should apply on the appropriate form to the court office out of which the writ was issued.
In some cases, the plaintiff must apply by summons before a master/district judge for leave. The law on this subject is complex and should be researched in the common practitioners' handbooks.

9.03.06   If the defendant has not returned the acknowledgement of service, the plaintiff must prove service of the writ (usually by affidavit).

9.03.07   If the defendant has returned the acknowledgement of service but has failed to serve a defence, the plaintiff may apply, without leave, for judgment in default.

Setting aside a judgment in default

9.03.08   The defendant should issue an *inter partes* summons returnable before a master/district judge supported by affidavit.

If the judgment has been entered irregularly (for example, it has been entered too soon or where the writ was never received by the defendant), the judgment will be set aside, as of right. Costs will usually be the defendant's in any event, see **20.03.10–11.** **9.03.09**

If the judgment has been entered regularly, the defendant must show that there is a triable issue, see **9.03.31**, and explain any failure to return the acknowledgement of service or serve a defence. Costs will usually be the plaintiff's in any event, see **20.03.10–11.** **9.03.10**

Judgment entered in default may be set aside on such terms as the court thinks fit. **9.03.11**

Notice of intention to defend

If the defendant gives notice that he intends to defend and the plaintiff considers there is no real defence to the claim, the plaintiff may apply for summary judgment (Order 14 proceedings). **9.03.12**

A defendant may also apply for summary judgment where there is no real defence to his counterclaim.

Summary judgment is not available in any case which includes a claim by the plaintiff for libel, slander, malicious prosecution, false imprisonment or a claim based on an allegation of fraud or Admiralty actions *in rem*. **9.03.13**

The purpose of making an application for summary judgment is to enable the plaintiff to obtain the relief he claims without a full trial of the action in a case where the defendant has no real defence. The plaintiff will therefore avoid the necessary procedural steps before the full trial and attendant costs. **9.03.14**

Making the application

The plaintiff should issue an *inter partes* summons for summary judgment on the claim returnable before the master/district judge. **9.03.15**

The summons must be supported by an affidavit, see **9.02.04–07,** which must: **9.03.16**

(a) Verify the facts set out in the statement of claim and give such additional information as appropriate.
(b) State that the plaintiff believes there is no real defence to the claim (or part of it). (This is often omitted from affidavits, which is a fatal defect.)

9.03.17 The summons and affidavit in support must be served by the plaintiff on the defendant at least 10 days (High Court) or 7 days (county court) before the date fixed for the hearing.

9.03.18 If the plaintiff serves an affidavit in support without making reference to the details of the claim, he should serve his affidavit in sufficient time to enable:

(a) The defendant to respond, and
(b) The plaintiff to serve an affidavit in reply.

9.03.19 If a party fails to give sufficient time to the other party to prepare an affidavit, the master will often allow an adjournment (with costs against that party).

9.03.20 In a case where the plaintiff believes that the defendant will not attend the hearing, the plaintiff should prepare an affidavit of service.

Opposing the application

9.03.21 The application can be made either before service of the defence or after service of the defence where no real defence is disclosed.

In either case, where the defendant opposes the application for summary judgement he must show that there is a triable issue.

9.03.22 The defendant should serve an affidavit, see **9.02.08**, and/or proposed pleading on the plaintiff not less than 3 days (High Court) before the date fixed for the hearing.

There is no time limit in the county court. The defendant should serve an affidavit and/or proposed pleading on the plaintiff a reasonable time before the date fixed for the hearing. If he fails to do so there is usually an order for costs thrown away, see **20.03.12–13**.

9.03.23 If the defendant alleges that there is a sufficient defence disclosed on the pleadings, the defendant's affidavit should detail all matters that show there is a triable issue.

9.03.24 If the application is made on the basis that the defence is insufficient, the defence may prepare a full(er) defence setting out the issues more clearly. It is prudent to support this by affidavit but not always essential.

Practice

9.03.25 Follow the practice before the master on an interlocutory application, see **9.02.29–37**.

The plaintiff's case

The plaintiff (or the party making the application) will usually intro- **9.03.26**
duce the parties to the master/district judge.

The plaintiff may then say: **9.03.27**

"This is an application for summary judgment (pursuant to Order 14). The writ and the statement of claim have been served and a defence has been filed."

(A defence will often not have been filed as service of the Order 14 summons extends time for service of the defence till after the hearing).

"The writ alleges (*state nature of claim*). **The defence filed alleges** (*state nature of defence*).

The plaintiff's affidavit dated (*date*) **sworn by** (*name*) **states that he verily believes that there is no (real) defence to the claim.** (*State content of affidavit and/or read any relevant paragraph*)**."**

The plaintiff may then direct the master/district judge to: **9.03.28**

(a) Any other documents or affidavits.
(b) Any relevant law.

The defendant's case

If the defendant has served an affidavit in reply, the defendant will **9.03.29**
usually refer the master/district judge to the affidavit and defence (if served) in the same way as the plaintiff.

The defendant has to show only that there is a triable issue and **9.03.30**
should not enter into a lengthy argument on the merits of the case.

What is a triable issue?

Different masters/district judges take different views as to the level of **9.03.31**
dispute needed to show a triable issue.

As a general rule, if the defendant can show a real dispute as to the facts relevant to liability, a trial will be ordered (in particular, if there is an allegation of misrepresentation or misbehaviour).

The best test of whether any defence is genuine is to see if contem- **9.03.32**
porary documents/conversations/complaints support it.

Where a defence is raised for the first time in the defendant's affidavit, and there was an opportunity to raise it earlier but it was not so raised, the master/district judge is far less likely to accept it.

Submissions

9.03.33 The parties may then be invited by the master/district judge to address him on the merits of the application.
The order of submissions varies.

9.03.34 In submissions, a party will usually:

(a) Draw the court's attention to any relevant law in that party's favour and/or
(b) Distinguish any relevant law that is not in that party's favour.
(c) Sum up on the facts.

9.03.35 The plaintiff may conclude his submissions:

"In the circumstances, it is the plaintiff's case that there is no real defence or triable issue."

9.03.36 The defendant may conclude his submissions:

"It can be seen that there is a clear dispute of fact which, should be resolved by the hearing of evidence at trial."

The order

9.03.37 The master will endorse a minute of the order on the original summons, see **9.02.38**. The summons will then be handed to the plaintiff.
The most common orders are:

(a) Judgment for the whole or part of the plaintiff's claim (if the plaintiff's claim is for an unliquidated sum, with damages to be assessed) (**J,Pl**).
(b) Order with (unconditional) leave to defend (**O2**).
(c) Order with (conditional) leave to defend on payment into court of part or all of the claim (**O3/4**).

Other orders (including directions) may also be made by the master/district judge.

Costs

9.03.38 The usual orders for costs are:
See **9.03.37(a):**   Plaintiff's costs or costs to be taxed.
See **9.03.37(b)** or **(c):**   Costs in cause, if payment is made or unconditional leave to defend is given.

The master/district judge may also dismiss an application for sum- **9.03.39**
mary judgment with defence costs if it was obvious that there was a
defence.

Counsel should ask for a certificate for counsel, see **20.03.22–27**. **9.03.40**

Interest

A party should always work out the interest (and, if possible, agree it **9.03.41**
with the other side) before the hearing, see **9.06.92–95**.

Appeal

Either party may appeal to a judge in chambers against the order **9.03.42**
made by the master/district judge, see **9.02.48–52**.
The time limit for the service of the Notice of Appeal is 5 days.

4. DIRECTIONS

Introduction

Directions may be _iven at any stage after the commencement of **9.04.01**
proceedings for the purpose of permitting or compelling any party to
carry out the necessary procedural steps in an action, for example, see
9.04.10.

Directions may be given at an interlocutory hearing or on the hearing **9.04.02**
of a summons for directions.

A summons for directions is usually issued by the plaintiff after the **9.04.03**
close of pleadings. There are automatic directions in:

(a) (High Court) all personal injury cases.
(b) (County court) all cases commenced by the issue of a default
summons.

The pleadings must be made available for the master/district judge to **9.04.04**
read and should be lodged when the summons is issued.

In the county court, the notice to the parties of the date fixed for the **9.04.05**
pre-trial review (PTR) states that the hearing will be informal and in
private. Its purpose is to:

(a) Make sure that all the parties and the court understand what the case is about.

(b) See if there is any possibility of settling the dispute and, if not, decide how it is going to be heard and how long the hearing will last.

(c) Decide what documents or other evidence are needed from both sides.

9.04.06   In the High Court, the hearing of a summons for directions will usually be before the master.

In the county court, the hearing of a pre-trial review will be before the district judge.

Right of audience and dress

9.04.07   See **5.02.11 & 12.**

Mode of Address

9.04.08   High Court:

Master:	**Master** (both sexes)
District judge:	**Sir/madam**

County Court:

District judge:	**Sir/madam**

Conduct

9.04.09   In the High Court, the hearing is in chambers. All parties stand.

In the county court, the hearing is usually in the district judge's room (or it may be in the court room). The parties are usually seated.

If it is not clear from the arrangement of the seats, a party should stand until invited to sit.

Directions

9.04.10   The parties should give general consideration to the pleadings and the evidence required at the trial and, in particular, to the directions listed on the standard High Court form for a summons for directions:

(a) Consolidation of the action with others.

(b) Trial by an official referee (district judge in the county court, by arbitration).

(c) Transfer of the proceedings to the High Court or to the county court.

(d) Amendments to pleading(s).

(e) Applications for further and better particulars of any pleading(s).
(f) Discovery and inspection of documents.
(g) Exchange of experts' reports, see **9.06.56.**
(h) Exchange of witnesses' statements, see **9.06.04.**
(i) Interrogatories.
(j) Evidence to be taken by deposition/examiner or on commission.
(k) Place of trial.
(l) Mode of trial (judge alone or judge and jury).
(m)Category of case (in descending order of importance): A, B or C (usually "B").
(n) Estimate of length of trial.
(o) Date for setting down time.

This list is not exhaustive and the parties may need to supplement it depending on the circumstances of an individual case. In particular, the parties should consider whether the case is suitable for a split trial (for example, the trial of a single issue, usually liability, separately from other issues).

Practice

Obtaining the order

In most cases directions are agreed before the hearing and the plaintiff only will attend the hearing to obtain the order by consent. If directions are not agreed before the hearing, the parties should attempt to agree the order outside court. **9.04.11**

If the order is agreed, the party (usually the plaintiff) may say: **9.04.12**

> **"Master/sir, we/the parties are agreed as to directions in this case. They are contained in a letter dated (*date*)."**

or (If the parties attend):

> **"We have put the agreed directions in writing. We would ask you to make a consent order."**

The party may (if the directions are not in writing) dictate the directions to the master/district judge. **9.04.13**

If directions are not agreed, after the case has been called, the plaintiff will usually introduce the application to the master/district judge as follows: **9.04.14**

> **"Master/sir, this is the hearing of the summons for directions/ pre-trial review of this case. This case is (*describe nature of case*).**

We are agreed as to most directions but (*name of party*) **does not agree** (*state nature of application*)."

9.04.15 The parties may then argue the application. The application may be argued on the pleadings, for example:

"A request for further and better particulars of the (defence) dated (*dated*) **was served on the (defendant) on** (*date*)**. To date, no reply has been given."**

A copy of the request should be handed to the court.

"The following matters are requested (*state the matters requested in such detail as required*)**.**
It is the (plaintiff's) contention that he is entitled to the information requested (*state reasons*)**."**

The (defendant) may reply on both law and fact.

9.04.16 Where either party is seeking amendments to pleadings, further particulars or interrogatories, the party should ensure that the master/district judge initials the pleadings which he orders or approves.

Directions given at an interlocutory hearing

9.04.17 At an interlocutory hearing it may be necessary for directions to be given to carry out immediate necessary procedural steps.
The party or parties should be ready to ask for the directions required (usually at the time the order is made) to expedite the hearing of the case, for example:

"(And) I ask for the following directions:
That the plaintiff be ordered to amend the statement of claim within 7 days.
That the defence be filed within 14 days thereafter. Reply, if so advised, 14 days thereafter. Mutual discovery by lists, 14 days thereafter. Inspection, 7 days thereafter.
And that the case be set down, 7 days thereafter, Category (–), with a time estimate of (*state time estimate*)**."**

Costs

9.04.18 Costs on an agreed hearing will normally be in the cause, see **20.03.08–09.**
Costs on a contested hearing (or where the order was substantially agreed but attendance was caused by a party not agreeing one or more items) are likely to be awarded to the successful party.

Costs when directions are given at any other hearing, see **9.04.17**, are not normally dealt with as a separate issue.

Family proceedings

In proceedings other than family proceedings, a summons for direc-   **9.04.19**
tions or a pre-trial review is often dealt with by post by agreement, and
the parties (if represented) do not usually attend.
This is not the case in family matters.
In divorce, ancillary relief and children matters, the court attempts to
conciliate as much as possible for the benefit of the parties. In these
cases, the parties should attend in order to reach agreement, if possible,
and/or to narrow the issues in dispute, see **10.06.29–36.**

5. DISCOVERY

Introduction

The purpose of discovery

The parties to any action will usually have documents and corres-   **9.05.01**
pondence which have a bearing on the issues. The purpose of discovery is to enable a party to an action to know what documents are in the
possession of the other party.
These documents are disclosed to the other parties on discovery.

As a general rule, every document in the possession of a party which   **9.05.02**
has a bearing on the case must be disclosed.
This does not entitle the other party to inspect (or take copies of)
every document but each document must be identified in sufficient
detail to enable that party to know the nature of the document and
whether that party is entitled to inspect the document.

Discovery may be made in the High Court and county court and in   **9.05.03**
some tribunals, for example, **14.02.11.**
For Rule 2.63, Questionnaires in ancillary relief applications, see
10.05.10.

Obtaining discovery

In actions begun by writ in the High Court there are provisions for   **9.05.04**
automatic discovery after the close of pleadings. (There are special
rules in personal injury cases, see **9.04.03**).

9.05.05   Where automatic discovery is not made, a party may make an application for discovery at an interlocutory application or at the hearing of a summons for directions or pre-trial review.

Order for discovery

9.05.06   The court may order (usually on an interlocutory application) any party to serve on any other party a list of documents, for example:
    Discovery by lists within (–) days.
    Inspection (–) days thereafter.

Lists

9.05.07   A party making discovery must serve a list of relevant documents (usually by post) on the other parties within the period ordered.

9.05.08   The list must be in the prescribed form and is divided into schedules as follows:
Schedule 1:
Documents relevant to the issue which the party has in his possession, custody or power at the time he serves the list:
Part I:
    And which that party does not object to produce to the other parties.
Part II:
    And which that party objects (on the grounds of privilege) to produce to the other parties. These documents are usually described in general terms.

Schedule 2:
Documents relevant to the issue which the party has had (but no longer has) in his possession, custody or power, setting out where they are now and when they left his possession.

Verification of the list

9.05.09   In the High Court (but not usually in the county court) a party may be ordered to verify the list of documents by affidavit deposing to the accuracy of the list.

Specific discovery

9.05.10   If a party believes that a party serving a list of documents has not disclosed a document, he may request in writing for that document to be disclosed.

If that document is not disclosed or the other party states that the document is not relevant, the party may make an application to the master for specific discovery.

The application should be supported by an affidavit.

Follow the practice in a master's private room, see **9.02.29–37.**　　**9.05.11**

Inspection

Inspection usually takes place within 7 days of the delivery of the list.　**9.05.12**
A party who has served a list of documents should allow the other party to inspect the documents listed in Schedule 1, Part I although, in practice, the other party will usually ask for copies of the documents. The party will be expected to pay for these copies.

Effect of discovery

The general rules are:　　**9.05.13**
If a document has been disclosed, it may be used in the course of the proceedings by any party to the action (subject to admissibility).

If a document has not been disclosed, the High Court is unlikely to permit the party to use that document in the course of the proceedings and may grant an adjournment (with costs) to a party prejudiced by late or defective discovery.

Discovery in the county court

Discovery and inspection may be made:　　**9.05.14**

(a) By agreement, or
(b) By order of the district judge (usually in a pre-trial review).

Where discovery is made, the rule in **9.05.13** applies except that the　**9.05.15** rule is generally less strictly enforced in the county court than in the High Court, see **8.03.17.**

6. TRIAL

Introduction

In practice, the trial of an action in the High Court is the final　**9.06.01** determination of the issues between the parties which commenced with the issue of proceedings by:

(a) Writ
(b) Originating summons
(c) Originating motion
(d) Petition.

Interlocutory applications

9.06.02   There are likely to have been interlocutory applications between the issue of proceedings and the trial, see **9.02**.

Directions

9.06.03   The conduct of the trial will have been determined by the giving of directions, see **9.04**, made on the application of any party or by the court of its own motion.

9.06.04   The exchange of witnesses' statements/proofs of evidence is required in the High Court. It is likely that there will have been an order on directions for the exchange of witnesses' statements/proofs of evidence and the party preparing the case for trial will be in possession of both his own and any other party's witnesses' statements/proofs of evidence.

9.06.05   In addition, all relevant documents should have been disclosed on discovery, see **9.05**.

Preparing the case

9.06.06   After considering any orders made by the court, the statements of the witnesses and any other evidence, the party preparing the case for trial should organise the following documents in bundles for use at the trial:

(a) Formal documents (usually in the possession of the court) for example, pleadings and orders of the court.
(b) Evidential documents (not usually in the possession of the court, for example, correspondence between the parties) which tend to prove the facts alleged in the pleadings.
(c) Lists of authorities.

Formal documents

9.06.07   The party preparing the bundle(s) for a case should assemble the formal ("court") documents, see **9.06.08–11**, in chronological order in a bundle, see **9.06.17**.

Action commenced by writ and statement of claim in the High Court or by summons and particulars of claim in the county court

The parties to an action commenced by writ/summons are required **9.06.08** to serve pleadings.

The parties will have the following pleadings:

(a) Statement/Particulars of claim, by the plaintiff, setting out the facts relied on in support of his claim and the relief sought.
(b) Defence, by the defendant, answering the facts relied on by the plaintiff and setting out any new facts on which the defence relies.

The parties may also have the following pleadings:
(c) Counterclaim, by defence.
(d) Reply (to defence), by plaintiff.
(e) Defence to counterclaim, by plaintiff.
(f) Reply to defence to counterclaim, by defence.
(g) Third party notice, by defence.
(h) Defence to third party notice, by third party.

The pleadings may also be clarified by:
(i) Request for further and better particulars of (any pleading), by either party.
(j) Further and better particulars of (any pleading), by either party.

Action commenced by originating summons or petition

The parties will have the following documents: **9.06.09**

(a) Originating summons, by the plaintiff, setting out the relief sought.
(b) Affidavit(s) in support of the originating summons, by the plaintiff, setting out the facts relied on in support of the relief sought.
The parties may also have the following documents:
(c) Affidavit(s) in reply, by defence.
(d) Other affidavits, by or for either party.

In an action commenced by originating summons it may be ordered **9.06.10** on directions that the originating summons be treated as a statement of claim, for example, where there is a substantial dispute on the facts requiring pleadings.

Orders

The parties should have copies of any interlocutory orders made **9.06.11** before trial, for example:

(a) Order for service of any pleading and/or particulars.
(b) Order made on application for summary judgment.
(c) Order(s) made on directions.
(d) Order(s) for discovery.

Evidential documents

9.06.12 The party should also assemble the evidential documents, see **9.06.13–16**, in chronological order in a bundle, see **9.06.17**.

Documents between the parties created before the cause of action

9.06.13 For example:

(a) Pre-contract enquiries/representations.
(b) Contracts.
(c) Title deeds.
(d) Advertising material.

Documents between the parties created after the cause of action

9.06.14 For example:

(a) Correspondence (including the letter before action).
(b) Invoices.

Agreed documents

9.06.15 For example:

(a) Reports.
(b) Schedules.
(c) Photographs.
(d) Plans.

Privileged documents

9.06.16 Privileged documents may only be put in a bundle by agreement between the parties.
For example:

(a) "Without prejudice" correspondence between the parties.
(b) Correspondence with a party's own lawyers.

(c) Medical records or experts' reports that have not been disclosed and upon which a party does not wish to rely.

Presentation of documents in a bundle

The bundle of documents is usually prepared by the plaintiff. The bundle may be divided into sections for ease of reference. **9.06.17**

The sections may follow the paragraph numbers in **9.06.08–16.**

The documents in the bundle must be: **9.06.18**

(a) Firmly secured together.
(b) Arranged in chronological order, beginning with the earliest.
(c) Page numbered (paginated) consecutively at centre bottom.
(d) Fully and easily legible. If not, a typed copy should also be included.
(e) The bundle should also have an index.

In the absence of any order on directions or agreement to the contrary, copies of the bundle should be served on all parties to the action and the court. **9.06.19**

A copy or copies of the bundle should also be made available for witnesses and, in particular, where a document (for example, a plan) is likely to be marked by witness(es), extra copies should be made available.

If a bundle has not been served in advance, the party taken by surprise may apply for an adjournment.

Where there is likely to be an argument in relation to the admissibility of a document tending to establish any fact alleged in the pleadings, that document is usually included in the bundle and "argued out" (except where the judge is hearing the case with a jury). **9.06.20**

For example:

(a) A letter alleged to have been sent but not received.
(b) A receipt which is said to be a forgery.

If a document is excluded from the bundle at the request of a party, its admissibility can be argued at any stage or, if appropriate, in a preliminary application at the trial, see **9.06.36.** **9.06.21**

Lists of authorities

A party intending to raise a matter of law should serve a list of authorities on all the parties and the court at least 24 hours before the **9.06.22** hearing, see **22.01.06–07**. A party taken by surprise may ask for an adjournment.

9.06.23   If it has not been possible to follow the rule in **9.06.22**, the party should serve sufficient (photo)copies of the authorities on all the parties and the court at the hearing.

In the county court, even where the rule in **9.06.22** has been followed, the advocate is advised to take sufficient (photo)copies of the authorities to court wherever possible because many county courts and parties have limited access to legal works at short notice.

9.06.24   If not otherwise ordered on directions, see **9.04.10**, the parties should also consider the following (where, in any action, it might save time at the trial of the action):

(a) Serving a chronology of relevant events (a "chronology"), see **22.01.04**.
(b) Serving an outline submission of legal argument (a "skeleton argument"), see **22.01.03**.

Practice

Introduction

9.06.25   For right of audience, dress, mode of address and conduct generally, see **9.01.13–18**.

Conduct of the trial

9.06.26   The trial of an action is held in open court before a single judge of the High Court.

If the public are excluded and the court is sitting *in camera*, the conduct of the trial and mode of address are the same as in open court. The advocates are usually robed.

A trial may be heard with a jury in the following circumstances:

(a) Defamation.
(b) Actions (against the police) for malicious prosecution or false imprisonment.
(c) Actions where there is an allegation of fraud.

Application for a jury trial should be made on directions, see **9.04.10(l)**.

Calling the case

The associate will (usually) stand and read out the name of the case. **9.06.27**
The parties should be present in court ready for the case to be called.
If the parties are not present:
In the Queen's Bench Division: The case will usually be called
outside court.
In the Chancery Division: The case may not be called outside court
and the action may be struck out.

Presence of the parties and/or witnesses in court

The parties and/or witnesses will usually be present in court throug- **9.06.28**
hout the proceedings and/or the day or part of the day on which the
party and/or witness gives evidence.
A party may make an application to exclude a witness where, for
example, there is an allegation of misconduct by that witness.

Introduction of the parties

The plaintiff usually introduces the parties to the court: **9.06.29**

"In this action I appear for the plaintiff. My learned friend,
(*name*), appears for the (*name of defendant/party*) or (*Name*)
appears in person."

Where a party appears in person, the judge may ask if the unrepresented party is content not to be represented.

- OMIT **9.06.30–35** if all parties attend.

Attendance of the parties

A party giving material evidence in his case should attend. If he does **9.06.30**
not attend or appear by his legal representative, the court may proceed
with the trial or adjourn the case (usually with costs thrown away), as
appropriate.
A party not giving material evidence in his case need not attend but
must appear by his legal representative.

If a defendant or party does not attend, the plaintiff may say: **9.06.31**

"(*Name of party*) does not appear and is not represented today. I
am instructed that a notice giving this date was sent to all parties
on (*date*). I would, therefore, seek to prove my case in the
absence of (*name of party*)."

Unless the judge indicates that it is unnecessary, the plaintiff will then call evidence, see **9.06.34.**

9.06.32   If the plaintiff does not attend and the defendant has not served a counterclaim, the defendant may say:

> **"The plaintiff does not appear and is not represented today. I would therefore seek to have the claim dismissed for want of prosecution. And for costs."**

9.06.33   If there is a counterclaim, the defendant may also say:

> **"I would seek to prove the counterclaim in the absence of the plaintiff."**

Unless the judge indicates that it is unnecessary, the defendant will then call evidence on the counterclaim, see **9.06.34.**

9.06.34   A party seeking to prove his case in the absence of another party should call evidence only from witnesses limited to the matters essential to prove his case against that party. He may prove his case by the use of affidavit evidence, with the leave of the court, provided he can establish that the affidavits have been served.

9.06.35   The evidence may be treated briefly and the advocate should note with care any indication from the judge to shorten the case.

- OMIT **9.06.36** if there are no preliminary applications.

Preliminary applications

9.06.36   Preliminary applications may include:

(a) Amendments to pleadings.
(b) Argument as to admissibility of evidence.
(c) Holding a split trial.
(d) Holding a view.
(e) Administrative matters, for example, timing.
(f) Where the judge is hearing the case with a jury, questions of the admissibility of evidence may be determined before the plaintiff opens, see also **5.04.16–17**.
(g) See also **9.04.10**.

9.06.37   If the judge is sitting with a jury, the jury will then be called to the jury box and sworn, see also **5.04.21**.

Order of presentation and speeches

The plaintiff will usually present his case to the court first except where **9.06.38** all of the burden of proving the case falls on another party, for example:

(a) Where the plaintiff's claim has been struck out on an interlocutory application and there is a counterclaim.
(b) Where the plaintiff's case is agreed and there is a dispute over contribution between the defendant and other parties.

The party who is to open the case may then say: **9.06.39**

"Due to the fact that the plaintiff's claim was struck out/is agreed, the burden of proof in this case falls on the defendant. Therefore I propose to open the case, subject to (*the court's*) agreement."

In the absence of any ruling by the court and/or agreement between **9.06.40** the parties, the order of presentation and speeches is as follows:

Where the plaintiff and the defendant both call evidence: **9.06.41**
    Plaintiff opens.
    Plaintiff's evidence.
    Defendant opens.
    Defendant's evidence.
    Defendant closes.
    Plaintiff closes.
    Defendant's response (if permitted).

Where the plaintiff calls evidence and the defendant calls no **9.06.42** evidence:
    Plaintiff opens.
    Plaintiff's evidence.
    Plaintiff closes.
    Defendant closes.
    Plaintiff's response (if permitted).

Where there are two or more defendants and/or parties and, the **9.06.43** plaintiff calls evidence and the defendants and/or parties call no evidence:
    Plaintiff opens.
    Plaintiff's evidence.
    Plaintiff closes.
    Defendants and/or parties close in order of title.
    Plaintiff's response (if permitted).

9.06.44   Where there are two or more defendants and/or parties and, the plaintiff and the defendants and/or parties all call evidence:
> Plaintiff opens.
> Plaintiff's evidence.
> First defendant opens.
> First defendant's evidence.
>>   Continue in order of title.
> Defendants and/or other parties close in order of title.
> Plaintiff closes.
> Defendants' and/or other parties' response (if permitted, in such order as determined by the court).

9.06.45   Where there are two or more defendants and/or parties and, the plaintiff calls evidence and one or more, but not all, of the defendants and/or parties call evidence:
> Plaintiff opens.
> Plaintiff's evidence.
> Defendant and/or party calling evidence opens.
> Defendant and/or party calls evidence.
>>   Continue in order of title.
> Defendant and/or party calling evidence close in the order that they presented their cases.
> Plaintiff closes.
> Defendant and/or party not calling evidence close in order of title.
> Response by any party (if permitted, in such order as determined by the court).

The case on behalf of the plaintiff

Plaintiff's opening

9.06.46   The plaintiff will usually open the case. The opening should be carefully prepared, see **22.03.01–06.**

The opening is important because it enables the plaintiff to "set the scene" and to predispose the court in the plaintiff's favour by:

(a) Directing the judge's attention to the better points in the plaintiff's case.

(b) Explaining, in a manner favourable to the plaintiff, any contentious points in the defendant's case as disclosed in the pleadings.

9.06.47   The plaintiff's opening should contain:

(a) An explanation of the nature of the case, for example:

"**This is an action for** (*state nature of relief sought*) **for** (*state cause of action*)."

(b) A summary of the relevant pleadings, with reference to the plaintiff's case, for example:

"**The** (*state cause of action*) **is set out in paragraph(s) (–) of the statement of claim as follows** (*state nature of claim*)."

"**The defendant contends in paragraph(s) (–) of the defence that** (*state nature of defence*)."

"(*The court*) **may be assisted on** (*state issue*) **if I were to draw** (*the court's*) **attention to the document at page (–) in the bundle.**"

(c) A summary of the points of agreement and/or dispute between the parties.

(d) An outline of the evidence upon which the plaintiff intends to rely and/or whether it is live evidence or in documentary form.

(e) An outline of the contents of the bundle of documents (in such detail as necessary) describing the documents upon which the plaintiff relies and any documents which may be the subject of argument.

(f) A summary of the relevant law upon which the plaintiff relies (if not agreed).

The judge may clarify any matters raised in the opening with any other party, for example: **9.06.48**

"(*Name of defendant and/or party*) **do you accept the law as put forward by** (*name*) **for the plaintiff?**"

The plaintiff may conclude the opening by saying: **9.06.49**

"**Unless I can assist you further, I now propose to call the evidence. And I call (the plaintiff in this action).**"

Evidence on behalf of the plaintiff

Witnesses

The plaintiff and/or any witness(es) on behalf of the plaintiff is then called and identified.   **9.06.50**

A witness may also be asked to describe his relationship to the plaintiff and/or the action.

9.06.51 The usual rules as to the examination, cross-examination and re-examination of witnesses apply, see **Chapter 21**, Examination of Witnesses, except that where there has been an exchange of witness statements, a witness may (with the leave of the judge) affirm the statement and then be tendered for cross-examination.

Order of cross-examination

9.06.52 The order of cross-examination of the plaintiff's witnesses, where there is more than one defendant and/or party, is in order of title. The plaintiff may re-examine.

Questions of admissibility

9.06.53 The relevant law in relation to the admissibility of evidence should be researched. The following is a brief guide to the practice:

Where there is an argument about admissibility, the order of submissions is usually as follows:

(a) Either party (usually the defendant) identifies the evidence to which an objection is taken:
    (i) If the objection can be considered without hearing/reading the disputed evidence, the party may make his objection without reference to the disputed evidence.
    (ii) If the objection cannot be considered without hearing/reading the disputed evidence, the defendant should draw the judge's attention to the disputed evidence.
(b) The defendant then gives reasons for the objection and refers to any relevant law.
(c) Reply by the plaintiff.
(d) Response by the defendant, with the leave of the judge, see **9.06.86**, dealing with any points of law raised by the plaintiff or the judge, but not repeating the submissions in (b).
(e) Decision by the judge. Where (a)(ii) applies and the judge rules against the party intending to call the disputed evidence, the judge will usually state in the summing up that he has not taken that evidence into account.

9.06.54 Where the judge is hearing the case with a jury, questions of admissibility are decided in the absence of the jury, see also **5.04.40.**

Affidavit evidence

9.06.55 A witness who has given evidence on affidavit (for example, in interlocutory proceedings before trial) may be called, see **21.06.**

Expert evidence

The report/witness statement of an expert should be disclosed to all **9.06.56**
parties following directions, see **9.04.10(g).**

If agreed, the report will usually be part of the bundle, see **9.06.12 &
15(a)**, and may be opened by any party or it may be referred to at an
appropriate time during the evidence.

If not agreed, the expert must be called, see **21.03.**

Evidence under the Civil Evidence Acts

The Civil Evidence Acts enable a party to introduce hearsay evidence **9.06.57**
contained in statements or documents; for example, maps, photographs, plans, computer records.

The relevant law should be researched. The following is a brief guide
to the practice under the Civil Evidence Acts.

The party seeking to introduce hearsay evidence under the Civil **9.06.58**
Evidence Acts must serve a notice on all other parties (in practice) a
reasonable time before the trial.

The notice will usually contain particulars of:

(a) The person by whom a statement or document was made and to
    whom it was made.
(b) The circumstances in which the statement or document was
    made.
(c) Particulars of the statement or a copy of the document.
(d) The reason(s) that the statement or document is admissible under
    the Civil Evidence Acts, see **9.06.59.**

A statement or document may be admissible under the Civil Evid- **9.06.59**
ence Acts where the person who made the statement or document is:

(a) Dead
(b) Beyond the seas
(c) Unfit to attend the trial
(d) Unidentifiable
(e) Untraceable
(f) Unlikely to be able to remember

A party may serve a counternotice requiring the party serving notice **9.06.60**
to call the maker of the statement or document where the reason(s)
given in **9.06.58(d)** and **9.06.59** is not substantiated.

If a counternotice is not served, the party may introduce the evidence
described in **9.06.58(c)** at the trial.

The party introducing the evidence may say: **9.06.61**

"The evidence of the next witness has been served by notice under the Civil Evidence Act on (*date*)**. The relevant document is at page (–) of the bundle.**

The notice states (*state reason in* **9.06.58(d)** *and refer the court to any supporting evidence*)**."**

9.06.62   If a counternotice has been served, the party may then say:

"A counternotice was served on (*date*)**. And we would therefore seek your ruling on whether this evidence can be adduced."**

The argument will follow the order of submissions in **9.06.53**.

Oral admissions

9.06.63   An oral admission may be made at the hearing by agreement between the parties, for example:

"I have been asked to admit that (*state admission*)**. And I make that admission."**

Written admissions and notices to admit facts

9.06.64   A written admission (including any admission made in the pleadings) is usually made before the hearing. The party seeking the admission may serve a notice to admit facts.

The failure by a party on whom the notice to admit facts has been served to serve a counternotice usually within 7 days (or any extended time) is deemed to be an admission of the fact alleged.

9.06.65   At the trial, the party must prove service of the notice, for example:

"On (*date*) **the plaintiff's solicitors served a notice on the defendant to admit that** (*state nature of admission*)**.**

The defendant was asked to serve any counter notice within 14 days and has not done so.

A copy of the notice is to be found at page (–) of the bundle."

Agreements

9.06.66   The parties to an action may make any agreement which the court is satisfied is a lawful agreement. Where a party making an agreement is under a disability (for example, a child), the court must also be satisfied that it is a reasonable agreement.

An agreement may be made at any stage and, if necessary, put in writing for the judge.

A view

If a view is considered appropriate, an application should be made **9.06.67** by any party on directions, see **9.04**, or as a preliminary application, see **9.06.36(d)**, or it may be made at any convenient time.

A view may be made either before, during or after the evidence is heard.

On a view, the parties may point out, for example; objects, site lines, **9.06.68** landmarks and obstructions to the judge, but should not discuss them.

Close of the plaintiff's case

When the plaintiff and/or the party calling evidence, see **9.06.69** **9.06.38—39**, has called and/or read all the evidence and any admission and/or agreement has been made, the case is said to be closed. The usual form of words is:

"That is the case for the plaintiff."

Submission of no case to answer

The grounds on which a submission of no case to answer may be made **9.06.70** and the relevant law should be researched. As a general rule, the judge will not hear a submission of no case to answer if there is more than one defendant and/or party.

In practice, a submission is very rarely made because the court will **9.06.71** usually "put the defendant to his election". This means that the court will only hear the submission of no case to answer if the defendant elects not to call evidence in support of his case.

The practice of the judge should be clarified with him, for example: **9.06.72**

"I am considering a submission of no case to answer. I would be grateful if you would indicate whether, if I make a submission and it is not upheld, I would be permitted to call evidence on behalf of the defendant."

The judge may indicate that the defendant will be "put to his **9.06.73** election" for example:

"No, (*name of advocate***), the usual rule must apply."**

In practice, if a submission of no case to answer is made, the order of **9.06.74** submissions is as follows:

(a) The defendant may begin:

"I submit that there is no case to answer on the ground that the plaintiff has failed in law to establish any case against the defendant for the following reasons (*state reasons*)**."**

(b) The defendant should identify the evidence to which he refers and direct the judge to any relevant law.
(c) Reply by the plaintiff.
(d) Response by the defendant, with the leave of the judge.
(e) Decision by the judge.

9.06.75   For the procedure in a case where the judge is hearing the case with a jury, see **5.04.57–59.**

The case for the defendant and/or other party

Introduction

9.06.76   For preparation, see **9.06.06–24**. For order of presentation and speeches, see **9.06.40–45.**

Calling no evidence

9.06.77   Where a defendant and/or other party is not calling evidence, he should state this in clear terms:

"I call no evidence on behalf of (*name of defendant and/or party*)**."**

Defendant's and/or other party's opening

9.06.78   The defendant and/or other party has the right to open the case if he is calling evidence, see also **22.03.01–06.**

9.06.79   The opening may contain:

(a) A summary of the defendant's and/or other party's pleadings (usually where the pleadings were not opened by the plaintiff).
(b) Where there is a counterclaim, an explanation of the nature of the counterclaim if it has not become clear from cross-examination.
(c) A criticism of the plaintiff's case (usually where it has been discredited by cross-examination).
(d) An outline of the documents in the bundle on which the defendant and/or other party relies.

(e) A summary of the relevant law on which the defendant and/or other party relies (if not agreed).

The defendant and/or other party may conclude the opening by saying: **9.06.80**

> **"Unless I can assist you further, I now propose to call the evidence. And I now call** (*name of defendant or party or witness*)**."**

Evidence on behalf of the defendant and/or other parties

The evidence on behalf of the defendant and/or other parties is subject to the same rules and is presented in the same way as the evidence on behalf of the plaintiff, see **9.06.50–69.** **9.06.81**

A submission of no case to answer by the plaintiff on a defendant's counterclaim may be, but in practice is never, made. **9.06.82**

Speeches

For the order of speeches, see **9.06.40–45.** **9.06.83**

Content of closing speeches

See also, **22.03.09–12.** In closing, a party will usually: **9.06.84**

(a) Sum up the basic points of his case in so far as those points will assist the judge to give judgment for him.
(b) Compare the evidence of the parties and the character and motives of the witnesses (if relevant).
(c) Refer the court to any relevant law, see **9.06.22–24.**

The judge will listen to the submissions of the parties in turn but may interrupt to indicate agreement or otherwise on any point, for example: **9.06.85**

> **"I need not trouble you on that point, but I would like to hear you on** (*state issue*)**."**

Note: The party addressing the judge should address the judge on the issue indicated by the judge before continuing his speech.

Response

9.06.86   A party may respond, on a matter of law only, with the leave, or by invitation, of the judge, for example:

> "(*Name of party*) **has referred to the case of** (*name of case*) **on which I have not addressed you. I would be grateful if I could address you on that point.**"

or the judge may say:

> "**What do you say about** (*state issues raised by other party in closing*), (*name of party*)?"

Judgment

9.06.87   The judge may:

(a) Deliver a full judgment.
(b) Deliver a short judgment with reasons to follow.
(c) Reserve judgment (usually to another day).

9.06.88   The judgment will usually contain:

(a) A description of the parties.
(b) A summary of the nature of the case.
(c) A summary of the issues.
(d) A summary of the evidence.
(e) A description of the manner in which the judge intends to approach the relevant evidence.
(f) A summary of the legal argument and his ruling thereon.
(g) A determination of the facts, with reference to any documentary evidence (if appropriate).

9.06.89   The parties should (and, if counsel, are obliged to) take a full note of the judgment in order that it can be considered before an appeal is lodged.

Judgment order

9.06.90   The judgment order will usually follow the judge's determination of the facts. If the judge has not announced the judgment order at the conclusion of his judgment, the successful party may say:

> "**I ask for judgment for the** (*state name of party*) **for/on** (*state nature of relief sought*) **in the sum of** (*state sum*).

> And that the (*name of unsuccessful party's*) (*relief sought*) be dismissed.
> And, for interest on (*state sum*) at the rate of (–)% per annum from (*appropriate date*) to today (*see* **9.06.92–95**).
> And, for costs (*see* **9.06.96**)."

Where, on an order for a split trial, the question of liability is tried first, the successful party may say: **9.06.91**

> "I ask for judgment for the (plaintiff) for damages to be assessed."

Interest

Interest is only obtainable where it has been claimed in the pleadings. The total interest due should have been calculated by each party in advance. **9.06.92**

If the case relates to an agreement in which a rate of interest is specified, then that rate will normally apply. The plaintiff may say: **9.06.93**

> "The plaintiff's claim includes a claim for interest which is set at (–) % per annum in clause (–) of the contract and I would submit that this is the appropriate rate."

In other cases, the rate will be such as may be approved by the judge. The plaintiff may say: **9.06.94**

> "Interest is claimed at the rate of (–) %. That has been the prevailing rate throughout most of the time these proceedings have been in existence.
> And I would submit that interest at (–)% would be the appropriate rate."

Interest on general damages for pain and suffering in personal injury cases is awarded at a lower rate. **9.06.95**

Costs

It is not unusual for there to be an argument on the question of costs, in particular, where there have been a number of interlocutory applications, see **20.03.03–21 & 28**. **9.06.96**

Appeal

Appeal from a judgment of the High Court is to the Court of Appeal (Civil Division). The notice of appeal must be served on the parties and the court within 28 days, see **12.01.17–18**. **9.06.97**

7. COMPANIES COURT

Introduction

9.07.01 There is no separate court which deals with matters arising from the operation of a company, although where a matter is within the jurisdiction of the companies registrar in the Chancery Division it is often said to be in the companies court.

9.07.02 As a general rule, the practice will follow the practice described in the preceding sections of this chapter.

The practice on an uncontested winding up of a company is distinct. The following is a brief guide.

WINDING UP A COMPANY

Preparation

9.07.03 A person who wishes to obtain satisfaction of a debt owed by a company may apply to wind up that company.

9.07.04 In order for a creditor to petition to wind up a company, the company must be indebted to that person for a sum in excess of the current financial limit.

9.07.05 The petitioner is usually described as either:
A trade creditor (see **9.07.06**), or
A judgment creditor (see **5.07.07**).

9.07.06 A trade creditor is a person who is owed money by the company; it does not necessarily have to be a trade debt in the normal sense of the word "trade".

9.07.07 A judgment creditor is a person who has an unsatisfied judgment outstanding against the company and whose attempts to enforce that judgment in other ways have failed.

The statutory demand

9.07.08 Before a petition is presented and filed it is usual for there to be a statutory demand. This is a formal written demand for the sum due.

A statutory demand sets out the amount of the debt, the way it arises and full particulars of how it is calculated. It also sets out the purpose and effect of the document and how to comply with it. It is signed by the creditor or a person authorised to sign on his behalf.

Whether or not a statutory demand has been served, it is necessary that the company's debt should be undisputed. The companies court is not the proper forum for trying disputed debts.

If an alleged creditor threatens to present a winding up petition based upon a disputed debt, the company may seek an injunction to restrain presentation of the petition. In such a case, the process is instituted by originating motion in the companies court, see **9.02.54.**

If it is too late, the company may apply to restrain advertisement of the petition. An ordinary notice of motion in the petition may then be used.

The petition

The petition must contain full details of the debt and any statutory **9.07.09** demand. Three copies of the petition must be filed with an affidavit (which must be filed not later than 7 days after the petition) verifying the facts contained in the petition.

The petition and affidavit are filed in the office of the registrar. A date and time for the hearing will be fixed.

The affidavit verifying the petition

The affidavit must be made by the petitioner or an officer or servant of **9.07.10** the petitioner or other authorised person (usually the petitioner's solicitor). If the deponent is not the petitioner, that person should state his capacity and authority.

Service

The petition must be served on the company at the company's **9.07.11** registered office:

(a) on a person known to be a director, officer or employee of the company, or

(b) on a person adknowledging himself to be a person named in (a), or

(c) by leaving the petition at the company's registered office.

(a) or (b) are recommended.

Affidavit of service

9.07.12   An affidavit of service of the petition (setting out the manner of service) must be made.

Advertisement

9.07.13   The petition must be advertised, usually in the London Gazette. It should appear not less than 7 days before the hearing and not less than 7 days after service.

The court can give leave for an alternative publication for the advertisement.

The advertisement should contain:

(a) All information required for any interested party to identify the company and the petitioner(s)
(b) The date of the hearing
(c) The name of the petitioner's solicitor (if appropriate)
(d) A statement that any party wishing to appear at the hearing must give notice.

Certificate of compliance

9.07.14   At least 5 days before the hearing the petitioner or his solicitor must serve on the court a certificate of compliance with the rules as to service and advertisement.

The certificate of compliance must show:

(a) The date of presentation of the petition
(b) The date fixed for the hearing
(c) The date of service of the petition
(d) The date of publication of the advertisement (with a copy of the advertisement).

List of supporting/opposing creditors

9.07.15   By the day of the hearing the party or his solicitor should serve on the court a list of all creditors who have given notice that they support or oppose the petition. This is the "list" in **9.07.29 & 32**. If no one has given notice, the list is described as negative.

Time limits

9.07.16   The Insolvency Rules set out the time limits applied in **9.07.08–15**.

In some limited circumstances (for example, where the advertisement was published a day late) leave can be given by the court, at the hearing, to dispense with that formality but only if there is no possibility of an injustice being occasioned to any interested party.

Practice

Introduction

All unopposed petitions are listed before the registrar of the compan-   **9.07.17**
ies court on Wednesdays. The hearing is in open court.

A party addressing the court should do so standing. The party should be brief and to the point.

Mode of address

The registrar is addressed as **Sir.**   **9.07.18**

Right of audience

Barristers, solicitors, petitioners in person.   **9.07.19**

Dress

Barristers and solicitors should be robed. Petitioners in person should   **9.07.20**
be respectably dressed.

The cases are listed in the Daily Cause List in half hour groups at   **9.07.21**
10.30 am, 11.00 am, 11.30 am, etc.

The court room will probably be very full throughout the day, see   **9.07.22**
9.07.27, and it is up to the advocate to make sure he is in court at the right time.

The ushers do not take the names of the parties or call the cases.   **9.07.23**

If there are any other interested parties (for example, the company or   **9.07.24**
any supporting or opposing creditor) the petitioner's advocate should take the names of their advocates.

The advocate may call out the name of the case outside court or ask   **9.07.25**
in court if attending before 10.30 am.

The parties may then negotiate or discuss any compromise of the petition.

If there are any queries as to the state of the court file these will be   **9.07.26**
very difficult, if not impossible, to deal with once the court has started.

The associate or his assistant is normally in court early and may be consulted.

The hearing

9.07.27   The registrar enters and all stand.

Once the registrar sits, those who can find a seat sit down. It is very likely that there will be insufficient seating, so some advocates may have to stand in the side aisles.

9.07.28   The cases will be called on in the order shown on the Daily Cause List.

The case is called by the associate by number and name. If nobody responds to the call it will be repeated. If there is still no response the petition will be dismissed.

The advocate for the petitioner, on hearing the case called, should stand to address the court.

9.07.29   In a straightforward case, the advocate may say:

> **"This is a trade creditor's petition in the sum of £15,525 odd** (*Note: Figures are rounded to omit pence and called "odd"*) **(pursuant to a statutory demand).**
>
> **The debtor company is not/is represented by** (*name*)**. (I believe that) The list** (*of supporting creditors*) **is negative (or, there is (–) supporting creditor represented by** (*name*)**). (As far as I am aware) The documents are in order** (*all relevant documents have been served within the time limits and comply with the rules*)**.**
>
> **I therefore ask for the usual compulsory order** (*see* **9.07.30**)**."**

The advocate may use the phrases **"I believe"** and **"as far as I am aware"** if he has not had the opportunity to check the relevant documents.

The "usual compulsory order"

9.07.30   Order that:

(a) The company be wound up, and
(b) The company pay the petitioner's costs (see **20.03.03**).

9.07.31   **9.07.32–44** apply in a less straightforward case.

The list is not negative

The advocate may say: **9.07.32**

"The (opposing) creditor does not appear and is not represented (so far as I am aware). In the circumstances, I ask for the usual compulsory order."

Late advertisement

The advocate may say: **9.07.33**

"The documents are in order save that the advertisement was published a day late."

If the company does not appear:

"Would you waive that defect."

If the company appears:

"The company is represented today. I would be grateful if you would waive that defect and dispense with the need to readvertise."

The affidavit of service is defective

The advocate may say: **9.07.34**

"Might I have 7 days (*to file a fresh affidavit*)."

Payment of the debt

If the debt has been paid (or arrangements have been made accord- **9.07.35**
ingly) before the hearing, the petition may be dismissed.
When the petition is called the advocate may say:

"Payment has been made/Suitable arrangements for payment have been made. Accordingly, would you dismiss the petition with/without costs."

Adjournments in the list

It sometimes happens that an offer of settlement is made at the door of **9.07.36**
the court and negotiations are still taking place when the petition is
called on.

The petitioner may say (after introducing the parties):

"We are talking. May it be mentioned next time around/at a convenient moment."

Or, simply:

"Next time around, please. (See 9.07.37–39)."

"Next time around"

9.07.37   When the list (or a group of cases in the list) has been finished, the associate will usually read out the names of the cases not dealt with first time around. These cases may then be dealt with in the same way as they could have been, first time around.

A "convenient moment"

9.07.38   Unless there is a gap caused by a half hour group of cases finishing before the next group starts, a "convenient moment" will usually be at the end of the list.

How to get a case mentioned

9.07.39   (a) Pass a note to the associate who may fit the case in at a convenient moment.
(b) When there is a natural break in the proceedings, the advocate may say:

"May I mention case (–). This case is now agreed/to be stood out."

Adjournments to another day

9.07.40   If the parties (are negotiating and) agree to ask for an adjournment, either party may apply for the case to be stood out.
A case will be stood out for 7 days or a multiple of weeks.
Either party may say:

"(We are talking and) I would apply to stand the case out for two weeks."

Substitution

9.07.41   Substitution may occur:

(a) Where the petitioner has been paid his debt but a supporting creditor has not.

(b) Where the petitioner has failed to prosecute the petition.

A supporting creditor may attend and seek to be substituted as the petitioner. The court has a general discretion to permit substitution and may give an order on such terms as it thinks just.   **9.07.42**

Opposed petitions

A company opposing the petition must serve an affidavit not less than 7 days before the hearing. The company will normally be represented at the hearing.   **9.07.43**

The petition will usually be taken out of the registrar's list and put into the judge's list which is heard on Mondays.

If the petition is in the registrar's list and there is opposition, there may be argument but if the argument is longer than a few minutes, the petition will be stood out to the judge's list.

Hearing of an opposed petition

The hearing of an opposed petition will follow the general practice in **9.06** Trial.   **9.07.44**

CHAPTER 10

Family Proceedings in the County Court and High Court

1. INTRODUCTION

Introduction

10.01.01 In practice there are no significant differences between the practice of the county court and the High Court in family proceedings.

Family proceedings

10.01.02 A party may commence proceedings for divorce or judicial separation at a designated county court or in the Divorce Registry of the High Court.

10.01.03 The petitioner or a respondent, who files an answer, in proceedings for divorce or judicial separation, may apply for ancillary relief (*i.e.* relief which is ancillary to the proceedings).

A party to a marriage and, in some cases, a party living with a co-habitee, may apply for an injunction restraining the other party from molesting that party or a child of the family (or dealing with any property intending to defeat a claim for ancillary relief). **10.01.04**

Applications in relation to children are made principally under the Children Act 1989. They may be made by persons who have a sufficient interest in the welfare of the child and those who have a particular interest such as adoption, legitimacy or maintenance of the child or its return to its country of residence. **10.01.05**

They may be between private individuals (private law cases) or a local authority and private individuals (public law cases).

The court

Proceedings will be heard: **10.01.06**

    (a) In open court before a judge of the High Court.
    (b) In open court before a judge of the county court.
    (c) In chambers.

In practice, all applications in the family division are in chambers except committals for breach of an order or undertaking, defended petitions, Children Act appeals, judicial review and declarations as to status.

Judgments are sometimes delivered in open court.

Proceedings in open court before a judge of the High Court

Right of audience

Barristers, parties in person. **10.01.07**

Dress

Barristers are robed. Parties in person should be respectably dressed. **10.01.08**

Mode of address

Judge: **My lord/my lady** **10.01.09**

Proceedings in open court before a judge of the county court

Right of audience

10.01.10   Barristers, solicitors, parties in person.

Dress

10.01.11   Barristers and solicitors are robed. Parties in person should be respectably dressed.

Mode of address

10.01.12   Judge: **Your honour**

Proceedings in chambers before:

(a) A judge of the High Court
(b) A judge of the county court
(c) A district judge of the High Court or county court

Right of audience

10.01.13   Barristers, solicitors, experienced solicitors' clerks, parties in person.

Dress

10.01.14   Barristers and solicitors are not robed. All parties should be respectably dressed.

Mode of address

10.01.15   High Court judge and
deputy High Court judge: **My lord/my lady**
County court judge: **Your Honour**
District judge: **Sir/Madam**

Conduct in open court and in chambers

10.01.16   Although the system of resolving disputes between the parties is adversarial, the parties should (and are actively encouraged to) settle disputes by compromise and negotiation.

Referring to the parties or witnesses

In any application, the parties are advised to agree, before the hearing, **10.01.17** how to refer to the parties or witnesses, particularly in the following situations:

(a) Where the parties have remarried.
(b) Where the court is considering an application in which the respondent to the petition is the applicant.

A useful form of words is for the parties to refer to **the husband, the wife, the child** or **children**, and to the new spouse as **Mr** or **Mrs** (name).

2. PETITIONS

Introduction

Proceedings for divorce and judicial separation are commenced by **10.02.01** petition. A petition is issued out of:

(a) The divorce registry in London
(b) Any county court, which is designated to accept divorce business.

The petition

The petition will contain: **10.02.02**

(a) The names of the parties.
(b) The addresses of the parties (and the address at which they last lived).
(c) The date of the marriage.
(d) The names and dates of birth of any children of the parties.
(e) The particulars upon which the petitioner relies.

The petition will also contain a prayer, claiming the following relief: **10.02.03**
For the petitioner only:

(a) A decree of divorce.
(b) A decree of judicial separation.

For the petitioner and/or children:

(c) A property adjustment order.

(d) A periodical payments order.

(e) A lump sum order.

(f) A secured periodical payments order.

(g) Any order relating to the children of the marriage.

(h) Costs.

Special procedure

10.02.04   Where a divorce is not contested it can proceed by way of special procedure in which most matters, except those relating to children are dealt with by post.

Defended petitions

10.02.05   If the respondent to a petition files an answer, the petition is treated as defended. A defended petition is rare.

10.02.06   A defended petition may be heard by:

(a) A judge of the family division.

(b) A county court judge, sitting as a judge of the High Court.

(c) A county court judge in a county court designated as a divorce trial court.

Practice

10.02.07   The trial of a defended petition will follow the practice in **9.06** Trial in the High Court.

3. INJUNCTIONS IN FAMILY PROCEEDINGS

Introduction

10.03.01   All county courts have jurisdiction to grant injunctions against molestation and/or to order a spouse or cohabitee to leave (or not return) to the parties' home.

Injunctions may also be granted ancillary to an application under the Children Act.

Non-molestation order

A non-molestation order may be granted: **10.03.02**

(a) To protect a party to divorce proceedings or a child of the family.
(b) To protect spouses, cohabitees and their children pursuant to the
     Domestic Violence Act.

The order will often be granted *ex parte*. A return date may be fixed,   **10.03.03**
see **10.03.32–33.**

The usual terms of the order are: **10.03.04**

> **"That the respondent do not assault, molest or otherwise inter-
> fere with the applicant/petitioner** (*state name*) **or** (*state names of
> children*) **by himself, his servants or agents."**

Exclusion order

An exclusion order may be granted in similar circumstances to a non-   **10.03.05**
molestation order either under the Domestic Violence and Matrimonial
Proceedings Act (DVMPA) or the Matrimonial Homes Act (MHA).

The order may be granted *ex parte*, usually where the judge is   **10.03.06**
satisfied that the respondent has left the parties' home. A return date
may be fixed, see **10.03.32–33.**

The usual terms of the order are: **10.03.07**

> **"That the respondent do not return to/approach, enter or
> attempt to enter** (*address*)**."**

Ouster

An ouster may be granted where the applicant is able to show that the   **10.03.08**
other party has caused actual bodily harm to the applicant or a child.

The order will only be granted *ex parte* in the most exceptional   **10.03.09**
circumstances, see **10.03.24.** A return date will usually be fixed, see
10.03.32–33.

The usual terms of the order are: **10.03.10**

> **"That the respondent vacate** (*address*) (*or* **the former matrimo-
> nial home at** (*address*)**) by** (*date and time*) **and do not return
> thereto (save as may be agreed in writing for the purposes of
> access to** (*name(s) of children*)**)."**

Power of arrest

10.03.11   A power of arrest may be attached to a non-molestation or exclusion order or an ouster, for the protection of the applicant, only where the application is made under the DVMPA.

It may be granted only where the applicant is able to show that:

(a) the other party has caused actual bodily harm to the applicant or a child, and
(b) the other party is likely to do so again.

Preparation

10.03.12   If the application is made other than under the DVMPA or the MHA a plaint or petition should be issued.

10.03.13   In all applications the applicant should have:

(a) Notice of application.
(b) Affidavit in support (if *ex parte*, reasons must be given).
(c) Draft order (optional).

10.03.14   The relevant forms must be submitted. If the application is *ex parte* (usually in an urgent case) the minimum practical requirement is an application and an affidavit, see **10.03.25**.

The advocate is advised to check the practice of the court because some courts will not hear the application until all the documents are available however urgent the case.

Practice

Introduction

10.03.15   The hearing is before a judge or district judge. Barristers, solicitors and qualified legal executives (in some courts) have a right of audience.

10.03.16   The hearing is in chambers. It may take place in the judge's or district judge's room or in the court room. In the judge's or district judge's room the parties will sit. In the court room the parties will stand to address the judge or district judge.

Advocates are not robed.

Presentation of the application

The advocate should always bear in mind that an order for non-molestation, exclusion or ouster affects both the liberty and property rights of the parties. It is therefore imperative that the court has all the information it needs to make a proper decision. This includes information which may not put the applicant in the best light. **10.03.17**

For the purposes of **10.03.19–41** it is assumed that the applicant is the wife or female cohabitee in family proceedings. **10.03.18**

Ex parte applications

A party making an urgent *ex parte* application will usually telephone the court to find out when a judge can hear the application. **10.03.19**
If a judge is available and the party is able to attend court, the hearing will usually take place at a convenient time at the beginning or end of the judge's morning or afternoon list.

In a High Court case, if the party is able to attend the High Court, there is a High Court judge available during court hours to hear *ex parte* applications. A party need not telephone in advance but is advised to do so. **10.03.20**
In cases of extreme urgency, he may telephone out of court hours. Contact is made through the emergency duty officer of the RCJ.
In a Divorce Registry case, there is a county court judge sitting at the RCJ to hear such applications.

Attendance of the applicant

The applicant must attend court unless there is a good reason for her absence (for example, she is in hospital). **10.03.21**

The hearing

On arrival at court, the party should give his name to the usher or clerk and hand in any documentation, see **10.03.12–14.** **10.03.22**
The party will then wait to be called in to see the judge.

The party making the application may say: **10.03.23**

> **"This is my application for** (*state order sought*)**."**

The party should make it clear what order is sought, for example: **10.03.24**

> **"The application is for a non-molestation order and ouster. However, I accept that today the court will not order the respondent to leave the matrimonial home. Therefore, the application is for a non-molestation order only."**

10.03.25   If **10.03.14** applies, the party may then say:

> **"At present, there is no formal application/proceedings have not yet been commenced. And I undertake to issue within** (*for example, 24 hours*)**."**

10.03.26   The party may then refer the judge to the affidavit (in such detail as required), for example:

> **"There is a (draft) affidavit of** (*name of applicant*)**."**

10.03.27   The judge may indicate that he wishes to read the affidavit. He may then ask some questions to clarify matters.

10.03.28   The application will then usually proceed informally (often in the nature of a discussion between the advocate and the judge as to the merits of the application).

10.03.29   If there are matters which have arisen since the affidavit was drafted (or sworn), the advocate will usually call the applicant to give evidence, see **21.06.**

10.03.30   If the affidavit is defective, the advocate may be required to undertake to file an additional affidavit.

The order

10.03.31   The judge may:

(a) Grant the application and make an order.
(b) Refuse the application.
(c) Adjourn the case for further evidence and/or argument.

If the judge makes an order and **10.03.14 & 25** apply, the order will have no effect until such time as any conditions (for example, the issuing of proceedings) have been complied with.

The return date

10.03.32   If the application is granted or adjourned, a return date may be fixed (which is the date on which the case returns to court *inter partes*). The return date may be 7 days or (less frequently) up to 3 weeks.

In some courts which do not sit regularly, a return date is often not fixed. In which case, the respondent may apply for a date to be heard on the application. The order will state that the respondent has "liberty to apply". **10.03.33**

Costs

If the applicant is legally aided, the advocate should ask for legal aid taxation and a certificate for counsel (if appropriate), see **20.03.22–27**. **10.03.34**

Inter partes

The hearing will be *inter partes*: **10.03.35**

(a) On the return date of an *ex parte* application, see **10.03.32–33**.
(b) On the first hearing where the application has been made on notice.
(c) On any subsequent hearing.

Attendance of the parties

The respondent should attend court unless he intends to submit to the application in full or his solicitors have negotiated an agreement with the applicant in advance. **10.03.36**

Conduct

Applications for non-molestation, exclusion or ouster are often made at, or very soon after, the break-up of a relationship. The feelings of the parties are likely to be strong. **10.03.37**

The advocates should therefore try to assist their respective parties to come to a settlement of their affairs that each can live with. If there is a trial of the issues, it can often make the situation between the parties worse.

The respective advocates should be ready to discuss the issues sensibly and, if possible, to negotiate an agreed order (or a party may give an undertaking to the court).

Undertakings

If a party gives an undertaking to the court, the undertaking is a solemn promise to the court. It has the same effect as if an order had been made. **10.03.38**

Agreed orders

10.03.39   An agreed order may be put in writing in order that it can be handed to the judge for him to agree or amend. (It may be signed by the advocates).

The draft order must be in the specified form. The judge must approve the terms of any draft order or undertakings.

The effect of any breach must be explained to the party.

Practice at the hearing

10.03.40   Where there is a contested hearing, the practice is likely to follow the practice in **10.05.21–41** (with appropriate amendments).

Breach of an order or undertaking

10.03.41   A breach of an order or undertaking can be punished by the court as a contempt, see **10.04** Enforcement of injunctions.

4. ENFORCEMENT OF INJUNCTIONS

Introduction

10.04.01   Breach of an order made by, or an undertaking made to, the court is punishable as a contempt. This can be by reprimand, fine or committal to prison.

It is for this reason that an application for the enforcement of an injunction or undertaking is often known as a committal application.

The rules of evidence and procedure have to be strictly adhered to. The standard of proof is "beyond reasonable doubt" and not "on the balance of probabilities".

10.04.02   The party seeking to prove the contempt must prove:

(a) That the order was made and had a penal notice attached.
(b) That the order was duly served upon the person against whom the committal is sought.
(c) That the person is in breach.
(d) That service of notice "to show cause" (the application to commit) has been made.

Preparation

The advocate should prepare or ensure that he has the following: **10.04.03**

(a) A copy of the order, see also **10.04.04.**
(b) Affidavit of service of the order.
(c) Affidavit (of the applicant) of breach of the order.
(d) Affidavit of service of the application to commit.

The advocate should check that the court has a copy of the order on   **10.04.04**
the court file. If not, the advocate should ensure that he is able to prove
the order (usually by affidavit).

The court may dispense with this requirement if the respondent gave
an undertaking to the court, of which he is alleged to be in breach. He
will be assumed to know the terms of his own undertaking. It will have
been usual for him to sign a written undertaking at the time it was made
and this will be kept on the court file.

Conduct and dress in open court

A committal application is always before a judge in open court (even   **10.04.05**
though most committal applications relate to family, domestic or
matrimonial matters). The advocate is robed.

For the purposes of **10.04.07–13** it is assumed that the applicant is   **10.04.06**
the petitioning wife or female cohabitee in domestic proceedings.

Presence of the parties in court

The applicant must be present in court to be cross-examined on her   **10.04.07**
affidavit. The respondent should be, but is often not, present in court or
represented at the hearing.

If the respondent is not present it is essential that the applicant
proves:

(a) Service of the original order.
(b) Service of the notice of the committal hearing and affidavit(s).

If the respondent attends but is not represented, the judge will usually
warn him of the possible outcome of the case and ask him if he is
content not to be represented.

Practice

Opening

The applicant may open, as follows: **10.04.08**

233

> **"I appear for the petitioner in this case on her application to commit the respondent for contempt. The respondent is represented by (*name*)/the respondent appears in person."**

> **"On the (*date*) his honour judge (name) made an order as follows (*state as fully as necessary*). The order was served on (*date*) as proved by the affidavit of (*name*) sworn on (*date*)."**

or

> **"On the (*date*) the respondent gave an undertaking to his honour judge (*name*) that (*state as fully as necessary*). He signed a form setting out the terms of that undertaking."**

> **"It is the petitioner's case that, in clear breach of that order/ undertaking, the respondent (*state facts*), as proved by the evidence of the petitioner whose affidavit dated (*date*) is before the court and the affidavits of (*state others*)."**

10.04.09   No judge actually wants to put a person in prison. The judge may interrupt at any stage to see if a committal is the only remedy sought or if the application can be dealt with in any other way.

Evidence of the applicant

10.04.10   The applicant is called and sworn, see **21.06**. The applicant may be cross-examined in the usual way.

Evidence on behalf of the applicant

10.04.11   The applicant may call and/or read, see **21.06**, any other evidence to prove the breach of the order.

Close of the applicant's case

10.04.12   The advocate may say:

> **"That is the case. And, it is upon that evidence that I would invite (*the court*) to find the respondent to have breached the order and make an order for committal accordingly."**

Evidence on behalf of the respondent

10.04.13   The respondent and/or any witnesses on his behalf may be called, and any evidence read, see **21.06**, to prove that he was not in breach of the order.

Speeches

Order of speeches

The usual order of speeches is: **10.04.14**

(a) Respondent.
(b) Petitioner.
(c) Response (by respondent) if permitted.

Judgment

The judgment will usually contain: **10.04.15**

(a) The judge's findings of fact.
(b) A finding as to whether there is a breach.
(c) The pronouncement of the order.

It may be that after having made his finding as to whether there is a breach, the judge will invite the parties to address him as to what order he should make.

"Purging contempt"

A person committed to prison may apply to the court for his dis- **10.04.16**
charge. He must show that he has purged or desires to purge his contempt.
The notice of application to discharge must be served on the committing party not less than one day before the application is to be heard.

5. ANCILLARY RELIEF APPLICATIONS

Introduction

Ancillary relief is financial relief which is ancillary to the matrimonial **10.05.01**
proceedings.
Ancillary relief includes the payment of maintenance, the payment of a lump sum and property transfer orders.

As a general rule, the courts will enforce a party's obligations to the **10.05.02**
children of the marriage.
In all other cases, the principles upon which the court will exercise its powers to make an order for ancillary relief and the orders which are

available are complex and should be researched in the common practitioners' handbooks.

Application for ancillary relief

10.05.03   The application should be made in the petition, see **10.02.03**, or answer or it can be made at any other time, with the leave of the court, except where the party making the application has remarried.

10.05.04   The application is made on a standard form which is filed in the court in which the cause is proceeding.
The party making the application should file:

(a) The notice of application (in duplicate).
(b) An affidavit in support of the application.

10.05.05   A copy of the notice of application and affidavit in support should be served on the respondent(s) within 4 days of filing.
Where any order may affect another person, for example, a mortgagee, the application should also be served on him.

Affidavit

10.05.06   The affidavit in support is usually made by the applicant (petitioner), see **9.02.04–07**.
The affidavit should contain:

(a) The name, address and status of the deponent.
(b) The purpose of the affidavit, for example:

> **"I make this affidavit in support of my application for** (*state relief sought*)**."**

(c) The matters upon which the applicant relies in support of the application.
(d) The details of any real property (including any mortgage), if the application relates to land.
(e) The details of any personal property (including income).

10.05.07   The affidavit should not contain unnecessary reference to the behaviour of the respondent, except where the applicant is claiming that such behaviour should be taken into account.

Affidavit in reply

10.05.08   The respondent to the application must serve an affidavit in reply. The affidavit should be served within 28 days of receipt of the notice of application and affidavit in support, see **9.02.08**. For the content of the affidavit, see **10.05.06.**

Full disclosure in the affidavits

Both parties are under a duty to make full disclosure of all relevant matters including an intention to remarry or co-habit. **10.05.09**

Rule 2.63 Questionnaires

In an application for ancillary relief, a Rule 2.63 Questionnaire is a mixture of a request for further and better particulars, discovery and interrogatories combined. **10.05.10**

It may be in the form of a letter, setting out the information requested in numbered paragraphs.

If a party fails to reply, adequately or at all, the court may make such directions as are necessary.

The court is also empowered by means of a "production appointment" to order that any person attend court to produce documents and be examined or cross-examined (at or before the trial of the main application). **10.05.11**

Practitioners should always bear in mind the cost of making extensive enquiries of the other party and acquaint their client with the costs implications.

Directions

A party may apply by summons on notice for directions, see **9.04**, or discovery, see **9.05**, or directions may be given at the hearing of an interlocutory application, for example, an application for maintenance pending suit, see **10.05.14.** **10.05.12**

The following matters may be considered on directions: **10.05.13**

(a) Affidavit(s) of means.
(b) Valuation(s) of property.
(c) Filing of copies of Land Registry entries.
(d) List(s) of documents and inspection, see **9.05.07–12.**
(e) Length of hearing.

Maintenance pending suit

A party may apply to the district judge for maintenance pending suit. **10.05.14**
The hearing is on affidavit evidence, see **21.06**. A party may be permitted to give additional evidence.

An order made on an application for maintenance pending suit will last until the decree absolute or the hearing of the application.

Preparation

10.05.15 All affidavits and documents should be filed at least 14 days before the hearing.

Any document filed less than 14 days before the hearing may not be included in the court file. The advocate should therefore take extra copies to court.

Bundles

10.05.16 Where there is substantial correspondence and/or documents a bundle should be prepared (usually by the applicant) and agreed, see **9.06.17–21.**

It is common practice in a substantial case (and good practice in any case) to prepare and produce a chronology of events, see **22.01.04**, schedule of income and expenditure and assets.

Costs estimate

10.05.17 The parties should prepare an estimate of any costs which should be taken into consideration in the court's assessment of the award. The estimate may include:

(a) An estimate of the legal costs up to the date of the hearing and for each day thereafter.
(b) The costs of the sale or purchase of any properties.
(c) The costs of discharging any mortgages.

Assessment of tax implications

10.05.18 If an award may have tax implications, the parties should be prepared to explain to the court the effect of any reduction (or increase) in a party's tax liability.

The date of the hearing

10.05.19 The hearing may be fixed by the court (in a simple case) or by application of the parties, on filing certificates of readiness and time estimates.

Referring to the parties or witnesses

The parties are advised to agree, before the hearing, how to refer to the parties or witnesses, see **10.01.17.**   **10.05.20**

Practice

The conduct of the hearing of an application for ancillary relief varies greatly. One court may treat the hearing more informally than another. The following is intended as a guide: **10.05.21**

The hearing will be in chambers usually before a district judge. In both the High Court and the county court, the district judge may refer the case to a judge if he considers it complex.   **10.05.22**

For right of audience, dress and mode of address generally, see **10.01.13–15.**   **10.05.23**

Conduct

If the hearing is before the judge, it will usually be in a court room. The advocates and any party should stand to address the court. The judge may invite the advocates to sit but this is unusual.   **10.05.24**

If the hearing is before the district judge, it will usually be in the district judge's room. The advocates and parties will usually be seated at a table.

A party or witness taking the oath should do so standing.

Presence of witnesses in court

A judge (but not usually a district judge) may expect the witnesses to remain in court throughout the proceedings although practice varies.   **10.05.25**

Order of presentation and opening

The party having the burden of proof or, where both parties have an application before the court, the party who was first in time to make an application, will usually open.   **10.05.26**

The party opening may ask the court whether it has read the papers in advance, for example: **10.05.27**

> **"May I ask whether (***the court***) has had the opportunity to read the papers?"**

10.05.28   The party opening may also ask the court what papers are on the court file, for example:

> **"May I ask whether you have the following affidavits** (*state name of person(s) making the affidavit and date sworn*) **and reports** (*state name of person(s) making the report and date*)."

10.05.29   If the court has read the papers, the party opening may omit **10.05.31(e)–(g)**.

10.05.30   The party opening may also refer to a written chronology of events where the party has served the chronology on the court and the other parties beforehand, see **22.01.04**.

10.05.31   The opening may contain:

(a) An explanation of the nature of the application, for example:

> **"This an application for** (*state nature of relief sought*)."

(b) An explanation of the facts giving rise to the application.
(c) The names, ages and dates of birth of the parties.
(d) The names, ages and dates of birth of the children.
(e) The history of the marriage.
(f) A summary of any affidavit or part thereof.
(g) A summary of the evidence that the party is intending to call.
(h) A reference to the statutory criteria in section 25 MCA 1973.

The party should refer to any relevant law.

10.05.32   The advocate must be prepared to adapt his opening to the requirements of the court.

10.05.33   If the court has not read the papers, after **10.05.31(a)–(d)**, the judge may say:

> **"Now that I know the basic issues, I shall read the affidavits."**

Evidence on behalf of the applicant

10.05.34   The evidence is usually on affidavit, see **21.06**.
The party may read and/or call the evidence in any convenient order but will usually read the evidence of (and/or call) the applicant first.

Order of cross-examination

10.05.35   The order of cross-examination follows the title order of the application.

Close of the applicant's case

The party may say: **10.05.36**

"That is the case on behalf of the applicant (petitioner)."

In practice, a submission of no case to answer is never made. An   **10.05.37**
application to strike out could be made where there is a technical defect
in the case although, as a general rule, it should be made as a
preliminary issue.

The case for the respondent

As a general rule, the respondent does not make an opening speech,   **10.05.38**
see **8.06.16A.**
The evidence on behalf of the respondent will follow the practice in
10.05.34.

Submissions

The parties will make their submissions in such order as the court   **10.05.39**
directs (or, as agreed between the parties and the court).
The usual order of speeches is that the party who opened the case
will make his speech last, for example:

(a) Respondent.
(b) Applicant.

The parties may address the court on the facts and on any relevant   **10.05.40**
law in their closing submissions.
The parties may also prepare and submit written skeleton arguments
to the court, see **22.01.03**. The parties may refer to these skeleton
arguments in submissions.

Decision

The court will then give judgment making such findings of fact and/or   **10.05.41**
law as are appropriate.
The court may:

(a) Grant the application (in whole or in part).
(b) Refuse the application.
(c) Adjourn the case for further evidence and/or argument, usually
    after inviting the parties to address the court further.
(d) Deal with the costs of the application.

10.05.42   *Note*: Only at this stage is the court to be invited to consider any correspondence written "without prejudice save as to costs" ("Calderbank letters").

6. APPLICATIONS IN RELATION TO CHILDREN

Introduction

10.06.01   Applications in relation to the status, welfare, upbringing and maintenance of children are complex and reference should be made to the statutes, rules and practitioners' textbooks.

10.06.02   This section is principally concerned with proceedings in the county court and High Court under the Children Act 1989.
The following are also considered:

Issued out of the High Court, transferable to the county court:
(a) Wardship proceedings.
High Court only:
(b) The inherent jurisdiction of the High Court.
High Court and county court:
(c) Adoption

10.06.03   The jurisdiction of the county court and the High Court overlaps with that of the family proceedings court, see **Chapter 3**, Family Proceedings Court, and, in private law proceedings, the parties are able to choose the court to hear the case (subject to certain limitations).
In practice, all care proceedings commence in the family proceedings court (although there are some exceptions).

10.06.04   The proceedings are conducted in chambers (usually only the parties, their legal representatives and the welfare agencies attend). Other persons may be present during the hearing, with the permission of the court.

Proceedings under the Children Act

10.06.05   Under section 4, Children Act 1989

● Parental responsibility orders.

10.06.06   Under section 8, Children Act 1989

- (a) Residence orders.
- (b) Contact orders.
- (c) Prohibited steps orders.
- (d) Specific issue orders.

Applicants who may apply as of right:

(i) Parent or guardian
(ii) (b)(c) or (d) only: Any person who has a residence order in relation to the child.

Applicants who may apply with leave:

(i) Anyone else including the child.
(ii) (a) and (b) only: Foster parents with the leave of the local authority.

Under section 31, Children Act 1989   **10.06.07**

- Care orders and supervision orders.

Under sections 44–45, Children Act 1989

- Emergency protection orders.

  Only the local authority or an "authorised person" (at present only the NSPCC) may apply for a care order or a supervision order.

  Under Schedule 1, Children Act 1989   **10.06.08**

- Financial provision for a child.

  A parent, guardian or person in whose favour a residence order is in force may apply.

The parties should note that, in applications under section 8 and in   **10.06.09** some other cases, where an application is before the court, the court may exercise any of its powers under the Children Act (even if not the subject of the application).

Parental responsibility

Persons (usually the parents of a child) who have parental responsi-   **10.06.10** bility are responsible for the child's care and upbringing. In certain circumstances, a local authority can acquire parental responsibility for the child in care proceedings, see **10.06.07.**

The following person(s) have parental responsibility: **10.06.11**

(a) The married or adoptive parents of the child.

243

(b) A person who is granted a residence order.

(c) A peron who is appointed guardian of the child.

(d) An unmarried father in favour of whom a parental responsibility order is made.

The principles

10.06.12   The following principles apply in applications for orders under the Children Act, wardship and invoking the inherent jurisdiction of the court. In order to avoid protracted hearings, generating animosity between the parties, it is important to bear these principles in mind at each stage:

(A) The welfare of the child

When a court determines any question with respect to the upbringing/property/income from property of a child, the child's welfare shall be the court's paramount consideration.

(B) Welfare checklist

In an opposed application to make/vary/discharge a section 8 order or care or supervision order, the court shall have regard to:

(a) the ascertainable wishes and feeling of the child concerned (considered in the light of his age and understanding);

(b) his physical, emotional and educational needs;

(c) the likely effect on him of any change in his circumstances;

(d) his age, sex, background and any characteristics of his which the court considers relevant;

(e) any harm which he has suffered or is at risk of suffering;

(f) how capable each of his parents, and any other person in relation to whom the court considers the question to be relevant, is of meeting his needs;

(g) the range of powers available to the court under the Act in the proceedings in question.

(C) Without delay

Any delay in determining questions with respect to the upbringing of a child is likely to prejudice the welfare of the child, but:

(D) Making an order

The court may not make an order under the Act unless it considers that doing so would be better for the child than making no order at all.

Commencement of proceedings under the Children Act

Proceedings are commenced by completing a standard application **10.06.13** form and serving a copy of that form on each of the respondents together with a notice of hearing of a directions appointment, see **10.06.29.**

Where leave is required, the applicant must apply (on a standard **10.06.14** form) to the court stating reasons why leave should be given. Leave may be granted without an oral hearing.

In most cases the respondent(s) must serve an answer, usually on a **10.06.15** standard from.

Other proceedings in relation to children

Wardship proceedings

Proceedings are commenced by the issue of an originating summons **10.06.16** supported by an affidavit. Upon issue of the summons the minor becomes a ward of court.

Anyone, except a local authority, can make a child (who is not the subject of a care order) a ward of court. The applicant is known as the plaintiff. The child is referred to as a "minor".

The summons should be served on the person or persons, known as **10.06.17** the defendant(s), who have an immediate interest in the welfare of the minor.

The minor will cease to be a ward unless, within 21 days of issue of **10.06.18** the originating summons, a hearing date before a district judge for a first appointment is obtained.

On the first appointment the court decides whether to confirm the wardship. The court will give directions, see **10.06.33.**

Invoking the inherent jurisdiction of the High Court

Anyone who has a sufficient interest in the welfare of the minor may **10.06.19** apply to invoke the inherent jurisdiction, for example to sanction medical treatment or to restrain the publication of information relating to a child. A local authority requires leave, see **10.06.14.**

No practice or procedure has been laid down for applications apart from those by local authorities.

Adoption

10.06.20   Proceedings are commenced by completing a standard application form. Children Act applications can also be made within these proceedings.

The case will be given a serial number where the adopters require their identity and the whereabouts of the child not to be disclosed.

10.06.21   In the High Court the child must be a party. The child may be represented by a guardian *ad litem* who will file a report. The local authority in whose area the child lives (and who must be given notice of the application) must also provide a report.

10.06.22   There is provision for other parties (including local authorities) to apply to be made parties.

Preparation and practice in proceedings in relation to children generally

10.06.23   The preparation for hearing and the hearing of wardship proceedings, proceedings invoking the inherent jurisdiction of the High Court and adoption proceedings are likely to be similar to the practice in Children Act cases.

The practice in proceedings under the Child Abduction and Custody Act 1985 does not fit conveniently into the practice considered in this section and is condidered in **10.07.** For applications for child maintenace under Schedule 1 of the Children Act, see **10.05** Ancillary Relief applications.

Service of evidence

10.06.24   After the application has been made, the rules provide for the service of evidence (in rule 4.17 statement form) by one party on the other and on the court, in practice, in all cases.

This should be done as soon as practicable.

In section 8 applications, the statements and documents should be **10.06.25** served on the other parties and filed with the court before a directions appointment.

The following documents are likely to be served (not necessarily all at **10.06.26** the same time):

(a) Statements of evidence, signed and dated with the declaration that:

"(Name of person making the statement) **believes the statement to be true and understands that it may be placed before the court."**

(b) Welfare reports.
(c) Guardian *ad litem* reports.
(d) Statements of means (in some cases).
(e) Any other document that the party proposes to use at the hearing.

Welfare and guardian *ad litem* reports

A welfare report (private law proceedings) is likely to be requested **10.06.27** where there is concern for the welfare of a child or there is a dispute about with whom the child should live or with whom the child should have contact.

In care proceedings (public law proceedings) a guardian *ad litem* will be appointed and he will prepare a report for the court.

Both welfare reports and the reports of guardians *ad litem* generally carry significant weight with the court.

The court encourages mediation and conciliation either through the **10.06.28** court with the assistance of a welfare officer or through various privately run schemes. What takes place during conciliation is usually privileged from disclosure.

Directions appointments

Where the court receives an application under the Children Act, it will **10.06.29** consider (either of its own motion or at the request of either party) whether a directions appointment should be held in advance of the hearing.

In practice, at least one directions appointment is almost always held.

The parties should attend, unless excused. The welfare officer and guardian *ad litem* will also usually be present.

10.06.30 A directions appointment is usually held by the district judge, although it may be referred to a judge in complex and difficult cases.

The directions appointment may be in the courtroom or the district judge's room.

The emphasis is on the informal.

Conduct

10.06.31 For right of audience, dress, mode of address and conduct generally, see **10.01.13–15.**

Referring to the parties or witnesses

10.06.32 The parties are advised to agree, before the hearing, how to refer to the parties or witnesses, see **10.01.17.**

The parties are likely to be referred to as **the applicant** or **the respondent** or **the mother, the father,** etc.

Specimen directions

10.06.33 Directions which may be given may include any of the following matters:

(a) Timetable for the proceedings.
(b) Time limits for complying with the rules.
(c) Attendance of the child.
(d) Appointment of a guardian *ad litem* or solicitor.
(e) Service of documents.
(f) Submission of evidence (in statement form), including experts' reports (and, in a case where paternity is in dispute, blood tests and/or DNA fingerprinting) and statements of means.
(g) Preparation of welfare reports.
(h) Transfer of proceedings.
(i) Consolidation with other proceedings (which may include transfer).

10.06.34 The list is not exhaustive and the emphasis is on "sorting out" as much as possible at the directions appointment. It is the focal point of the applications procedure and it is advisable that the advocate who is proposing to attend the full hearing also attends the directions appointment.

Negotiations at the directions appointment may lead to pre-hearing conciliation.

If a party has not seen the welfare officer or guardian *ad litem*, the court may take the oportunity of advising that party to do so and ordering a report. The court may then fix a further directions appointment. **10.06.35**

If the case is going to be contested there may be a further directions appointment. **10.06.36**

Appeal

Appeal from the decision of a district judge at a directions appointment is to the judge, as of right. **10.06.37**

Preparation for the hearing

All statements and documents should be filed in good time before the hearing. **10.06.38**
Any statement or document filed shortly before the hearing may not be included in the court file. The advocate should therefore take extra copies to court.

Bundles

Where there is substantial correspondence and/or documents a bundle should be prepared (usually by the applicant) and agreed, see **9.06.17–21.** **10.06.39**
It is common practice in a substantial case (and good practice in any case) to prepare and produce a chronology of events and skeleton arguments, see **22.01.03–04.**

The date of the hearing

The hearing may be fixed by the court (in a simple case) or by application of the parties, on filing certificates of readiness and time estimates. **10.06.40**

Practice

Introduction

There are no hard and fast rules. The procedure has been deliberately designed to be flexible. **10.06.41**

The following is intended as a guide:

10.06.42   The hearing will be in chambers usually before a district judge. In both the High Court and the county court, the district judge may refer the case to a judge if he considers it complex.

10.06.43   For right of audience, dress and mode of address generally, see **10.01.13–15.**

Conduct

10.06.44   If the hearing is before the district judge, it will usually be in the district judge's room. The advocates and parties will usually be seated at a table.

If the hearing is before the judge, it will usually be in a court room. Practice varies widely as to whether the advocate should stand or sit to address the court. If it is not possible to ascertain the practice of the court in advance, the advocate should stand, although he may later be invited by the court to sit.

Attendance of the parties at court

10.06.45   The parties should attend, unless excused.

If the applicant appears, but one of the respondents is absent, the court may proceed with the case.

If one or more of the respondents appear, but the applicant does not, the court may refuse the application or, if sufficient evidence has already been received, carry on with the case.

Order of presentation and opening

10.06.46   The party having the burden of proof usually opens.

The advocates should agree the order of presentation. If the advocates are unable to agree the order of presentation, the advocates should invite the court to determine the matter.

10.06.47   In a simple case (for example, an application for contact by a father) where directions may not have been given, the likely order of presentation is:

(a) Applicant.
(b) Any person with parental responsibility.
(c) Other respondents, in order.
(d) Guardian *ad litem.*
(e) Child (if not represented by a guardian *ad litem*).

The advocate should assume that the court has read all the statements and reports in advance. **10.06.48**

Applicant's opening

The applicant will usually open the case. The applicant may say: **10.06.49**

> **"I appear for the applicant who is** (*name*)**. The other parties present are** (*names*) **and are represented by** (*names of advocates*)**."**

The applicant may then: **10.06.50**

(a) Give a general account to the court of the nature of the application.
(b) Summarise the history of the application.
(c) Refer the court to any order made on directions, for example:

> **"The following directions were given on** (*date*) **namely . . . "**

(d) Indicate the issues which are in dispute and those which are not in dispute.
(e) Refer the court to any law.

The party opening may also refer to a written chronology of events where the party has served the chronology on the court and the other parties beforehand. **10.06.51**

The advocate must be prepared to adapt his opening to the requirements of the court. **10.06.52**

The parties will then call witnesses in order of presentation on the issue(s) in dispute. **10.06.53**
The evidence in the case may take the form of: (**10.06.54–58**)

Evidence on behalf of the applicant

The evidence of the parties will be in the form of statements filed in accordance with the rules. **10.06.54**
The party may call, read or summarise the evidence in any convenient order but will usually call the evidence of the applicant and any witness(es) on behalf of the applicant first.

Witnesses

The advocate may only call a witness (without leave) whose statement has been served in accordance with the rules, see **10.06.33(f)**. **10.06.55**

Witnesses should stand to take the oath but may later be invited by the court to sit to give evidence.

Order of cross-examination

10.06.56   The order of cross-examination may follow the title order of the application or may be agreed at **10.06.46.**

Written evidence

10.06.57   The written evidence will be in the form of reports and statements. The evidence should not be read to the court but it may be referred to in submissions after the conclusion of all the (live) evidence.

Admitted facts

10.06.58   A party need not call evidence in respect of stated facts which are admitted and not in dispute but it may be referred to in submissions after the conclusion of all the (live) evidence.

Close of the applicant's case

10.06.59   The party may say:

"That is the case on behalf of the (applicant)."

10.06.60   In practice, a submission of no case to answer is never made.

The case(s) for the respondent(s)

10.06.61   As a general rule, the respondent does not make an opening speech, see **8.06.16A.**

10.06.62   The evidence on behalf of the respondent(s) is subject to the same rules and is presented in the same way as the evidence on behalf of the applicant, see **10.06.54–58.**

Submissions

10.06.63   The parties will make their submissions in such order as the court directs (or, as agreed between the parties and the court).

The usual order of speeches is that the party who opened the case will make his speech last, for example:

(a) Respondent(s) in order.

(b) Applicant.

(c) Submissions by guardian *ad litem*/official solicitor.

The parties may address the court on the facts and on any relevant law in their closing submissions. **10.06.64**

The advocates may have been ordered on a directions application or during the hearing to prepare and submit skeleton arguments/draft orders to which they may refer in closing submissions. **10.06.65**

Decision

The court will then give judgment making such findings of fact and/or law as are appropriate. **10.06.66**
The court may:

(a) Grant the application (in whole or in part).
(b) Refuse the application.
(c) Adjourn the case for further evidence and/or argument, usually after inviting the parties to address the court further.
(d) (If appropriate) deal with the costs of the application.

Costs

Costs in childrens' cases are rarely awarded save for the Official Solicitor's costs which are nearly always provided for. **10.06.67**

Appeal

Appeal from the district judge is to a judge in chambers on notice. Time limits vary depending on whether the case is a county court or High Court case. **10.06.68**
Appeal of a final decision of the county court judge or High Court judge is to the Court of Appeal, on notice with grounds of appeal, within 4 weeks of the date on which the order is sealed.

7. CHILD ABDUCTION

"Child snatching"

It sometimes happens that a child is removed from a person having parental responsibility for that child abroad and brought to the UK. **10.07.01**

In a case where the European or Hague Conventions apply that person may make an application to the High Court through the Lord **10.07.02**

Chancellor's Department, acting as Central Authority for the non-removing parent, for an order for the return of the child to the country from which it was removed. Applications may also be made for the enforcement of certain foreign orders.

10.07.03   The application is made under the Child Abduction and Custody Act, 1985, by originating summons supported by affidavit. The hearing will be before a High Court judge in chambers.

10.07.04   A child abduction case is unusual in that the welfare of the child is not paramount. It is one of a number of factors that the court will take into consideration including the conduct of the parties and the ability of the country in question to protect the child or the removing parent.

Practice

10.07.05   At the hearing the judge will hear submissions on the affidavits/reports/statements of both parties on the following matters:

(a) The way in which the child was removed.
(b) What orders, if any, are currently affecting the child.

The parties are also likely to obtain expert evidence as to the law in the country of origin. It is rare for oral evidence to be given.

10.07.06   The practice at the hearing will be similar to **9.02.29–37.**

10.07.07   If there is an order in respect of the child in the country of origin, it is likely to be enforced in the UK.

CHAPTER 11

Court of Appeal (Criminal Division)

1. INTRODUCTION

Introduction

An appeal against conviction or sentence on indictment by the Crown **11.01.01**
Court is made to the Court of Appeal, Criminal Division.

An appeal against a decision of the Crown Court on any other matter
is made to the Divisional Court of the Queen's Bench Division, see
13.02 & 13.04, although such appeals will be rare.

Leave to appeal

An appellant may appeal against conviction, as of right, to the Court **11.01.02**
of Appeal, Criminal Division:

   (a) If the ground(s) on which the appellant relies involves a question
       of law only, or
   (b) (In an exceptional case) if the trial judge has granted a certificate
       of fitness for appeal.

In all other cases the appellant must obtain the leave of the Court of
Appeal.

As a general rule, an appellant to the Court of Appeal against **11.01.03**
sentence must obtain the leave of the court.

Time limits

11.01.04   The appellant must serve notice of appeal or notice of application for leave to appeal (on a standard form) on the Crown Court within 28 days of the conviction, order or sentence appealed.

11.01.05   The notice must be accompanied by grounds of appeal, see **11.01.08.**

The effect of the time limit is that, if conviction is being appealed and sentence is delayed (for example, for the preparation of pre-sentence reports), the appellant must nevertheless serve notice of appeal of the conviction.

If sentence is later appealed, the appeals may be consolidated.

The decision to appeal

11.01.06   The defence advocate must always consider and advise on the merits of an appeal.

This should first be done by giving provisional advice immediately after conviction or sentence at court. As a general rule, counsel should not wait to be asked by the defendant for any provisional view on appeal.

Advice on appeal

11.01.07   The initial advice on appeal should be followed by a written advice on appeal, if requested and, where appeal is advised, signed grounds of appeal.

Grounds of appeal

11.01.08   The grounds of appeal must identify the matters relied on and state reasons for the appeal. It is not sufficient for counsel drafting the grounds of appeal to state only that "the conviction is unsafe and unsatisfactory".

The advice on appeal and grounds of appeal should be sent to the solicitor, usually within 14 days, to enable the solicitor to consider the prospects of the appeal with the appellant.

Service of the notice of appeal

11.01.09   If counsel has advised an appeal, the solicitor should send the notice of application, the signed grounds of appeal and the advice on appeal to the Crown Court.

The Crown Court will forward these to the Registrar for Criminal Appeals.

Transcripts

Counsel may include in the advice on appeal (or in a subsequent note to the Registrar) a request for a transcript of any relevant part(s) of the evidence/summing up. **11.01.10**

The Registrar may order that a transcript be obtained of any part of the proceedings.

If the Registrar is of the opinion that part or all of the transcript requested is not necessary, he may refer the request to a single judge of the Court of Appeal for his consideration.

Bail pending appeal

An application for bail pending appeal may be made to a single judge of the Court of Appeal, sitting in chambers, on service of the grounds of appeal, see **4.04.10**. **11.01.11**

The advocate should remember that the primary test for bail pending appeal is: What are the chances of the appeal being successful?

The single judge may consider leave, see **11.01.17**, on an application for bail, usually in an appeal which has some prospect of success. If bail is refused, the single judge may order an expedited hearing. **11.01.12**

Perfecting the grounds of appeal

If a transcript is obtained, the Registrar will usually invite counsel to perfect his grounds of appeal in the light of the transcript. **11.01.13**

When perfecting the grounds of appeal, counsel may alter, amend or abandon any drafted ground of appeal.

Counsel may also refer (usually in margin note), in respect of any ground of appeal, to: **11.01.14**

(a) The appropriate page and section letter of the transcript.
(b) Any document.
(c) Any exhibit.
(d) Any authority on which he intends to rely.

Leave to call fresh evidence

If the appellant wishes to call fresh evidence, he should apply on a standard form to the Registrar enclosing the following documents (for the consideration of the single judge): **11.01.15**

(a) A (section 9 CJA) statement from the witness.

(b) An affidavit (usually sworn by the appellant's solicitor) stating why the witness was not available at the trial.

Copies of the statement and affidavit should be served on the Crown. The full court will consider the application for leave to call the witness, see **11.02.09.**

11.01.16   At the hearing of the appeal, the appellant must show special grounds, namely:

(a) That the evidence was not available at the trial.

(b) That, if the evidence had been available at the trial, it would have been likely to have influenced the decision.

(c) That the evidence appears to be admissible and truthful.

Obtaining leave

11.01.17   The (perfected) grounds of appeal and any other relevant document are then placed by the Registrar before a single judge of the Court of Appeal for his consideration.

The single judge may grant the application for leave to appeal, refuse it or refer it to the court.

The Registrar has no power to grant leave.

Leave granted

11.01.18   If the single judge grants leave to appeal or refers the application to the court (or where the appeal is by certificate of the trial judge), the single judge will usually grant legal aid for the hearing.

The Registrar will then instruct counsel (who will usually be the counsel who appeared at the Crown Court).

Leave refused

11.01.19   If the single judge refuses leave, the Registrar will send a notification of the refusal (and any observations made by the single judge) to the appellant and his solicitors.

If the appellant wishes to pursue the appeal further, he (or his solicitor) must give notice of intention to renew the application before the full Court of Appeal within 14 days. The renewed application for leave will usually be heard as part of the appeal, see **11.02.06.**

The Registrar will not usually grant legal aid to renew the application.

11.01.20   If the appellant wishes to pursue the appeal and he is serving a custodial sentence, he may be at risk of the full court ordering that the time spent in custody pending appeal not count against the sentence if it dismisses the application for leave.

Preparation for the hearing of the appeal/renewed application for leave

The appellant (usually after consultation with the Registrar) may provide to the court any additional material which he considers would be of assistance to the court when considering the appeal.   **11.01.21**

The appellant may also further perfect the grounds of appeal, if appropriate.

Skeleton arguments/chronologies

In a conviction appeal, the Court of Appeal requires skeleton arguments, see **22.01.03**. A skeleton argument may be accompanied by a chronology of events relevant to the appeal, see **22.01.04**.   **11.01.22**

The appellant must provide to the court, in advance of the hearing, at least three copies of the skeleton argument (and chronology). A copy should also be provided to any other party to the appeal, see **22.01.08**.

Lists of authorities

The appellant should provide a list of cases and/or authorities to the court and the other parties in advance of the hearing, see **22.01.06**.   **11.01.23**

It is recommended that the list should be provided to the court and any other party to the appeal (at the very latest) by 4.00 pm on the day preceeding the hearing.

The court has extensive reports available but if the authority to be used is not a common work, it is recommended that the appellant have sufficient (photo)copies available for the court and any opponent(s).

Practice

Right of audience

Barristers, appellant(s) in person.   **11.01.24**

Conduct and dress

The hearing of an appeal is in open court. Any person addressing the court does so standing.   **11.01.25**

Barristers are robed. Appellants in person should be respectably dressed.

Mode of address

11.01.26   The court is addressed as **my lords/your lordships** although when one judge addresses the advocate, the advocate should reply to that judge as **my lord/lady.**

Role of the Crown

11.01.27   If the appeal is against conviction, the Crown will usually be represented.

If the appeal is against sentence, the Crown will not usually be represented.

If present, it is the duty of the Crown to assist the court.

Presence of the appellant

11.01.28   If the appellant is in custody, he will usually be produced for the hearing of his appeal.

2. APPEAL AGAINST CONVICTION

Calling the case

11.02.01   The associate will stand and read out the name of the case.

The presiding judge will then indicate to the appellant that he may begin and/or may direct the appellant's attention to a particular ground of appeal, see **11.02.11.**

The case for the appellant

Appellant's introduction

11.02.02   The appellant may say:

> **"This is an appeal against/application for leave to appeal the conviction of (***name***) before His Honour Judge (***name***) sitting at the (***name***) Crown Court on (***date***). My learned friend, (***name***), appears for the Crown."**

The advocate should assume that the court has read all the papers in advance.　　**11.02.03**

Content of the introduction

The introduction may contain:　　**11.02.04**

(a) A statement of the offences of which the appellant was convicted.
(b) A brief summary of the evidence against the defendant relevant to the appeal.

The appellant may then say:　　**11.02.05**

"I seek to persuade the court that the conviction is unsafe and unsatisfactory for the reasons set out in the grounds of appeal."

Application for leave to appeal

On an application for leave to appeal, usually in a straightforward　　**11.02.06**
case or where the Registrar has asked for the Crown to be represented, the court may say:

"If we are minded to grant leave, do you have instructions to treat this as a full hearing?"

The appellant is advised to obtain instructions before the hearing, see **11.02.16.**

Presentation

After the introduction, the appellant may present the appeal in as　　**11.02.07**
much detail as the appellant feels is necessary (or as indicated by the court).

The appellant may refer the court to the events leading up to the (i) arrest, (ii) trial and (iii) appeal with reference to the chronology, see **11.01.22.**

The appellant may then refer the court to each ground of appeal in　　**11.02.08**
order of merit.

In respect of each ground of appeal, the appellant may:

(a) Read or refer the court to any part of the transcript of evidence.
(b) Read or refer the court to any part of the transcript of the judge's summing up.
(c) Refer the court (with reference to any document) to the issues raised in that ground of appeal.

(d) Set out the law on which the appellant relies with reference to the skeleton argument, see **11.01.22**, and list of authorities, see **11.01.23**.

Fresh evidence

11.02.09   The appellant may, either after introducing the case or when referring the court to the evidence, apply for leave to call fresh evidence. If the court grants leave, the appellant may call the witness (or read the evidence).

The usual rules as to the examination, cross-examination and re-examination of witnesses apply, see **Chapter 21**, Examination of witnesses.

Intervention by the court

11.02.10   A party presenting his case to the court should never expect to do so without interruption or intervention by the court.

11.02.11   The court is very likely to direct the appellant's attention to certain areas of the case.

The court will usually indicate if it considers certain grounds of appeal to be without merit. The appellant should note such indications carefully and be ready to move to another argument if necessary.

The case for the Crown

11.02.12   If the appellant has not established any ground of appeal, the court will usually dismiss the appeal without hearing the Crown. The usual form of words is:

"We need not trouble you, (*name of counsel*)."

11.02.13   If the appellant has established any ground of appeal, the court will usually indicate to the Crown the grounds on which he should address the court.

11.02.14   The Crown may then present his case to the court in the same way as the appellant, see **11.02.07–08**.

Reply

11.02.15   The appellant may reply to any new matter raised by the Crown or the court.

The appellant should not (and usually will not be permitted to) repeat his submissions.

Judgment

In an application for leave to appeal against conviction

The court may: **11.02.16**

(a) Dismiss the application for leave.
(b) Grant the application for leave and stand the case out for a full hearing.
(c) Grant the application and invite the appellant to address the court for a second time, for example:

"Is there any other matter on which you would wish to address us?"

Note: If leave is granted after a full hearing, the court may be minded to allow the appeal and the appellant will often decline to address the court for a second time.

In an appeal (where leave has been granted)

The court may: **11.02.17**

(a) Dismiss the appeal.
(b) Allow the appeal in full and direct an acquittal.
(c) Allow the appeal and substitute a conviction for another offence that would have been open to the jury.

Costs

The majority of appeals are legally aided and costs are not usually **11.02.18**
considered.

A successful appellant who is privately represented may apply for a defendant's costs order, see **20.02.22(b).**

3. APPEAL AGAINST SENTENCE

Calling the case

The associate will stand and read out the name of the case.   **11.03.01**

The presiding judge will then indicate to the appellant that he may begin and/or may direct the appellant's attention to a particular ground of appeal, see **11.02.11**.

The case for the appellant

Appellant's introduction

11.03.02 After the case has been called, the appellant may say:

> **"This is an appeal against/application for leave to appeal the sentence imposed on** (*name*) **by His Honour Judge** (*name*) **sitting at the** (*name*) **Crown Court on** (*date*)"**

Content of the introduction

11.03.03 The introduction may contain:

(a) A statement of the offences for which the appellant was sentenced.
(b) A summary of any mitigating/aggravating features.

11.03.04 The appellant may then say:

> **"I seek to persuade the court that the sentence is wrong in principle and/or excessive, for the reasons set out in the grounds of appeal."**

Presentation of the appeal

11.03.05 The appellant may then refer the court to each ground of appeal in order of merit, see **11.02.07–08**.

If the appeal is complex or on a new point of law, the appellant will be expected to have prepared and served a skeleton argument and chronology. In any other case, where the appellant is referring to authorities, he will be expected to have provided the court with a list of authorities, see **11.01.23**.

If a transcript of the judge's remarks on sentence is available, the appellant may refer the court to any part of the transcript.

Mitigation

11.03.06 The appellant may, when referring the court to each ground of appeal, address the court in mitigation, see **7.04.01–15**.

The court may intervene, see **11.02.10–11**.

The appellant should remember that an appeal against sentence is **11.03.07** not a re-hearing of the sentencing of the appellant at the Crown Court. The criteria to be addressed are whether the sentence was wrong in principle and/or manifestly excessive.

For example, if the sentence imposed was imprisonment: Was it correct to do so in the circumstances of the case and, if so, was the sentence far too long?

Judgment

In an application for leave to appeal sentence

11.02.16 applies.   **11.03.08**

In an appeal (where leave has been granted)

The court may: **11.03.09**

(a) Dismiss the appeal.
(b) Allow the appeal and substitute any sentence which the Crown Court could have passed.

Costs

Where the appeal against sentence is allowed, the court may make a **11.03.10** defendant's costs order, see **20.02.22(b).**

CHAPTER 12

Court of Appeal (Civil Division)

1. INTRODUCTION

Introduction

12.01.01   An appeal from a decision of a judge of the High Court or the county court may be made to the Court of Appeal, Civil Division.

12.01.02   If a party is intending to appeal a decision of the county court, the party should consider an application for a retrial. The county court has wide powers to order a retrial (for example, where there is new evidence). A retrial is quicker and cheaper than an appeal to the Court of Appeal.

12.01.03   An appeal to the Court of Appeal is often in two stages:

(a) Application for leave to appeal.
(b) Full hearing of the appeal.

Application for leave to appeal

12.01.04   Leave to appeal a decision of the High Court or county court is required in certain cases, namely:

(a) Interlocutory judgments and orders except:
    (i) Where an injunction is granted or refused.

(ii) Where the liberty of the subject is concerned.

(iii) In other specified cases.

(b) An order made by consent of the parties.

(c) An order as to costs only.

(d) An order of a judge in chambers in the Family Division or the Chancery Division.

(e) A determination by a Divisional Court of an appeal (see **13.03.13**).

(f) County court only: on a financial claim (but not the award) which is less than £5,000.

In most cases the party may (and in **12.01.04(b) & (c)** must) make the application for leave to the judge whose order that party is appealing. **12.01.05**

Application for leave to the judge

The party intending to appeal may say: **12.01.06**

"It is the plaintiff's/defendant's intention to appeal the order made against him.

It is clear that there is some conflict between the leading cases which should be resolved. And in the circumstances, I ask for leave to appeal."

Application for leave to the Court of Appeal

If leave to appeal is refused or the application is not made to the judge whose order the party is appealing, the party must apply for leave to a single judge of the Court of Appeal. **12.01.07**

The appellant must file a notice of appeal within 4 weeks (or any shorter period in an interlocutory appeal) of the judgment or order (although an application for an extension of time may be made to the Registrar of Civil Appeals). **12.01.08**

The notice of appeal must state the grounds of appeal and the nature of relief sought on appeal. **12.01.09**

No grounds can be raised at the hearing of the appeal that are not contained in the notice of appeal (although leave to amend may be sought).

The notice of appeal will not be effective until leave to appeal has been granted.

The notice of application for leave should be lodged with the Civil Appeals Office (CAO). **12.01.10**

The following documents are usually filed with the notice:

(a) The order which is the subject of the appeal.
(b) The order refusing leave, see **12.01.05**.
(c) Draft grounds of appeal.
(d) Any affidavit(s) in support.

12.01.11   The application for leave is usually determined by a single judge of the Court of Appeal on the papers although the parties may be heard on the application, see **12.01.13–16**.
The Registrar cannot give leave to appeal.

12.01.12   The single judge may refer the application for leave for hearing in open court or either party may appeal to the Court of Appeal the refusal or granting of leave, if determined on the papers, see **12.01.11** (within 7 days of the notice).

Practice on the application for leave

12.01.13   The appellant may say:

> **"This is my application for leave to appeal the order of** (*name of judge*) **at** (*name of court*) (*sitting in chambers*) **on** (*date*). **Mr** (*name*) **now appears on behalf of the defendant/plaintiff** (*if the proposed respondent is represented*)**."**

12.01.14   The appellant will then usually:

(a) Outline the nature of the case.
(b) Outline the facts as proved at the hearing.
(c) Outline the issues in dispute and/or any relevant law.

The appellant may follow the practice in **9.02.29–37**.
On an application for leave, the appellant only has to show that he has an arguable case.

12.01.15   The single judge will:

(a) Grant leave to appeal, or
(b) Adjourn the hearing for the case to be argued *inter partes* (if appropriate), or
(c) Refuse leave to appeal. There is no appeal from that decision.

12.01.16   If leave to appeal is granted the party must serve notice of appeal, if this has not already been served, see **12.01.08–09**.

Service of the notice of appeal

12.01.17   The notice of appeal should be served on all parties (and, if appropriate, the county court) within 4 weeks of the date of judgment or order being appealed.

If a party has applied for legal aid, the legal aid application is unlikely **12.01.18** to have been considered within the time limit of 4 weeks. An application for an extension of time is unlikely to be granted pending consideration of the application. The notice of appeal should be served.

Respondent's notice

If the respondent is seeking a variation of the order or to cross-appeal **12.01.19** he must serve a respondent's notice on the parties within 21 days (or 7 days in an interlocutory appeal) of receipt of the notice of appeal.

Effect of giving notice of appeal

A notice of appeal does not act as an automatic stay of execution. **12.01.20**

The parties may agree to take no steps to enforce the judgment until the appeal is heard. If the parties do not agree, the appellant must apply for a stay of execution to the judge or to a single judge of the Court of Appeal on notice (*inter partes*).

Leave to call fresh evidence

An application to call fresh evidence may be made on summons **12.01.21** (after leave to appeal is granted, if appropriate) to the Registrar. The application should be supported by affidavit.

If the application to call fresh evidence is granted, the court, at the hearing of the appeal, may order a new trial.

The party making the application must show special grounds, **12.01.22** namely:

(a) That the evidence was not readily available at the trial.
(b) That, if the evidence had been available at the trial, it would have been likely to have influenced the decision.
(c) That the evidence appears to be admissible and truthful.

Preparation for appeal

Documents

The following documents must be deposited at the CAO within 7 **12.01.23** days of service:

(a) Copy of the judgment order, see **9.06.90.**
(b) Two copies of the notice of appeal.

(c) List of exhibits.

Listing the appeal

12.01.24   The court will then set down the appeal in the appropriate list according to the court from which the appeal is made and the nature of the appeal.

The appellant must, within 2 days of setting down, give notice of setting down to all parties.

12.01.25   The case will eventually appear in the List of Forthcoming Appeals.

If the appeal is short it may be placed in the Short Warned List (SWL) which means that it may come on at 1 or 2 day's notice. A party may apply by summons to the Registrar to take the case out of the SWL.

Other cases (and cases taken out of the SWL) are likely to be given a fixed date for hearing.

12.01.26   The appellant must then, within 14 days, lodge at the CAO 3 bundles each containing copies of the following documents:

(a) Notice of appeal.
(b) Respondent's notice.
(c) Any further or amended notices.
(d) Judgment order appealed.
(e) All pleadings.
(f) List of exhibits.
(g) Any relevant affidavit.
(h) Any other relevant documents (including correspondence)
(i) A note or transcript of the judgment and, if appropriate, of any relevant part(s) of the evidence, see **12.01.27.**

Agreed note

12.01.27   There is no official shorthand note made of proceedings in the county court. The parties should have a note of the evidence and the judgment. (Counsel is under a duty to take a note).

The note should be agreed by the parties, if possible, and submitted to the judge who may agree the note (with or without comment). The judge may be asked to provide copies of his note.

If the note made by the parties and the judge's note of his judgment differ, the judge's note is final.

The note signed by the judge can be used in the appeal.

12.01.28   In an appeal from an interlocutory order in the High Court, **12.01.27** also applies.

Transcripts

In the High Court the proceedings will have been tape recorded and **12.01.29** there may also be a shorthand note.

The appellant must arrange (and pay) for the tape or shorthand note to be typed and certified. The typed copy will usually be sent direct to the CAO.

Skeleton arguments/chronologies

The Court of Appeal requires the use of skeleton arguments, see **12.01.30** **22.01.03.**

A skeleton argument must be accompanied by a chronology of events relevant to the the appeal (except in urgent cases or where the court orders otherwise).

A skeleton argument should be lodged by all parties to the appeal. A respondent who seeks to uphold the decision of the court below for the reasons given in that court may simply send a letter to that effect to the Court of Appeal.

At least three copies of the skeleton argument and chronology of **12.01.31** events must be lodged with the CAO (and a copy each delivered to the other parties):

Fixed date appeals: Not less than 4 weeks before the date of the hearing.

Short warned list appeals: Not less than 10 days before the case becomes "on call".

The skeleton argument should: **12.01.32**

(a) Identify (not argue) any point of law, with reference to the principal authorities in support.
(b) Identify any finding of fact in the transcript or notes of evidence and state briefly the basis on which it is contended that the court can interfere with that finding of fact.

Lists of authorities

The parties should exchange lists of authorities in advance of the **12.01.33** hearing in order that each party can properly prepare his argument(s).

The parties should also hand to the court the lists of authorities in advance of the hearing (not later than 5.30 pm on the day before the hearing although, sometimes, before 10.00 am on the day of the hearing).

Practice

Right of audience

12.01.34   Barristers and parties in person.

Dress

12.01.35   Barristers are robed, parties in person should be respectably dressed.

Mode of address

12.01.36   The court is addressed as **my lords/your lordships** but where a party is responding to an individual judge, the judge is addressed as **my lord** or **my lady.**

Conduct

12.01.37   The hearing is in open court. In appeals from the High Court there are usually 3 judges. In appeals from the county court there are usually 2 judges.

A party addressing the court should do so standing.

2. PRACTICE AT THE HEARING

Calling the case

12.02.01   The associate will usually stand and read out the name of the case. The presiding judge will then indicate to the appellant that he may begin.

The case for the appellant

Appellant's introduction

12.02.02   The appellant may say:

> **"This is an appeal from the judgment/order of Mr Justice/Judge** (*name of*) **sitting in the** (*name of*) **division/**(*name of*) **court. My learned friend** (*name*) **appears for the respondent."**

The presiding judge (or the judge who has given consideration to the **12.02.03**
appeal) may indicate that the court has read all the papers in advance.

If the court does not give any indication, the appellant may say:

**"Before I present the appeal may I ask whether (*the court*) has
had the opportunity to read the papers?"**

If the court has read the papers, the appellant may omit the opening,
see **12.02.05**, and argue the main points of the appeal.

If the court has not read the papers, the appellant may open the **12.02.04**
appeal in as much detail as the appellant feels is necessary (or as
indicated by the court).

Appellant's opening

The opening should contain: **12.02.05**

(a) An outline of the nature of the case.
(b) A summary of the issues in dispute, with reference to the skeleton
    argument.

Presentation of the appeal

After opening the appellant may: **12.02.06**

(a) Refer to the events leading up to the issue of proceedings with
    reference to the chronology (if appropriate).
(b) Read or refer the court to any agreed note of evidence.
(c) Read or refer the court to any relevant part of the transcript of
    evidence.
(d) Read any relevant affidavit.
(e) Read or refer the court to any part(s) of the agreed note or
    transcript of the judgment.
(f) Refer the court (with reference to any document) to the issues in
    dispute and whether the issues in dispute are of law only or mixed
    law and fact.
(g) Set out the law on which the appellant relies with reference to the
    skeleton argument and refer the court to any authorities.

The court may indicate that it has considered and agrees/disagrees **12.02.07**
with any of (a)–(g). The appellant may then argue each disputed point.

The appellant may, either after introducing the case or when refer- **12.02.08**
ring the court to the evidence, call or read any fresh evidence if leave
has previously been obtained to call it, see **12.01.21–22**.

Leave to call fresh evidence will not be given at the hearing.

12.02.09   A party presenting his case to the court should never expect to do so without interruption or intervention from the court.

12.02.10   The court will usually indicate if it considers certain grounds of appeal to be without merit and direct the party's attention to other grounds of appeal/areas of the case.

The party should note such indication carefully and be ready to move to another argument if necessary.

The case for the respondent

12.02.11   If the appellant has not established any of the grounds of appeal, the court may dismiss the appeal before hearing the respondent. The usual form of words is:

"We need not trouble you, (*name of respondent*)**."**

12.02.12   If the appellant has established one or more of the grounds of appeal, the court will usually indicate to the respondent the grounds on which the respondent should address the court.

12.02.13   The respondent should note any indication of the court carefully.

12.02.14   The respondent may then present his case to the court in the same way as the appellant, see **12.02.06–10.**

12.02.15   The usual order of response is in the title order of the action (although this may be varied by the direction of the court or by agreement of the parties).

Reply

12.02.16   The appellant may reply to any new matter raised by the respondent (or other party) or the court. The appellant should not (and will usually not be permitted to) repeat his submissions.

Judgment

12.02.17   The court may:

  (a) Deliver a full judgment.
  (b) Deliver a short judgment, with reasons to follow.
  (c) Reserve judgment.

In judgment the court may: **12.02.18**

(a) Allow the appeal in full (or in part).
(b) Dismiss the appeal.
(c) Make any order which could have been made by the lower court.
(d) Order a new trial in the lower court (usually where fresh evidence has been admitted).

Costs

As a general rule, costs follow the event, see **20.03.03.**   **12.02.19**
A successful legally aided party has an obligation to apply for costs against a non-legally aided party to indemnify the legal aid fund.
A successful non-legally aided party may apply for costs against a legally aided party although the court will usually order that costs are not to be enforced without leave of the court, see **20.03.18.**
If both parties are legally aided there will usually be no order for costs save legal aid taxation, see **20.03.16.**

CHAPTER 13

Appeals to the High Court and the Divisional Court

1. INTRODUCTION

Introduction

13.01.01   An appeal to the High Court from a decision of a court of lower jurisdiction, tribunal or person (for example, an arbitrator or inspector) may be made to:

(a) The Divisional Court of the Queen's Bench Division where the relevant statute describes the decision as final.
(b) A single judge of the High Court where the relevant statute describes the manner in which an appeal may be made.

13.01.02   The preparation and practice in the following situations are considered in this section:

- Application for judicial review, see **13.02.**
- Appeals to the High Court under statute, see **13.03.**
- Appeals by case stated, see **13.04.**

13.01.03   As a guide:

(a) Judicial review is a review of the decision making process of a court, tribunal or person (or body of persons) charged with a public duty.

276

(b) Appeals to the High Court under statute are directed by the relevant statute.

(c) Appeals by case stated are made where a court, tribunal or person (or body of persons) charged with a public duty has made a decision on the wrong principles of law.

2. APPLICATION FOR JUDICIAL REVIEW

Introduction

As a general rule, judicial review may be obtained against:　　　　**13.02.01**

(a) A court of lower jurisdiction.
(b) A tribunal.
(c) A person or body of persons charged with a public duty.

As a general rule, judicial review may be obtained where the court, **13.02.02** tribunal or person:

(a) Acted without jurisdiction or exceeded its jurisdiction.
(b) Acted in breach of the rules of natural justice.
(c) Acted unreasonably.
    Or, where in respect of the court, tribunal or person:
(d) There is an error of law on the face of the record.

Orders

The applicant may apply for the following prerogative orders:　　**13.02.03**

(a) *Mandamus*: An order directing a court, tribunal or person to do an act where it has refused or neglected to do so, for example, where a magistrates' court has refused, on demand, to state a case, see **13.04.06.**
(b) *Prohibition*: An order restraining a court, tribunal or person from exceeding its jurisdiction.
(c) *Certiorari*: An order removing the proceedings of the court, tribunal or person into the Divisional Court for the purpose of quashing the proceedings.

and/or the following non-prerogative orders:

(d) A *declaration*.
(e) *Damages*.
(f) An *injunction*.

The law on this subject is complex. The practitioner is advised to consult the Rules of the Supreme Court.

Application for leave

13.02.04   An applicant for judicial review must first obtain leave.

An application for leave must be made as soon as possible after the decision complained of and, in any event, within 3 months.

This is an unusual time limit because, if the court is of the opinion that a period shorter than 3 months is sufficient, it may refuse leave on that ground alone even though the application is within the 3 month time limit.

13.02.05   The application for leave is made *ex parte* to a single judge by filing in the Crown Office:

   (a) A standard form notice, stating:
      (i)   The name, address and description of the applicant.
      (ii) The name and address of the applicant's solicitors.
      (iii) The relief sought.
      (iv) The grounds on which the applicant claims to be entitled to that relief.
   (b) An affidavit (usually sworn by the applicant) verifying the facts in the notice (with any relevant exhibits).

13.02.06   The application for leave is usually determined on the documents by the single judge without a hearing (although a hearing may be requested. For the practice see, **12.01.11–16.**

The applicant is then notified of the decision of the single judge.

Renewing the application for leave

13.02.07   If leave is refused, the applicant may renew the application, to the court (specified in **13.02.08(a) or (b)**) on service of a standard form notice.

Preparation

Method of applying for judicial review

13.02.08   If the application for leave is granted, the applicant should make the application for judicial review by origination motion within 14 days:

   (a) In a criminal case, to the Divisional Court.
   (b) In any other case, to a single judge in open court.

The applicant should then serve the standard form notice, the **13.02.09** affidavit, see **13.02.05(a) & (b)**, and originating motion, see **13.02.08**, on the court, tribunal or person who made the decision.

An affidavit of service of the documents must be served before the **13.02.10** application can be entered for hearing.

A respondent wishing to file evidence should do so by affidavit **13.02.11** within 21 days of service on him of the originating motion.

The applicant should give notice (if appropriate) of his intention at **13.02.12** the hearing of the application for judicial review to:

(a) Amend the notice in support of the application.
(b) Rely on further affidavits.

Before the hearing, a party may make any interlocutory application **13.02.13** to a master of the QBD, see **9.02.29–37**, for example, for discovery or for leave to cross-examine the maker of an affidavit.

Agreed notes and transcripts

An agreed note and/or transcript should be obtained (as appropriate), **13.02.14** see **12.01.27–29.**

Lists of authorities, skeleton arguments/chronologies

For pre-hearing preparation, see **12.01.30–33** and **22.01.** **12.02.15**

Practice

Introduction

For right of audience, dress, mode of address and conduct generally, **13.02.16** see **12.01.34–37.**
The hearing is in open court. There will usually be 3 judges (but will often be only 2).

A party should note that the prerogative orders are discretionary **13.02.17** remedies. The application may be refused if there has been delay or misconduct.

The hearing

The practice at the hearing follows the practice in **12.02** Practice at **13.02.18** the hearing of the appeal.

The decision

13.02.19   In judgment, the court may:

(a) Allow the application for judicial review and grant the prerogative order sought in the originating motion.

(b) Dismiss the application.

(c) Where certiorari is granted, quash the decision and remit the
matter to the court, tribunal or person with a direction to reconsider it.

Costs

13.02.20   Costs are in the discretion of the court:
Criminal cases: See **20.02.12 & 30**
Non-criminal cases: See **20.03.03**

Appeal

13.02.21   Criminal cases: From the Divisional Court to the House of
Lords, with leave.

Non-criminal cases: From the single judge or the Divisional
Court to the Court of Appeal, as of right.

3. APPEALS TO THE HIGH COURT UNDER STATUTE

Introduction

13.03.01   Where the jurisdiction of a court, tribunal or person is founded on
statute, the statute may set out the method of appeal of the decision of
the court, tribunal or person. Leave may be required.

The preparation, practice and conduct of the appeal should, in each
case, be researched in the common practitioners' handbooks. The
following is intended as a brief guide:

Preparation

Method of appealing

13.03.02   Where the decision of the court, tribunal or person is final, the appeal
is heard by the Divisional Court. In all other cases, the appeal is heard
by a single judge.

The appeal is by originating motion, stating: **13.03.03**

(a) The grounds of appeal.
(b) Whether the appeal is against the whole or part of the decision.

The originating motion should be served on: **13.03.04**

(a) The court, tribunal or person against whose decision the appeal is made.
(b) Any other person affected by the appeal.

As a general rule, service and entry of the originating motion must be **13.03.05**
made within 28 days of the date of the decision.

Pre-hearing

For interlocutory applications, preparation of agreed notes and/or **13.03.06**
transcripts (as appropriate) and lists of authorities/skeleton arguments/
chronologies, see **12.01.27–33.**

Evidence at the hearing

The court will usually decide the appeal on the basis of the findings of **13.03.07**
fact by the court, tribunal or person. The court may also reconsider any
matter which, in the opinion of the court, is relevant.

The court may hear or read any other evidence in its discretion, but: **13.03.08**

(a) Fresh evidence will not be heard if the appeal is on law only.
(b) Affidavits and/or signed notes of a person attending the hearing
    before the court, tribunal or person, will not be considered unless
    they have been submitted to the court, tribunal or person whose
    decision is being appealed for signature and/or comment.

Practice

Introduction

For right of audience, dress, mode of address and conduct generally, **13.03.09**
see **12.01.34–37.**
The hearing is in open court. Where the appeal is heard by the
Divisional Court, see **13.03.02**, there will usually be 3 judges (but will
often be only 2).

The hearing

13.03.10   The practice at the hearing follows the practice in **12.02** Practice at the hearing of the appeal.

The decision

13.03.11   In judgment, the court may:

> (a) Give any judgment or decision which could have been made by the court, tribunal or person.
> (b) Remit the case for rehearing.

The court is not bound to interfere unless a substantial wrong or miscarriage of justice has been occasioned.

Costs

13.03.12   The court's power to award costs will usually be set out in the relevant statute.

Appeal

13.03.13   A right of appeal to the Court of Appeal, with leave, may be set out in the relevant statute.

4. APPEALS BY CASE STATED

Introduction

13.04.01   A decision, judgment or order of a court, tribunal or person may be challenged by any party affected by that decision on appeal by case stated, usually on the ground that it is wrong in law or in excess or jurisdiction.

The appellant will require the court, tribunal or person to state:

> (a) The findings of fact.
> (b) The principles of law applied.

13.04.02   Appeal by case stated is an appropriate form of appeal where the facts are not in dispute but the principles of law to be applied to the facts are in dispute.

If the facts are in dispute, the appellant should consider an alternative form of appeal where fresh evidence may be introduced (for example, an appeal from the magistrates' court to the Crown Court, see **5.06).**

The court

(a) In criminal cases (except any case heard on indictment) the appeal is to the Divisional Court of the QBD. **13.04.03**
(b) In any other case the appeal is to a single judge of the QBD, except
(c) Appeals from the family proceedings court by case stated are to the Divisional Court of the Family Division.

Appeal by case stated from the magistrates' court

The most common appeal by case stated is from the magistrates' court to the Divisional Court of the QBD. **13.04.04**

The application to state a case should be made in writing to the clerk to the justices (specifying **13.04.05(d)**) within 21 days of the decision or sentence.

The statement of case should contain: **13.04.05**

(a) The statement of facts.
(b) Any submissions made by the parties.
(c) The decision of the court.
(d) The question of law or jurisdiction on which the opinion of the High Court is sought.

If the clerk to the justices refuses to state a case he may be compelled (in a proper case) to do so by an order of mandamus, see **13.02.03(a).** **13.04.06**

The appellant must, within 10 days of receiving the statement of case, lodge it in the Crown Office. **13.04.07**

The procedure on case stated from the Crown Court (except **13.04.03(a)**), is similar to the procedure in **13.04.04–07.** **13.04.08**

Appeals by case stated from ministers, tribunals or other persons

The application to state a case will usually be made under statute which will prescribe the method and time limits for the application. **13.04.09**

The party making the application will usually apply to the court by originating motion for a case to be stated, stating: **13.04.10**

(a) The grounds of the application.

(b) The question of law on which it is sought to have the case stated.

13.04.11 The appellant must, within 14 days of receiving the statement of case, issue an originating motion together with a copy of the statement of case, see also **13.02.09.**

Pre-hearing

13.04.12 For interlocutory applications, preparation of agreed notes and/or transcripts (as appropriate) and lists of authorities/skeleton arguments/ chronologies, see **12.01.27–33.**

Practice

Introduction

13.04.13 For right of audience, dress, mode of address and conduct generally, see **12.01.34–37.**

The hearing is in open court. Where the appeal is heard by the Divisional Court, see **13.03.02**, there will usually be 3 judges (but will often be only 2).

The hearing

13.04.14 The practice at the hearing follows the practice in **12.02** Practice at the hearing of the appeal.

The decision

13.04.15 In judgment, the court may:

(a) Give any judgment or decision which could have been made by the court, tribunal or person.
(b) Remit the case for rehearing.

The court is not bound to interfere unless a substantial wrong or miscarriage of justice has been occasioned.

Costs

13.04.16 Costs are in the discretion of the court.
Criminal cases: See **20.02.12 & 30**
Non-criminal cases: See **20.03.03**

Appeal

Criminal cases:	None.	**13.04.17**
Non-criminal cases:	From the single judge or the Divisional Court to the Court of Appeal, as of right.	

CHAPTER 14

Industrial Tribunal

1. INTRODUCTION

Introduction

14.01.01　　The hearing of any matter before the industrial tribunal will usually take place in public. The industrial tribunal may sit *in camera*, on the application of either party, where it is hearing confidential information.

　　The hearing is likely to be informal. Parties are encouraged to conduct their own cases.

Right of audience

14.01.02　　Any person (often a trainee lawyer or trade union representative) may represent a party at the hearing. The representative may also be a witness.

Dress

14.01.03　　All parties should be respectably dressed. Barristers and solicitors are not robed.

Mode of address

14.01.04　　The tribunal usually comprises a chairman (who is a lawyer) and two lay members, usually one each from panels of employer and employee representatives.

The chairman of the tribunal is addressed as **sir** or **madam**. The lay   **14.01.05**
members of the tribunal may be referred to during the hearing as a
matter of courtesy as **your colleagues**, for example:

"Do you, sir, or your colleagues have any questions?"

If a person is addressed directly by one of the members, he may
reply, addressing that member as **sir** or **madam**.

Seating

The arrangement of the seating varies according to the facilities   **14.01.06**
available, but the parties will usually sit at tables facing the tribunal.

Addressing the tribunal

Any party addressing the tribunal will usually remain seated   **14.01.07**
(although witnesses taking the oath should do so standing). An advocate may stand if he prefers but should not do so if all other parties
remain seated.

Parties and witnesses attending the tribunal

Before the hearing, the applicant and respondent and their respective   **14.01.08**
lawyers/representatives and witnesses usually wait in separate rooms
until called into the room where the tribunal is being held.

When the case is called, the parties, their lawyers/representatives   **14.01.09**
and witnesses will usually enter the room together and remain in the
room until the conclusion of the case.

A party may ask the tribunal to exclude witness(es) from the room   **14.01.10**
where the presence of the witness(es) would affect the conduct of the
hearing.

After having given evidence, a witness should only leave the room   **14.01.11**
with the permission of the tribunal.

2. PRACTICE BEFORE THE HEARING

Introduction

The industrial tribunal may consider applications in relation to the   **14.02.01**
following matters:

(a) Unfair dismissal.

(b) Redundancy payments.

(c) Race and sex discrimination at work.

(d) Employment protection.

14.02.02   The following is a brief guide to an application for unfair dismissal.

Application (Form IT1)

14.02.03   The application must be made in writing within 3 months from the effective date of dismissal on Form IT1, to the Central Office of the Industrial Tribunals (COIT). A late application will only be considered if it was not "reasonably practicable" for it to be on time.

14.02.04   In some cases an employee may be awaiting a final decision of an appeal board or panel or criminal court which relates to the dismissal. He should make the application and apply in writing (stating reasons) to the tribunal to postpone the hearing.

Notice of appearance (Form IT3)

14.02.05   The COIT will send a copy of the Form IT1 to the respondent. The respondent must enter notice of appearance on Form IT3 within 14 days stating whether he intends to resist the application.

14.02.06   The COIT will then send a copy of the Form IT3 to the applicant.

Further particulars

14.02.07   A party may wish to apply for further particulars of another party's case. The application should be made in writing to the other party (with a copy to the tribunal) or to the tribunal where the other party does not reply or refuses the further particulars requested.

14.02.08   Further particulars should not be confused with discovery, see **14.02.11** and **9.05**.

A request for further particulars should be directed at obtaining a clearer exposition of the case of either the applicant or the respondent, whereas discovery should reveal the documentary evidence which will support that case.

For example, the respondent may state in Form IT3 that the reason for dismissal was misconduct. The applicant is entitled to know if a specific incident is being alleged (further particulars). If the incident is documented, the applicant will usually be entitled to see a copy of the document (discovery).

Documents

The applicant may have retained the following documents: **14.02.09**

(a) Letter of appointment.
(b) Contract of employment/statutory written terms.
(c) Employer's disciplinary rules and procedures.
(d) Any written warnings/minutes of disciplinary hearings.
(e) Letter of dismissal/written reasons for dismissal.

If the applicant does not have one or more of these documents he **14.02.10**
may ask to see (and require the respondent to produce) the documents
in the respondent's possession on discovery.

Discovery

If either party refuses to disclose a relevant document, a party may **14.02.11**
apply in writing to the tribunal for an order for discovery.

Presentation of documents in a bundle

The parties will usually assemble the documents in a bundle, see **14.02.12**
9.06.17–21. The bundle may be divided into sections for ease of
reference. The documents in the bundle should be numbered in date
order with an index.

If the bundle of documents is agreed, it is usually prepared by the
respondent. If the bundle is not agreed, both the applicant and the
respondent should prepare a bundle.

The party or parties should prepare three copies of the bundle for the **14.02.13**
tribunal and one copy for the other party. An extra copy of the bundle
should be made available for witnesses at the hearing.

The bundles should be served a reasonable time before the hearing.
Sometimes the tribunal directs that bundles should be lodged with it by
a specific date or not later than a number of days in advance of the
hearing.

List of authorities

A party intending to raise a matter of law should serve a list of **14.02.14**
authorities on the other party and the tribunal a reasonable time before
the hearing.

The party is advised to take sufficient (photo)copies of the authorities
to the hearing wherever possible because many tribunals and parties
have limited access to legal works at short notice.

Witness orders

14.02.15   The applicant should approach any witness he intends to call at the hearing. If the witness is reluctant to give evidence (for example, against his employer), the applicant may apply in writing to the tribunal for a witness order.

The tribunal may order that the witness gets paid for his time off work to attend the hearing.

Assessment of award

14.02.16   The parties should give consideration to conciliation and settlement, see **14.02.20–24**.

Conciliation and settlement are impractical unless the parties have made an assessment of how much a successful applicant is likely receive.

At the hearing, the parties may submit a reasoned estimate (written if complex) of the award, see **14.03.31(g)**. The tribunal may then correct or alter the parties' assessment of the award.

14.02.17   The following is intended as a brief guide to an assessment of the award.

The award has two separate elements:

14.02.18   The basic award is:

(a) Calculated according to applicant's age and length of service.
(b) Subject to a statutory ceiling on length of service.
(c) Subject to reduction for "contributory fault".

14.02.19   The compensatory award is:

(a) The amount of purely financial loss and expense "in consequence of the dismissal".
(b) Subject to a statutory ceiling expressed as a cash sum.
(c) Subject to reduction for "contributory fault".
(d) Subject to further reduction on failure to "mitigate loss" (usually to find a new job).
(e) Not an award for hurt feelings (unless sex or racial discrimination is involved).

Conciliation

14.02.20   Copies of forms IT1 and IT3 together with other correspondence to the tribunal are usually forwarded to the Advisory Conciliation and Arbitration Service (ACAS).

ACAS has a statutory duty to effect a settlement of the case. Settlements made through ACAS have the effect that neither party can later apply or reapply to the tribunal.

If the case is not settled, anything disclosed to ACAS is privileged and will not be disclosed to the tribunal. **14.02.21**

Settlement

The application can be withdrawn, with or without settlement, (usually by writing to the tribunal) at any time before the hearing, although the applicant may be liable for costs. **14.02.22**

The advantages to the applicant of settling and withdrawing a case are: **14.02.23**

(a) Costs will be reduced, and
(b) State benefits received by the applicant after dismissal, which are liable to be recouped from an award made by the tribunal, are not refundable from money received as a settlement.

The disadvantage to the applicant is that he will not have a written decision from the tribunal that he was unfairly dismissed and he is unlikely to receive that admission from the respondent as part of the settlement. **14.02.24**

Hearings before the full hearing

The following hearings may take place before the full hearing of the application: **14.02.25**

(a) Pre-hearing assessment.
(b) Preliminary hearing.
(c) Directions hearing.
(d) Interim relief hearing (not considered here).

A request for a pre-hearing assessment or a preliminary or directions hearing may be made by either party or may be ordered by the tribunal of its own motion.

Pre-hearing assessment (PHA)

At a pre-hearing assessment the tribunal will consider whether either party's case has any reasonable prospect of success. **14.02.26**

The parties may make written submissions, or attend to make submissions orally. The party with the weaker case usually attends.

The tribunal cannot dismiss the case, but it may issue a warning to the party pursuing the weaker case that it does so at risk as to costs and witness expenses at the full hearing.

14.02.27   At the full hearing, the tribunal:

(a) Must be differently constituted from the one at the PHA.
(b) Will have a copy of the tribunal's comments at the PHA, but is not bound to order costs, see **14.03.35(e).**

Preliminary hearing or preliminary point (PP)

14.02.28   At a preliminary hearing the tribunal will consider whether it has jurisdiction to hear the application.

It is usually the respondent who requests the hearing, if he considers that the applicant is not qualified to pursue the application where, for example:

(a) There has been a late application with no good excuse.
(b) The applicant has failed to meet the minimum period of continuous service to qualify for the right not be to unfairly dismissed.
(c) The respondent does not employ a sufficient number of staff for the Act to apply.
(d) The respondent is not based in the UK.

14.02.29   The practice at a preliminary hearing follows the practice at the full hearing but is limited to the preliminary issue. As the substantive application may be disposed of at this hearing, both parties usually attend, with witnesses (if appropriate).

The burden of proof is on the applicant, who will usually open the case.

Directions hearing

14.02.30   A directions hearing may be held, for example, to hear argument over whether discovery or further particulars should be ordered. In more complex cases an estimate of the length of the full hearing will be made to facilitate listing.

A directions hearing is usually conducted by a chairman sitting alone. He may also later preside at the full hearing.

Both parties will almost always attend.

3. PRACTICE AT THE HEARING

Introduction

For right of audience, dress, mode of address and conduct generally, see **14.01.01–11**.   **14.03.01**

The clerk to the tribunal will usually read out the name of the case. He will then identify the parties and their representatives, for example: **14.03.02**

> **"Are you** (*name of applicant*)**? And are you represented by** (*name*)**? And are you** (*name of respondent*)**? And are you represented by** (*name*)**?"**

Chairman's introduction

The chairman may introduce himself and his colleagues. The chairman may briefly explain the tribunal procedure.   **14.03.03**

The chairman may also state how much the tribunal knows about the case from the tribunal papers and the bundle(s) (if any). This will assist the party opening to know in how much detail he should open the case, see **14.03.16**.

Failure of a party to attend

The parties should attend. If either party fails to attend, the tribunal may: **14.03.04**

(a) Adjourn the case if a satisfactory explanation is given.
(b) Hear the case in the absence of either party and treat the contents of Form IT1 or Form IT3 (as appropriate) as written representations.
(c) Dismiss the case.

The party attending may invite the tribunal to hear the case if he is of the opinion that the other party is unlikely to apply to the tribunal to review the case if it is determined in his absence.   **14.03.05**

The party attending may apply for costs, see **14.03.35**.   **14.03.06**

Order of opening

The party who has the burden of proof usually opens (and also has the final closing speech). This is not a matter of law and the chairman may ask either party to open.   **14.03.07**

14.03.08   The following are some instances of the burden of proof:

Case	Burden: Party Opening
(a) Unfair dismissal (where the dismissal is denied, for example, where the respondent claims the applicant left of his own accord)	The applicant, (to prove dismissal)
(b) Unfair dismissal (where the dismissal is admitted but unfairness is denied)	The respondent, (to prove the fairness of the dismissal)
(c) Sex or Race Discrimination (where no dismissal is alleged)	The applicant

14.03.09   The practice in example (b), which is the most common example in the industrial tribunal, is followed in **14.03.15–32**.

14.03.10   In a case where dismissal and unfairness are both denied the tribunal may (but usually does not) order that the case should be heard in two stages:

(a) The applicant proves the dismissal.
(b) The respondent proves the fairness of the dismissal.

Preliminary applications

14.03.11   The tribunal may hear preliminary applications by either party, including an application to amend the Forms IT1 or IT3 or an application which could have been made at a preliminary hearing, see **14.02.28–29**, although the tribunal may grant the other party an adjournment with costs.

Opening speeches

14.03.12   Both parties may make an opening and closing speech, see **Chapter 22**, Speeches. In practice, only the party on whom there is the burden of proof makes an opening speech.

14.03.13   The party opening should help the tribunal to understand the evidence it is about to hear, usually with reference to the bundle(s).

14.03.14   The opening is important because it enables the party opening to "set the scene" and to pre-dispose the tribunal in that party's favour. If a party is intending to open the case, the opening should be carefully prepared.

The case on behalf of the respondent

The respondent's opening

The respondent will usually open the case unless the tribunal indi- **14.03.15**
cates that it has read and will treat the Forms IT1 and IT3 together with
any documents as a sufficient explanation of the issues.

The respondent's opening should contain: **14.03.16**

(a) An explanation of the nature of the case, for example:

   "This is a claim by (*name of applicant*) **for compensation for
   unfair dismissal on the grounds that** (*state grounds*)**. The dismissal took place on** (*date*) **and is not in dispute."**

(b) A summary of the allegations in Forms IT1 and IT3.
(c) An outline of the contents of the bundle(s) of documents (in such
    detail as necessary).
(d) An outline of the evidence on which the respondent intends to
    rely.
(e) An explanation of the structure of the business (if appropriate).
(f) An explanation of any specialised working practices/words (if
    appropriate).

Proof of reasons for dismissal

The respondent must prove: **14.03.17**

(a) That he had a reason for dismissal.
(b) That the reason for dismissal related to:
    (i) Capability.
    (ii) Conduct.
    (iii) Redundancy.
    (iv) Illegality (for example, a driver dismissed for losing his driving
         licence).
    (v) Any other substantial reason.
(c) That he acted reasonably, for example:
    (i) That he acted on reasonable evidence (and not mere gossip).
    (ii) That reasonable dismissal procedures were followed (includ-
         ing adherence to any relevant code of practice).
    (iii) That it was reasonable not to adopt any measure short of
          dismissal (for example, a final warning).

Evidence on behalf of the respondent

14.03.18 The respondent will then be called and/or any witness on behalf of the respondent. The respondent and/or witness is identified, as follows:

"Are you (*name*)? What is your address?"

The respondent and/or witness will usually be asked to describe his relationship to the applicant, for example:

"Are you the former employer of the (*name of applicant*)?"

14.03.19 The usual rules as to the examination, cross-examination and re-examination of witnesses applies, see **Chapter 21**. Examination of witnesses, except a party may be permitted to ask leading questions in examination in chief on non-contentious issues.

Admissibility of evidence

14.03.20 Rules concerning the admissibility of evidence in proceedings before the courts of law do not apply in the tribunal. As a general rule, all relevant evidence is admissible, although a party should be careful, for example:

(a) Where it is practicable to ask or compel a witness to attend, hearsay oral or written evidence will carry less weight, (for example, a letter "to whom it may concern").
(b) Where it is practicable to produce an original document, a photocopy of the document may carry less weight.

14.03.21 The parties may make oral or written admissions, without formal notice, and/or agreements in the usual way, see **9.06.63 & 66**.

14.03.22 If the parties agree, a party may read the statement(s) (in any form) of a witness without formal notice.

Close of the respondent's case

14.03.23 The usual form of words is:

"That is the case for the respondent."

Submission of no case to answer

14.03.24 The tribunal may express an informal view of the evidence called by the party having the burden of proof, see **14.02.26–27**.

In practice, except in the rare cases where the tribunal expresses a view, a submission of no case to answer is not be made.

For the practice on a submission of no case to answer, see **9.06.70–74**.

If a submission of no case to answer is rejected, the party making the submission is still entitled to call evidence in support of his case.   **14.03.25**

The case on behalf of the applicant

Applicant's opening

The applicant may (but usually does not) make an opening speech. If an opening speech is made, it should be concise and brief.   **14.03.26**

The applicant's opening may contain:

(a) An explanation of the nature of the case (if not fully explained by the respondent or made clear by the applicant in cross-examination).
(b) An explanation of the Form IT1 and/or any other document to which no previous reference has been been made by either party.
(c) An outline of the evidence upon which the applicant intends to rely (where the applicant is calling witnesses).

Evidence on behalf of the applicant

The evidence on behalf of the applicant is presented in the same way as the evidence on behalf of the respondent, see **14.03.18–22**.   **14.03.27**

Close of the applicant's case

The usual form of words is: **14.03.28**

> **"That is the case for the applicant."**

The tribunal may then invite speeches by saying: **14.03.29**

> **"Do you wish to address us on behalf of** (*name of applicant*)**?"**

Speeches

The party having the burden of proof will usually address the tribunal last.   **14.03.30**

In a case of unfair dismissal, where the dismissal is admitted but the unfairness is denied, see **14.03.08(b)**, the order of speeches is usually:

(a) Applicant.
(b) Respondent.

In a case of unfair dismissal, where both the dismissal and the unfairness are denied, see **14.03.08(a)**, the order of speeches is usually:

(a) Respondent.
(b) Applicant.

14.03.31   In closing, either party will usually:

(a) Sum up the principal points of his case in so far as these will persuade the tribunal to reach a decision in his favour.
(b) Explain, in relation to the evidence, any weaknesses in his case.
(c) Refer the tribunal to any weaknesses in the other party's case.
(d) Compare the evidence of the parties and the character and motives of the witnesses (if relevant).
(e) Deal with the issues (if raised) of the applicant's contributory fault and/or mitigation of loss.
(f) Refer the tribunal to any relevant law, see **14.02.14**.
(g) Provide the tribunal with an assessment (written, if complex) of the award sought by the applicant, see **14.02.16–19**. It is not thought presumptuous to do this, but the party should nevertheless do it with care. The applicant may say, for example:

"If you find in the applicant's favour, I am able to provide a calculation of the award sought, if that would be of assistance. I have made a copy available to (*name of respondent*)."

14.03.32   Where the respondent has the burden of proof, he should explain to the tribunal, with reference to the evidence, how he has discharged that burden in relation to the reasons for dismissal, see **14.03.17**.

The respondent may provide his own assessment of the award sought by the applicant.

Decision

14.03.33   The tribunal may retire (or ask the parties and their witnesses to leave the room) to consider their decision.

The tribunal may:

(a) Give a short judgment and issue written reasons later.

(b) Give a full judgment with reasons.

(c) Reserve judgment.

If a party intends to appeal, he must have full reasons. Certain types **14.03.34** of case (such as sex and racial discrimination) always have a fully reasoned decision.

Costs

The tribunal has no power to award costs to either party save in **14.03.35** exceptional circumstances. These are:

(a) Frivolousness, namely, if it is felt that a party has brought a hopeless case without himself believing it had any hope.

(b) Vexatiousness, namely, if it is felt that a party has been improperly motivated (for example, an applicant whose principal motive is adverse publicity for the respondent).

(c) Otherwise unreasonable behaviour, for example, prolonging the hearing unnecessarily.

(d) Occasioning avoidable adjournments and postponements.

(e) Where a warning has been issued at a PHA, see **14.02.26–27**.

The question of costs should not be raised until after the decision has **14.03.36** been given. If the decision is reserved, the matter of costs may be considered by the tribunal at a future hearing or by written representation, except where **14.03.35(c) & (d)** apply (where costs may be awarded against a successful party) when costs may be considered at the hearing.

Allowances

Allowances should not be confused with costs. Allowances are **14.03.37** usually paid to the parties and the witnesses (but not the representatives) out of public funds. Any party or witness may claim up to a modest maximum, regardless of success or failure. The allowance compensates for the expense of attending the hearing.

It should be noted that: **14.03.38**

(a) A party against whom costs are ordered may not claim.

(b) A party in whose favour costs are ordered may instead receive his own and his witnesses' expenses from the other party (not subject to any maximum).

Appeal

14.03.39   Appeal is to the Employment Appeal Tribunal (EAT) on a point of law only within 42 days of the date on which the full written reasons are sent to the party intending to appeal.

If the appeal discloses no point of law, it will be rejected by the EAT (without hearing either party). Any appeal against rejection must be made within 28 days.

CHAPTER 15

Other Tribunals

1. BASIC PRACTICE IN TRIBUNALS

Introduction

There are many other tribunals dealing, usually, with disputes between a person and the state or official bodies.   **15.01.01**

The procedure for the hearing of a case before most tribunals is rarely set out with any precision, although there are likely to be specific provisions in relation to the service of documents/evidence/medical reports which the representative is advised to check.   **15.01.02**

This can usually be done by obtaining from the tribunal the guidance notes which are issued by most tribunals.

In some cases the statute establishing the tribunal describes the practice at the hearing to be such as "is appropriate" or as the tribunal "thinks fit".   **15.01.03**

In most tribunals, including those considered in this chapter, the chairman will explain the practice that the tribunal will follow at the beginning of the hearing.

As a guide, the practice at the hearing of a case in most tribunals is likely to be similar to the practice in the industrial tribunal (often including provision for an application to the tribunal on a preliminary point, see **14.02.28**).   **15.01.04**

15.01.05   At the hearing of either a preliminary point or the full hearing, the party having the burden of proof *at that hearing* usually presents his case first.

Practice

15.01.06   The usual order of presentation and speeches at the full hearing is:

Opening:	Applicant/appellant (or party having the burden of proof) opens.
Evidence:	Evidence of applicant/appellant.
	NO submission of no case to answer.
	NO opening speech by the respondent.
	Evidence of respondent (or party not having the burden of proof).
Speeches/sub-missions:	(1)Respondent.
	(2)Applicant/appellant.
Decision.	

2. IMMIGRATION APPEAL TRIBUNAL

Introduction

Adjudicator appeals

15.02.01   An appeal to an adjudicator may be made against a administrative decision of:

(a) The Secretary of State.
(b) An immigration officer (IO) at ports of entry.
(c) An entry clearance officer (ECOs) abroad.

15.02.02   The decision of the adjudicator may be appealed, with the leave of the tribunal or the adjudicator, to the immigration appeal tribunal.

The practice at the hearing of an appeal before the adjudicator is the same as the practice at the hearing of an appeal before the immigration appeal tribunal.

The following may be used as a guide to practice in both:

15.02.03   The following administrative decisions may be appealed to the adjudicator:

(a) Exclusion from the UK.
(b) Any condition limiting leave to enter or remain in the UK.
(c) Deportation from the UK.
(d) Any direction for removal of an illegal immigrant from the UK.
(e) Any decision to remove a person to a particular country.

Any person making a decision specified in **15.02.03** against which there is a right of appeal must inform the appellant of the decision and of his right to appeal, the address to which the notice of appeal should be sent and the time limit(s) for appeal. **15.02.04**

A notice of deportation will be sent to a person's last known address. It will take effect whether or not the person has knowledge of it. **15.02.05**

An appellant who is in the UK should ensure that the application to extend his leave to remain in the the UK is made in good time. If leave is refused, the appellant must appeal within 28 days of the refusal. **15.02.06**

Time limits

Time limits for appeal vary, although the time limit is not shorter than 14 days. **15.02.07**
If an application for variation of leave is not made before the existing leave expires, the tribunal will not have jurisdiction.

Notice of appeal

The notice of appeal signed by the appellant must be served on the immigration authority named in the notice of decision. **15.02.08**
The notice of appeal must state:

(a) The name, address, date of birth and nationality of the appellant.
(b) The decision appealed against.
(c) The grounds of appeal.

The status of the appellant is frozen pending appeal. For example, an appellant making an application for variation of leave may remain in the UK on the same conditions as before. **15.02.09**

Statement of reasons for the decision

After service of the notice of appeal, the immigration authority will prepare a written statement of reasons for the decision which is served by the appellate authority on the appellant. **15.02.10**
The date of the appeal to the adjudicator is usually fixed and the appellant is informed of the date.

Presentation of documents in a bundle

15.02.11   The parties (usually the appellant) may present any documents in a bundle. The bundle may be divided into sections for ease of reference. The documents in the bundle should be numbered in date order, with an index, see **9.06.17–21**.

Copies of the bundle should be served on the immigration authority and the appellate authority a reasonable time before the hearing.

Pre-hearing procedures

15.02.12   Apart from the full hearing of the appeal by the adjudicator, there may be:

(a) Pre-trial review.
(b) Preliminary hearing.

Pre-trial review

15.02.13   A request for a pre-trial review may be made by either party or may be ordered by the appellate authority of its own motion (usually in a complex case).

The adjudicator may give directions for the hearing of the appeal.

Preliminary hearing

15.02.14   At a preliminary hearing the adjudicator will consider whether he has jurisdiction to hear the appeal.

It is usually the immigration authority which requests the hearing if it considers that the appellant is not qualified to pursue the appeal, for example, where the notice of appeal is out of time.

15.02.15   A preliminary issue is often decided by the adjudicator without an oral hearing. If there is an oral hearing the practice at a preliminary hearing follows the practice at the full hearing but the issue is limited to the preliminary point.

Practice at the hearing

Introduction

15.02.16   For right of audience, dress, mode of address and conduct generally, see **14.01.01–11**.

Before the hearing, the appellant and a representative of the immig- **15.02.17**
ration authority and their respective lawyers and witnesses usually wait
in separate rooms until called into the room where the appeal is heard.

Witnesses will usually wait outside the hearing room until called to **15.02.18**
give evidence and leave after having given evidence.

Wherever possible, the advocate on behalf of the appellant should **15.02.19**
ascertain from the presenting officer, before the hearing:

(a) How the presenting officer will put the facts.
(b) Whether the presenting officer is intending to call or adduce
    evidence in addition to the written statement, see **15.02.10**.

The presenting officer is likely to have all the relevant case law **15.02.20**
including any recent or unreported decisions (copies of which will
usually be made available).

Introduction of the appeal

The adjudicator will usually introduce himself and identify the **15.02.21**
parties and their legal representatives. He may also briefly explain the
procedure.
The adjudicator may also ask the presenting officer to explain any
matter in the written statement.

Attendance of the parties

The parties should attend. **15.02.22**
If either party fails to attend, the adjudicator will usually adjourn the
case except where the appellant has not provided any explanation of
his absence.

Preliminary applications

The adjudicator may hear an application for additional documentary **15.02.23**
evidence or any application which could have been made at a preliminary hearing, see **15.02.14–15** and, if appropriate, grant the other
party an adjournment.

Appellant's opening

The appellant has the burden of proof and usually opens (and also **15.02.24**
has the final closing speech) except where the burden of proof is on the
immigration authority (for example, where a decision to deport is made
on the ground that it is conducive to the public good).

If in doubt, the advocate should seek the guidance of the adjudicator.

15.02.25   The appellant will usually open the case except where the adjudicator indicates that he does not require to be taken through the documents.

15.02.26   The appellant's opening should contain:

(a) An explanation of the nature of the case, for example:

"This is an appeal against a decision of (*name of immigration authority*) **for** (*a refusal to vary the conditions of leave to stay in the UK*) **on the grounds that** (*state grounds*)."

(b) An outline of the written statement of reasons for the decision.
(c) An outline of the evidence on which the appellant intends to rely, with reference to the contents of the bundle(s) of documents (if appropriate).

Evidence on behalf of the appellant

15.02.27   The appellant and/or any witness on behalf of the appellant is called and identified. Where the appellant is giving evidence, he must be called first.

The usual rules as to the examination, cross-examination and re-examination of witnesses apply, see **Chapter 21**, Examination of witnesses, except a party may be permitted to ask leading questions in examination in chief.

Admissibility of evidence

15.02.28   In practice, all relevant evidence is admissible, although a party should be careful, for example:

(a) Where it is practicable to ask or compel a witness to attend, hearsay oral or written evidence will carry less weight, (for example, a letter "to whom it may concern").
(b) Where it is practicable to produce an original document, a photocopy of the document will carry less weight.

15.02.29   The parties may make oral or written admissions without formal notice, and/or agreements in the usual way, see **9.06.63 & 66**.

15.02.30   The parties may read the statement(s) (in any form) of a witness. The statement is usually read by agreement, without formal notice.

Close of the appellant's case

The usual form of words is: **15.02.31**

"That is the case for the appellant."

Submission of no case to answer

In practice, the presenting officer never makes a submission of no case **15.02.32** to answer.

The case on behalf of the immigration authority

Respondent's opening

The presenting officer may draw to the attention of the adjudicator **15.02.33** any matter in the written statement of reasons for the decision, in particular, where any matter has been established in cross-examination of the appellant and/or his witnesses.

It is unusual for the presenting officer to call or adduce evidence in **15.02.34** addition to the written statement of reasons for the decision. If he does so, the evidence on behalf of the respondent is presented in the same way and subject to the same rules as the evidence on behalf of the appellant, see **15.02.27–30**.

Speeches

The order of speeches is usually: **15.02.35**

(a) Respondent.
(b) Appellant.

This is not a matter of law and the adjudicator may ask the appellant to address him before the presenting officer (for example, if no oral evidence has been called by either party).

Decision

The adjudicator may: **15.02.36**

(a) Give a short judgment and issue written reasons later.

(b) Give a full judgment with reasons.

(c) Reserve judgment.

If a party intends to appeal, he must have full reasons.

Costs

15.02.37   The adjudicator has no power to award costs to either party.

Appeal

15.02.38   Appeal from the decision of the adjudicator is, with leave, to the immigration appeal tribunal, see **15.02.02**.

The application for leave should be made to the adjudicator as soon as he has given a full judgment.

3. SOCIAL SECURITY APPEAL TRIBUNAL

Introduction

15.03.01   An Adjudication Officer (AO), appointed by the Secretary of State, may consider a claim made by any person for benefit and determine whether that person is entitled to benefit.

In a complex case, the AO may refer the claim directly to the tribunal.

15.03.02   Any person who is dissatisfied with the decision of the AO may appeal to an independent Social Security Appeal Tribunal (SSAT) within 3 months by writing to the DSS office concerned.

15.03.03   An appeal to the SSAT can only be made against the decision of an AO. Other claims, for example housing benefit, are reviewed internally and are not independently appealed.

15.03.04   The clerk to the SSAT will acknowledge receipt of the notice of appeal and fix a date for hearing.

Statement of reasons for the decision

15.03.05   The AO will deliver to the SSAT and the appellant a written statement of the facts, a summary of the decision and any relevant law and the appellant's grounds of appeal.

Practice at the hearing

Introduction

For right of audience, dress, mode of address and conduct generally, **15.03.06**
see **14.01.01–11**.

It is unusual for either party to be legally represented (although the **15.03.07**
appellant may sometimes be represented by a trainee lawyer).
The AO's case is conducted by a presenting officer from the DSS.
This is not usually the same person as the AO.

The practice of the tribunal is informal (and usually more informal **15.03.08**
than the practice of the industrial tribunal).
The chairman decides the procedure at the hearing, which will vary
from case to case, see **15.01.03**.

The hearing is a rehearing of the claim before the AO. Any new facts **15.03.09**
or arguments may be heard if relevant to the claim.

The hearing is in the nature of an enquiry. It is not a contest. **15.03.10**
In practice, this means that the order of presenting cases is unimpor-
tant, provided both parties have the opportunity to address the tribunal
on the issues.
The usual rules of evidence do not apply and all relevant evidence is
admissible.

Chairman's opening

The chairman will usually: **15.03.11**

(a) Introduce the tribunal members by name.
(b) Emphasise the independence of the SSAT from the DSS.
(c) Describe the practice to be adopted at the hearing of the appeal.

Attendance of the parties

The tribunal may determine the appeal in the absence of either party, **15.03.12**
although in the case of the appellant, the tribunal must be satisfied that
he has been notified of the date of the hearing.

Order of presentation

The appellant is usually expected to open, and often does so. **15.03.13**
However, the chairman will often ask the appellant if he would prefer

the AO to open. In practice, the appellant will often prefer the AO to open.

The presenting officer's opening

15.03.14   In opening, the presenting officer (on behalf of the AO) will usually reiterate the AO's written statement, see **15.03.05**, and may expand upon it.

The presenting officer should not strive to persuade the tribunal to uphold the AO's decision.

The case for the adjudication officer

15.03.15   Often no further evidence is given, although the presenting officer may call the AO and/or any visiting officer, medical officer or counter-staff.

15.03.16   The presenting officer may tender any documentary evidence to the tribunal.

15.03.17   A submission of no case to answer is not made in the SSAT.

The case for the appellant

15.03.18   The appellant may make any oral representation or may tender a written statement made by him to the tribunal and/or call and/or read any other evidence or tender any document to the tribunal in the same way as the respondent.

15.03.19   If new matters are raised by either party, the other party is usually permitted to respond and/or call evidence, unless the chairman considers it would be unnecessary or unfair.

Addresses

15.03.20   Either party may address the tribunal, on either law or fact, in such order as invited to do so by the chairman.

Decision

15.03.21   The tribunal will usually ask the parties concerned in the case to leave the room in order to consider its decision.

The parties will be invited to return to hear the decision.

15.03.22   The tribunal may:

(a) Give a short judgment and issue written reasons later.

(b) Give a full judgment with reasons.

(c) Reserve judgment.

The decision of the tribunal must be recorded by the chairman (in practice, on a standard form) and is made available to the parties (usually together with a note of the evidence).

Costs/expenses

Costs are not awarded by the SSAT. However, parties, witnesses and representatives may claim their expenses from the clerk of the tribunal.

Expenses cover only attendance at the hearing (including travel, subsistence, loss of earnings and child minding).

15.03.23

Appeal

Either party may appeal to the Social Security Commissioners with the leave of the tribunal or the Commissioner on a point of law only.

Application for leave must be made orally at the end of the hearing or in writing within three months of being notified of the tribunal's decision.

15.03.24

CHAPTER 16

Lands Tribunal

1. INTRODUCTION

Introduction

16.01.01 The Lands Tribunal is enabled by statute to determine the following matters:

(a) Appeals against determinations specified by statute to be to the tribunal.
(b) Rating (and Council Tax) appeals from the Valuation Tribunal.
(c) References as to the payment of compensation in respect of land.
(d) Applications for the modification of restrictive covenants affecting land.
(e) Arbitrations.
(f) Various other matters, for example, rights of light etc.

16.01.02 The Lands Tribunal has nothing to do with Agricultural Land Tribunals or with planning inquiries or with rental arbitrations under landlord and tenant legislation.

The Tribunal

16.01.03 The Lands Tribunal is located at 48–49 Chancery Lane, London WC2A 1JR (071–936 7200) for the registrar, administration and several courts.

312

The tribunal consists of a president who is a lawyer. The other **16.01.04** members are either lawyers or persons of experience in the valuation of land. They are appointed after consultation with the President of the Royal Institution of Chartered Surveyors.

Members normally hear cases on their own although in some more **16.01.05** complex cases a legal member may sit with a surveyor member.

The tribunal may hold hearings locally to suit the parties, often in **16.01.06** spare court rooms although there is no obligation on the tribunal to hold hearings near the subject land.

Procedure

Procedure is governed by the: **16.01.07**

● Lands Tribunal Rules 1975–1989 (S.I.1975 No. 299 as amended).

It is important to refer to the 62 rules in their updated form for all **16.01.08** aspects of procedure. The rules prescribe the forms to be used for certain proceedings and set a schedule of fees. In addition the tribunal has, on occasion, produced practice directions.

The tribunal may determine all matters upon written representations **16.01.09** although this procedure is very rarely used.

Time limits

Different time limits apply to each matter before the tribunal:- **16.01.10**

(a) *Appeals against determinations*: Within 28 days of the determination appealed against unless the enactment specifically provides otherwise (Rule 4).
(b) *Rating (and Council Tax) appeals*: Within 28 days of the decision of the Valuation Tribunal (Rule 9(1)).
(c) *References and arbitrations*: In the case of the assessment of compensation for the compulsory acquisition of land not before the expiration of 28 days from service of the notice to treat; on a reference by consent to arbitration, not after six years; otherwise, unless the enactment specifically provides there is no time limit.
(d) *Restrictive covenants*: No time limits.
(e) *Rights of light*: No time limits.

The tribunal may extend the time limits specified in the rules. The **16.01.11** tribunal may not extend time limits specified by statute.

2. PRACTICE BEFORE THE HEARING

Introduction

Notice of appeal

16.02.01   Appeal to the Lands Tribunal must be made (usually) within 28 days of the determination appealed against by notice on a standard form.

16.02.02   The statement of case must be served on all parties and should include every valuation (including particulars and computations) in support and a description of any comparable hereditament to which the party intends to refer at the hearing.

In rating appeals notice of appearance must be given within 21 days of service of the notice of appeal.

16.02.03   A reply may be served within 28 days of receipt of the statement. This should contain similar details of facts, issues and valuations to be relied upon in reply at the hearing.

16.02.04   The tribunal may direct compliance under Rule 41 and may order an adjournment with costs against the party in default.

16.02.05   An appellant or applicant is limited to the grounds stated in the notice of appeal/statement of case/application at the hearing of the proceedings (except in references or rights of light applications).

Directions and discovery

16.02.06   The tribunal (by the registrar) may order discovery of its own motion or on the application of any party. The following may be required:

(a) Affidavits or lists of documents.
(b) Further and better particulars.
(c) Interrogatories.
(d) Statements of facts agreed and facts and issues remaining in dispute.

Expert witnesses

16.02.07   Only one expert witness may be called on either side without leave of the tribunal.

16.02.08   Where more than one party intends to call an expert, the registrar will usually request that every plan, valuation, statement of prices, costs or other particulars relating to other properties to be given in evidence (or a statement that none are to be relied upon), shall be served within 28 days of the request.

Extensions of time are also commonly given.

Interlocutory applications

Interlocutory applications may be made in writing to the registrar, either by consent or upon notice being given to the other parties. **16.02.09**

If an objection is made within 7 days of service and if an appearance is requested, the registrar will give the parties an opportunity to appear before him. **16.02.10**

The registrar may, and if requested must, refer the application to the president for decision. **16.02.11**

The following applications must be made to the president:

(a) A preliminary hearing of a point of law (Rule 49).
(b) Dismissal of proceedings otherwise than by consent (Rule 39).
(c) Leave to adduce evidence by affidavit (Rule 51).
(d) For substituted service (Rule 59).

For practice at the hearing of an interlocutory application, follow the practice in **9.02.29–37**.

A party may appeal from a decision of the registrar to the president within 7 days of receipt of the notice of decision. **16.02.12**

Pre-trial review

The tribunal or the registrar may hold a pre-trial review either of their own motion or on request. Directions may be given. **16.02.13**

Sealed offers

In appropriate cases a sealed offer may be sent to the registrar before the hearing or handed to the tribunal at the hearing. The offer shall not be disclosed to the tribunal until the award of compensation has been determined. **16.02.14**

A sealed offer should not include any element in respect of costs. A sealed or other offer may be considered in awarding costs and, in those cases to which section 4(1) of the Land Compensation Act 1961 applies, will determine the statutory incidence of costs. **16.02.15**

3. PRACTICE AT THE HEARING

Introduction

16.03.01   The parties may be represented by counsel, solicitor, valuation officer, or may appear in person.

Surveyors who are also witnesses and directors of companies which are parties are usually refused leave to represent parties.

16.03.02   All parties should be respectably dressed. Barristers and solicitors are not robed.

The tribunal sits in public. The conduct of the tribunal is formal (in contrast to **Chapter 14**, Industrial tribunals and **Chapter 15**, Other tribunals).

16.03.03   Advocates and witnesses stand to address the tribunal. The member is addressed as: **Sir**. Even a single member is usually referred to as: **the tribunal**.

Calling the case

16.03.04   The clerk will call on the case.

If an agreement is reached at the last minute the parties may submit a consent order before the case is opened thereby avoiding the fee payable once a case is called on.

16.03.05   There are no introductory remarks. The member will turn to the applicant or appellant immediately.

The case for the applicant/appellant

Applicant's opening speech

16.03.06   The applicant introduces his opponent. The applicant opens his case. The opening may include:

  (a) A description of the nature of the application.
  (b) The jurisdiction of the tribunal and the legal basis of the application.
  (c) The grounds of the application, the facts agreed and the facts not agreed, referring in particular to any statement of facts prepared or ordered in pre-trial proceedings, see **16.02.06**.
  (d) Any legal arguments.

(e) The valuations and the basis for them, identifying where the valuers agree and where they disagree.

(f) Any comparable properties or values relied upon and the reasons why they are either appropriate or inappropriate.

Witnesses on behalf of the applicant

The applicant may then call his witnesses. The evidence is given on oath. **16.03.07**

The usual rules as to the examination in chief, cross-examination and re-examination of witnesses apply, see **Chapter 21**, Examination of witnesses.

Admissibility of evidence

The rules of evidence are applied strictly. Where there is an argument as to admissibility, see **9.06.53**. **16.03.08**

Expert evidence

Opinion evidence is admissible only if the witness is able to establish that he is qualified to express an opinion on the subject matter concerned, see **21.03**. Expert evidence. **16.03.09**

An expert valuer may express his opinions on values, even though his opinion may have been formed in part on hearsay evidence, but he cannot give hearsay evidence as to the details of any transactions not within his personal knowledge in order to establish them as matters of fact. **16.03.10**

The expert may: **16.03.11**

(a) Express the opinions he has formed as to values, even though his opinion has been formed by matters of which he has no first-hand knowledge.

(b) Give evidence as to the details of any transaction within his personal knowledge, in order to establish them as matters of fact.

(c) Express his opinion as to the significance of any transactions which are, or will, be proved by admissible evidence (whether or not given by him) in relation to the valuation with which he is concerned.

An advocate who puts in a list of comparables is giving a warranty of his intention to tender admissible evidence of all that is shown in the list. **16.03.12**

The case for the respondent(s)

16.03.13   The respondent does not usually open his case.

16.03.14   The respondent calls his evidence in the same way as the appellant. The usual rules as to the examination in chief, cross-examination and re-examination of witnesses apply, see **Chapter 21**. Examination of witnesses.

16.03.15   If there is more than one respondent (for example, the rating authority or other parties with the benefit of a restrictive covenant opposed to its modification), the order of presentation of their witnesses will be determined by the member.

Closing speeches

16.03.16   The order of closing speeches is usually:

(a) Respondent(s) (in order).
(b) Applicant.

The speeches should summarise the issues, differences and outstanding disputes. The parties may also deal with any outstanding points of law, with reference (as appropriate or, if directed during the hearing) to a skeleton argument, see **22.01.03**.

Decision

16.03.17   The decision of the tribunal is usually reserved and given in writing. In cases where no injustice would arise the tribunal may give an oral decision but this is rare.
    Note: Decisions do not bind future tribunals and should be treated as persuasive only and not as precedents.

Awards

16.03.18   In most cases awards are made in money terms and relate to a valuation date. Whether the award is with interest depends upon the relevant statute. The tribunal has no general power to award interest.
    In other proceedings a form of declaration is given or a decision on the law.

Costs

In a case where a reserved written decision is given it is usually read **16.03.19** out. A party may then apply for costs.

There is no general rule as to costs in the Lands Tribunal, for **16.03.20** example:

In rating appeals costs follow the event subject to any sealed offer.

In applications to modify restrictive covenants, the old practice that the applicant paid all his costs has not been followed in recent years and there is no general rule.

In compulsory purchase cases and in some other compensation cases the authority pays the costs unless it has made an offer equal to or greater than the amount of the award.

The scale of legal and surveyor's costs are in the tribunal's discretion. **16.03.21** In some cases where the tribunal has accepted an argument that it has no jurisdiction it has also decided that it has no jurisdiction to award costs. Costs may form the sole matter in a reference.

Appeal

Appeal on a point of law is to the Court of Appeal by way of case stated, **16.03.22** see **13.04**.

A party must make a written request to the registrar for a case to be **16.03.23** stated within 4 weeks of the date of decision.

The tribunal will decline to state a case unless the question of law is **16.03.24** defined with reasonable precision. It will not, for example, accept a question in such terms as "whether upon the findings of fact, I came to a correct decision in law".

CHAPTER 17

Inquiries

1. INTRODUCTION

17.01.01 The following different types of inquiry are considered in this chapter:

17.02 Development Plan Inquiries into the Structure, Local or Unitary Development Plan at which a landowner or interested party may wish to protect or establish an interest.

17.03 Appeals against refusals of planning permission for development or against enforcement notices alleging a breach of planning control.

17.04–05 Other inquiries, for example, objections to compulsory purchase notices, to Department of Transport road orders, to power stations and transmission lines etc.

2. DEVELOPMENT PLAN INQUIRIES

Structure plan

Introduction

17.02.01 The Secretary of State will appoint a panel to hear representations into a structure plan and report to the promoting authority.

The hearing is called an examination in public. It considers only selected issues.

Development plan procedures are explained fully in *Development*   **17.02.02**
Plans — What you need to know, available from the Department of the Environment, PO Box 135, Bradford, West Yorkshire, BD9 4HU.

Pre-inquiry

At the pre-inquiry stage, a draft plan is placed on deposit and   **17.02.03**
advertised. Objections have to be made within a specified time and on a specified form. Participation is by invitation and objectors have no right to appear.

The pre-inquiry procedure is best ascertained from the panel sec-   **17.02.04**
retary or programme officer, who may be contacted at the offices of the promoting authority.

There is usually a preliminary meeting to discuss procedure and   **17.02.05**
timetables for considering issues or topics and for setting preliminary times for parties to appear and dates for submission of evidence will be set.

Examination in public

The practice at an examination in public should take the form of a   **17.02.06**
probing discussion led by the panel. Any objectors are usually allo-cated a single space at the round table discussion. If a more formal procedure is desired a specific request should be made in advance of appearance.

The participants may be accompanied by professional or other   **17.02.07**
advisors but, if it is intended that the participant's place at the table is to be taken, at any point, by an advisor, it should be by prior arrangement with the chairman of the panel.

No costs are awarded but participants may be able to reclaim   **17.02.08**
expenses of attendance from the promoting authority.

Local or unitary plan

The Secretary of State will appoint an inspector to hear objections to the   **17.02.09**
plan and to make recommendations to the promoting authority.

Pre-inquiry

17.02.10 At the pre-inquiry stage a draft plan is placed on deposit and advertised. Objections have to be made within six weeks from first publication of notice of deposit being placed in a local newspaper.

17.02.11 A person making an objection in writing in the prescribed way to new or changed policies or proposals (rather than to existing policies in previously adopted plans) is entitled to be heard at the inquiry.

17.02.12 A person making an objection other than in the prescribed way or a late objection may be heard at the discretion of the promoting authority or inspector.

An application to be heard may be made to the inspector as late as the pre-inquiry meeting but, in practice, the promoting authority usually select a cut-off date for objections before the pre-inquiry meeting.

17.02.13 At the pre-inquiry meeting the order of objections and a rough timetable for topics and appearances will be determined and directions will be given.

17.02.14 Proofs of evidence are exchanged in advance as directed at the pre-inquiry meeting. Late delivery may lead to postponement of appearance by the inspector.

The authority will prepare topic papers in advance of the inquiry and responses or rebuttals to each objection.

The inquiry

17.02.15 At the inquiry, appearances are usually topic or objection related rather than grouped by objector. This may necessitate repeated appearances. The programme officer, who is usually an employee of the promoting authority, will co-ordinate the timetable although it is likely to change from day to day.

17.02.16 The objectors should monitor any last minute modifications made to the deposit draft plan as these may be advertised and an additional objection period may run during the lead-up to the inquiry. This will enable those modifications to be considered at the inquiry.

17.02.17 Supporters of policies or proposals in a plan may appear at the inquiry at the inspector's discretion.

Order of presentation and speeches

17.02.18 The order of presentation and speeches is as follows:

(a) Opening by promoting authority.
(b) Opening by objectors.
(c) Evidence of objectors.
(d) Evidence of promoting authority.
  • Evidence of supporter.
(e) Closing speech by promoting authority.
  • Closing speech of supporter.
(f) Closing speech by objectors.
(g) Final short closing speech by promoting authority.

Parties may produce counter-objections to representations made. **17.02.19**
These will be heard at the inspector's discretion and as he directs.

No costs are awarded at these inquiries and no expenses are **17.02.20**
recoverable.

3. PLANNING INQUIRIES

Introduction

A developer or landowner who is aggrieved by a decision made against **17.03.01**
him by a planning authority may appeal against that decision to the
Secretary of State for the Environment.
  The appeal may be against:

(a) The refusal of an application for planning permission.
(b) The failure to determine an application for planning permission
    within the proper time allowed.
(c) The service of an enforcement notice.

A third party has no right of appeal to the Secretary of State against a **17.03.02**
grant of planning permission by a planning authority. Where an appeal
is before the Secretary of State, a third party may have a right to appear
at the inspector's discretion (according to the status of the objection
under the appropriate rules).

Although appeals may be by written representation, the statute **17.03.03**
usually obliges the Secretary of State to hold a hearing. The Secretary of
State will hold an inquiry if requested to do so.

The appropriate forms for appeal should be obtained from the **17.03.04**
Department of the Environment, Tollgate House, Houlton Street, Bris-
tol BS2 9DJ.

17.03.05   Planning appeals have to be made on the form required by Article 26 of the Town and Country Planning General Development Order 1988.

Enforcement notice appeals have to be made on the form contained with the publication *Enforcement Notice Appeals — a Guide to Procedure.*

A fee may be payable.

17.03.06   The Secretary of State will appoint an inspector to hear the appeal.

In most cases the decision will be delegated to the inspector to determine. In the more important cases the inspector will report to the Secretary of State and make recommendations.

17.03.07   Different rules of procedure apply, see:

- Town and Country (Inquiries Procedure) Rules 1992 (S.I.1992 No 2038).
- Town and Country Planning Appeals (Determination by Inspectors) (Inquiries Procedure) Rules 1992 (S.I.1992 No 2039).
- Town and Country Planning (Enforcement) (Inquiries Procedure) Rules 1992 (S.I.1992 No 1903).

Pre-inquiry procedure

Introduction

17.03.08   The aim of the pre-inquiry procedure is to identify the principal issues and material considerations upon which the public inquiry should concentrate.

Department of the Environment Circular 10/88 states "At a local inquiry there should be no place for surprise tactics". Circular 24/92 states " . . . the last minute introduction of a material consideration intended to catch an opposing party off-guard is not good practice".

Relevant date

17.03.09   Procedures run from the relevant date. This will be the date of the Secretary of State's written notice of the inquiry date.

Statements of case

17.03.10   Within 6 weeks of the relevant date, the local planning authority must serve on the appellant, on the Secretary of State and on any person holding an interest in the land concerned who is a statutory party, a written statement of its case. This is called a Rule 6 statement or a Rule 8 statement in the case of enforcement notices.

The appellant's statement of case must be served on all parties within 9 weeks of the relevant date. **17.03.11**

In either case the statement should be served no later than 4 weeks before the date of the inquiry. **17.03.12**

The written statements must contain full particulars of the arguments and a list of any documents, photographs, maps and plans that it is intended to refer to or put in evidence at the inquiry. **17.03.13**

Proofs of evidence

Proofs of evidence (and a summary if the proof is longer than 1,500 words) must be sent to the inspector not later than 3 weeks before the date fixed for the inquiry. **17.03.14**

Date and location of the inquiry

A date will be fixed for the inquiry which must be within 20 weeks of the relevant date. The inquiry will usually be held in a public room or hall in the locality of the site which is the subject of inquiry. **17.03.15**

There may be a pre-inquiry meeting but usually only in the most important appeals. **17.03.16**

The inquiry

Right of audience

Barrister, solicitor, consultant or any other person. **17.03.17**

Dress

Advocates are not robed. All parties should be respectably dressed. **17.03.18**

Mode of address

The inspector is addressed as **Sir** or **Madam** despite notice of the inspector's name being given before the inquiry and during the in-spector's introduction. **17.03.19**

Conduct

17.03.20   The inquiry is formal. An advocate addressing the inspector should do so standing.

Practice

Opening the inquiry

17.03.21   The inspector will open the inquiry. He will introduce himself and state his qualifications. He will inform the parties whether he will determine the appeal or merely pass on a recommendation to the Secretary of State for his decision.

17.03.22   He will ask that an attendance sheet be circulated and that all persons at the inquiry (including advocates) should sign. He will then take a note of the appearances.

The inspector will then ask who appears for the appellant.

The appellant

17.03.23   The advocate on behalf of the appellant should give his name and legal or other status (barrister/solicitor/consultant). If the advocate is a barrister, he should state the name and address of the solicitor instructing him or the professional client directly instructing him.

17.03.24   The advocate should then list the number and names of the witnesses he proposes to call, with a brief description of their professional qualifications (if appropriate). He may refer to their qualifications being set out in the proofs already delivered.

17.03.25   He should then identify the proofs and appendices previously sent to the Department of the Environment and check that they have all been passed to the inspector. He should say what topic each witness will cover and give a preliminary indication as to the order in which he intends to call them.

17.03.26   The advocate may say:

> "**I appear on behalf of the appellant. My name is** (*name*). **I am counsel, (directly) instructed by** (*name of solicitors or other professional client*). **Their address is** (*address to which the decision letter should be sent*).
>
> **I shall be calling (–) witnesses. They are** (*give the names of the witnesses and brief descriptions, as appropriate*).

Their qualifications appear on their respective proofs which should have been passed to you. (*Check that the inspector has all the proofs of evidence sent to the Department of the Environment*).

I shall be calling my witnesses in the order that I have read out their names."

The advocate should not introduce his opponents.   **17.03.27**

The local planning authority

The appearance of the local planning authority will be taken in the   **17.03.28**
same way, see **17.03.23–26**.

Interested parties

The inspector will ask if there are any other authorities, representa-   **17.03.29**
tive bodies or persons present who wish to be heard and who, at his
discretion, may ask questions of witnesses.

He will take their names and addresses and ask if they wish to be
notified of the decision. He will also ask them which party they support.

Opening remarks by the inspector

The inspector will outline the procedure he intends to follow and   **17.03.30**
may make any other remarks to facilitate the good conduct of the
inquiry. He may ask whether an advance notice of decision is required
should he subsequently find himself able to give one.

He will also warn the parties that if there is to be an application for   **17.03.31**
costs it must be made at the inquiry and not later.

He is then likely to ask the appellant's advocate to identify the plans   **17.03.32**
that he has before him and to confirm which plans form part of the
application or enforcement notice and which plans are purely
illustrative.

The case for the appellant

Appellant's opening address

The appellant may make an opening address. The appellant should   **17.03.33**
outline his case. The appellant's opening should contain:

(a) A brief description of the development.

(b) A short planning history of the site, giving relevant applications, dates and events.

(c) An identification of the development plan against which the development is to be determined and of the relevant policies.

(d) A summary of any environmental impact from the development.

(e) A summary of the reasons why the development should be allowed.

(f) A summary of the reasons why the objections of the planning authority (or any objectors) should not be allowed to stop the development.

(g) A summary of any relevant law.

17.03.34   The opening is an excellent opportunity to deal with, and reduce the impact of, any anticipated objections before they are made by the parties relying on them, see **22.03**.

Witnesses on behalf of the appellant

17.03.35   The witnesses for the appellant will then be called. They will go to a suitable desk and will remain seated while giving their evidence.

17.03.36   The witness may read his evidence from the written proof.

A supplementary proof is admissible and should be made available with a summary, if longer than 1,500 words, at the earliest possible opportunity.

17.03.37   The witness may only read a summary of any written proof that exceeds 1,500 words in length with suitable explanation adduced by his advocate's questions in chief. A shorter proof and/or oral evidence are not subject to restriction.

17.03.38   The advocate should ensure that sufficient copies of proofs and summaries are available for all parties expected to attend the inquiry.

17.03.39   In enforcement notice appeals the inspector will require the evidence as to fact to be on oath unless the parties agree otherwise.

17.03.40   Each witness for the appellant may be cross-examined by the local planning authority and by the statutory parties. Other parties may cross-examine with the permission of the inspector.

The inspector should protect witnesses from intimidating cross-examination. The inspector may also ask questions himself.

The witness may then be re-examined by the advocate for the appellant. See **Chapter 21**, Examination of witnesses.

Documentary evidence

Documentary evidence may be adduced. The documents should **17.03.41**
have been listed in the statement of case, see **17.03.10–13**.

As a general rule, a document is admissible if it is relevant. Where
documents, plans, drawings or reports are to be relied upon, copies
should be made available to all the other parties.

The case for the planning authority

The local planning authority will present its case next unless the **17.03.42**
inspector calls a representative of any government department present
at this point.

The planning authority does not make an opening statement. The
planning authority may call witnesses and present documentary evidence in the same way as the appellant, see **17.03.35–41**.

Arrangements for the conduct of the inquiry after the case of the planning authority

Before the closing the inspector is likely to discuss with the interested **17.03.43**
principal parties the terms of any conditions or agreements under
section 106 of the 1990 Act that he should have regard to if he is
minded to grant or recommend granting planning permission.

The items that cannot be agreed may then be dealt with in closing
addresses.

Where there are several objectors, the planning authority should **17.03.44**
make its closing speech first and immediately after calling its evidence.
However, inspectors often allow the planning authority to make the last
closing speech for the objectors, in which case, it will be immediately
before the appellant's speech.

Closing speech on behalf of the planning authority

The advocate on behalf of the planning authority will make a closing **17.03.45**
speech. The closing speech may contain:

(a) A summary of the authority's case.
(b) The reasons for objecting to the development.
(c) The basis upon which the authority states that those reasons are
    valid reasons.

329

The case for the other interested parties

17.03.46   The inspector must hear from other statutory bodies in the same way, see **17.03.35–41**.

He may also hear other interested parties. He will attempt to fit in short statements by objectors or supporters at times that are convenient to all parties.

Closing speech on behalf of any interested party

17.03.47   Any interested party may make a closing speech at the end of their evidence or at such other time as the inspector decides.

17.03.48   The closing speech on behalf of the planning authority may then be made at this stage, see **17.03.44–45**.

Closing speech on behalf of the appellant

17.03.49   The appellant may make a closing speech. The appellant's closing speech should contain:

(a) A summary of the issues.
(b) Reference to the development plan and how the development relates to it.
(c) A summary of the benefits of and points in favour of the development.
(d) A response to the objections of the local planning authority (on law, on fact and on policy).
(e) A response to the objections raised by other parties.

17.03.50   Increasingly, inspectors are requesting that closing speeches should be in writing, (in effect, an expanded skeleton argument, see **22.01.03**). Such speech notes should be legible, are not obligatory and may be departed from.

Note: Transcripts or notes should not be offered or sent to the inspector after the close of the inquiry.

Costs

17.03.51   If any party is to make an application for costs it must be made at the inquiry. The application is made after all the closing speeches. There is a right of response and a final reply.

17.03.52   As a general rule, each party bears its own costs of the appeal but if either the appellant, the planning authority or, more rarely, any other party consider that another party has acted unreasonably in the conduct of its case, they can apply for an order for full or partial costs to be awarded against that party.

The following is a brief guide:

Costs may be awarded against: **17.03.53**

(a) A planning authority which has refused planning permission with no reasonable grounds for doing so.
(b) A planning authority which was unable to support its grounds of refusal with evidence.
(c) An appellant making an appeal with no reasonable prospects of success (for example, where policy or previous decisions clearly support the decision appealed against).

Site inspection

In most cases the inspector will already have looked at the site,   **17.03.54** unaccompanied and from the public highway, usually before the inquiry.

At the close of the inquiry, the inspector will announce his intention of inspecting the site. The inspector will invite each party to send one nominated representative to accompany him if the site inspection is to be accompanied. Both principal parties must be represented at all times during the inspection. There is nothing to preclude an advocate from attending.

The representative is not entitled to give further evidence on the inspection since the inquiry will have been closed although any questions from the inspector may be answered.

Decision

The decision will be sent at a later date to the parties to the appeal and   **17.03.55** to any other interested party requesting it.

The decision will be in writing. It will also indicate how any appeal may be made.

Appeal

An appeal from the decision of an inspector can only be made on the   **17.03.56** grounds that the decision was outside the powers given by statute or that a procedural requirement was not complied with. The appeal is to the High Court, see **13.03**.

(a) *Planning appeals*: The appeal should be made within 6 weeks of the decision letter, by notice of motion to quash the decision (without leave).

(b) *Enforcement notice appeals*: The appeal should be made within 4 weeks of the date of the decision letter, by application for leave to appeal. There is no appeal from refusal of leave.

4. COMPULSORY PURCHASE INQUIRIES

Compulsory purchase notices

17.04.01 There are many bodies with compulsory powers of acquisition, for example, local authorites, development corporations, statutory undertakers or their private successors, and persons empowered by private Acts of Parliament.

A person receiving a compulsory purchase notice may appeal against it to the Secretary of State responsible for the acquiring authority.

Procedure

17.04.02 The procedure for inquiries is set out in the relevant rules:

- Compulsory Purchase by Non-Ministerial Acquiring Authorities (Inquiries Procedure) Rules 1990 (S.I. 1990 No. 512).
- Compulsory Purchase by Ministers (Inquiries Procedure) Rules 1967 (S.I. 1967 No. 720).

17.04.03 The procedure is similar to that set out for planning inquiries except an objector does not have to supply a statement of case or a proof of evidence in advance unless the inspector specifically so orders. There may only be a simple letter of objection from a particular objector.

The inquiry

17.04.04 The acquiring authority presents it case first. The acquiring authority will open its case justifying the whole of the order.

17.04.05 It is common for inspectors to hear objections to the principle of the whole order first since many objections are likely to be site specific.

When a site specific objection is heard the objector will call his **17.04.06** evidence first. The acquiring authority will usually be allowed to call rebuttal evidence particularly where it has had no prior sight of the objection.

The final word on the objection will be that of the objector but the acquiring authority will have the right to sum up at the end of the inquiry.

Valuation evidence

Evidence as to the compensation payable is not appropriate as that is **17.04.07** a matter for determination by the Lands Tribunal, (section 4(1) Acquisition of Land Act 1981), see **16.01.01(c)**.

Valuation evidence, see **16.03.09–12**, will be relevant to an objection that a more economical alternative exists.

Report

The inspector reports to the relevant Secretary of State. **17.04.08**

Costs

A successful appellant is entitled to costs. An application need not be **17.04.09** made until the result is known.

Appeal

There is a right of appeal to the high court on a point of law by notice **17.04.10** of motion without leave, within 6 weeks of the confirmation of the order, see **13.03**.

5. OTHER INQUIRIES

Department of Transport Road Orders

A person who objects to a road scheme may object to the compulsory **17.05.01** purchase orders for the road or to the various highways orders required. These may be line orders or side road stopping-up or variation orders.

Procedure

17.05.02 The procedure is set out in:

- Highways (Inquiries Procedure) Rules 1976 (S.I. 1976 No. 721).
- Notes for the Guidance of Independent Inquiry Inspectors Concerned with Orders and Special Road Schemes made under the Highways Act (1981).

17.05.03 The promoter's statement of case should be served 26 days before the inquiry. There is no requirement that objectors submit their proofs of evidence in advance but there may be a request for them to do so.

17.05.04 If an objector wishes to promote an alternative route, it cannot form the basis of a modification of the final order unless it has been advertised.

The Secretary of State may give notice that any objector intending to submit that the proposed road should follow an alternative route shall send him, within at least 14 days and at least 14 days before the inquiry, sufficient information to enable the route to be identified. This allows the promoter time to advertise the alternative.

The inquiry

17.05.05 The promoting authority presents its evidence in support of the orders first. The procedure is similar to that adopted in compulsory purchase cases.

The objections are likely to be site specific although they may challenge the principle but are not allowed to challenge government policy.

Report

17.05.06 The inspector reports to the Secretary of State for Transport.

Costs

17.05.07 There is power to award costs in these inquiries. There is no requirement to make an application at the inquiry.

Appeal

17.05.08 There is a right of appeal to the High Court on a point of law by notice of motion and without leave, within 6 weeks of the confirmation of the order, see **13.03**.

Power stations and transmission lines

The procedures are set out in: **17.05.09**

- Electricity Generating Stations and Overhead Lines (Inquiries Procedure) Rules 1990 (S.I. 1990 No. 528).

The procedures are similar to planning inquiries but should be **17.05.10** consulted for detailed differences, for example, the requirement for an outline statement of case and the definition of a qualifying objector.

CHAPTER 18

Coroner's Court

1. INTRODUCTION

Function of the coroner's court

18.01.01   The main function of the coroner's court is to inquire into the death of a person within the coroner's jurisdiction, who has:

(a) suffered a violent or unnatural death, or
(b) suffered a sudden death and/or from an unknown cause, or
(c) died in prison.

The purpose of an inquest

18.01.02   The purpose of the inquest is to determine how, when and where the deceased died. The inquest is an inquiry into the cause of death. It is not an inquiry to determine blame. The advocate should always bear this in mind and be careful to address his questions towards the issue of causation rather than blameworthiness.

18.01.03   An inquest may also be held (with a jury) in a case of treasure trove, see **18.02.04 & 40**.

18.01.04   The hearing is inquisitorial, not accusatorial. Therefore, there are no parties to an inquest.

Persons appearing at the inquest

18.01.05   The following persons, having an interest in questions of civil or criminal liability, may ask questions (either in person or by legal representative) at the inquest, namely:

336

(a) The parent, child, spouse or personal representative of the deceased.

(b) Any beneficiary under a policy of insurance on the life of the deceased.

(c) The insurer who issued such a policy of insurance.

(d) Any person whose act or omission or that of his servant or agent may, in the opinion of the coroner, have caused or contributed to the death of the deceased.

(e) Any person appointed by a trade union to which the deceased belonged, if the death of the deceased may have been caused during the course of his employment or by industrial disease.

(f) An inspector appointed by, or a representative of, an enforcing authority or any person appointed by a government department to attend the inquest.

(g) The chief officer of police.

(h) Any other person who, in the opinion of the coroner, is a properly interested person.

The advocate will probably represent someone (who may also be a witness) from one of the above categories.

Mode of address

Any person addressing the coroner does so standing and addresses him as **Sir**. **18.01.06**

Dress

Any person appearing at the inquest and their legal representatives should be respectably dressed. Advocates are not robed. **18.01.07**

Seating

There are no rules about seating in the coroner's court, although the advocate likely to have the most cross-examination should be seated prominently. If in doubt, the advocates should seek the guidance of the coroner's officer. **18.01.08**

The advocates may, at this stage, agree the order in which they will cross-examine, if it is not obvious.

The hearing

The coroner usually sits alone. For the circumstances in which a jury is required, see **18.02.04**. **18.01.09**

Unless there is an application for evidence to be heard *in camera*, an inquest takes place in open court.

Inquests are often tape recorded and the evidence and any argument transcribed. The advocate should therefore prepare his cross-examination with special care.

Conduct of the inquest

18.01.10   The usual rules of evidence do not apply and the coroner has the final say over what questions may or may not be asked. The advocate should bear this in mind before making an objection to evidence, see **18.02.17**.

The coroner determines what witnesses will be called and the order in which they will be called.

The advocate has no right to the statements of the witnesses.

2. PRACTICE AT THE HEARING

Opening and adjourning the inquest

18.02.01   There will often be a brief preliminary hearing, usually within a week of the death, at which the coroner:

(a) Opens the inquest.
(b) Takes evidence of identification, see **18.02.10**.
(c) Issues the order for burial/cremation.
(d) Adjourns to a convenient time and place.

The advocate will usually be instructed to attend the resumed hearing.

The hearing

18.02.02   At the resumed hearing the court is formally opened by the coroner's officer (who may also act an as usher) calling "silence" or by proclamation.

Preliminary applications

18.02.03   If any advocate is proposing to make any preliminary applications or legal submissions at the inquest which may affect the length of the inquest, he should inform the coroner's court in advance of the hearing.

The jury

A jury (numbering between 7 and 11 jurors) is required in the case of **18.02.04** death occurring in prison or police custody or where it has resulted from an accident, poisoning, or disease, notice of which is required to be given to a government department (*i.e.* accidents at work, on the railway or ships) or in circumstances the continuance or possible recurrence of which are prejudicial to the health or safety of the public.

A jury will also be required in a case of treasure trove, see **18.02.40**.

If there is a jury the coroner's officer calls the names of the jurors. **18.02.05**
The jurors are then sworn in by the coroner's officer either individually or en masse.

Challenging jurors

There is no right to challenge jurors although an advocate is entitled **18.02.06** to raise proper objections (in an exceptional case and usually in the absence of the jury) where the juror is ineligible or disqualified. The advocate may say:

> **"With your leave, I would like to raise objection to** (*name of juror*) **being empanelled on this jury on the grounds that** (*for example*)**:**
> **(a) he is an employee in the factory where** (*name of deceased*) **died, or**
> **(b) he is related to the driver of one of the vehicles involved in this accident, or**
> **(c) he is** (*in a specified way*) **partial."**

The advocate should give reasons for the objection. The coroner is under an obligation to take note of a proper objection.

Introductory remarks by the coroner

The coroner may welcome the jury. He may then say: **18.02.07**

> **"This is the resumed inquest into the death of** (*name and address of deceased*) **who died on** (*date of death*) **aged** (*state age in years*)**. The inquest was adjourned to this date on** (*state date*)**."**

The coroner may then:

(a) Introduce the advocates present.
(b) Give a brief introduction to the facts of the case, which may include mentioning or recalling evidence heard at the opening of the inquest, see **18.02.01**.

(c) Give the names of the witnesses he intends to call (as to fact and/
or medical evidence).

Formal evidence "setting the scene"

18.02.08   If plans have been prepared or photographs have been taken, the
coroner may wish to introduce these in evidence before calling any
other evidence in order to assist the advocates and the jury to follow the
case.

Witnesses attending court

18.02.09 Witnesses (of fact) attending court will usually remain out of court until
they are called to give evidence except where the cause of death is
obvious (for example, suicide by overdose) when they may be permitted to listen to the proceedings.

The coroner calls witness(es) to the witness box to be sworn. The oath
is usually administered by the coroner's officer.

Evidence of identification

18.02.10   It is customary for evidence identifying the body of the deceased to
be given first, unless this was done when the inquest was opened, see
18.02.01(b). The coroner may say:

> **"I call** (*name of witness*)**."**

> **"Your full name is** (*name of witness*) **and your address is** (*address
> of witness*). **You are the** (*relation of witness*) **of the deceased?"**

> **"**(*The deceased*) **was (–) years of age and I believe that on** (*date*)
> **at about** (*time*) **you attended at the** (*name of hospital*) **where you
> saw and identified** (*the deceased's*) **body?"**

> **"Thank you,** (*name of witness*). **Now, does anyone have any
> questions they would like to ask** (*name of witness*)**?"**

In practice, it is rare that any cross-examination arises out of formal
identification evidence.

Witnesses of fact

The coroner will usually call witnesses in such order as to give a clear account, in sequence, of the events leading up to the deceased's death. **18.02.11**

Where there is an individual who appears to have been responsible for the death, he will usually be called last.

The witness is sworn and identified. The coroner will then lead the witness through his statement (although, in practice, he will not lead on controversial matters). The coroner will usually adduce evidence of the witness's: **18.02.12**

(a) Relationship to or knowledge of the deceased.
(b) The events leading to or including the incident leading to death.
(c) The deceased's general state of health, etc.

The coroner may conclude by saying, for example:

> **"Thank you** (*name of witness*). **Now has anyone got any questions they would like to ask?"**

Cross-examination of witnesses

If there is an invitation from the coroner to cross-examine, the advocate(s) may cross-examine (in turn), see **18.02.14**. **18.02.13**

If there is no invitation from the coroner to cross-examine, the advocate may say:

> **"With your leave, may I ask some questions of this witness?"**

There is no rule as to the order of cross-examination except that, if a witness is represented at an inquest, he is examined last by his representative. In any other case, the persons attending the inquest and their legal representatives will either, by agreement, see **18.01.08** or, by application to the coroner determine the order of cross-examination. **18.02.14**

The advocate should be ready to defend the relevance of his questions if challenged by the coroner, and should always bear in mind the rule in **18.01.02**. **18.02.15**

Witnesses should remain in court after having given evidence until released by the coroner. **18.02.16**

Objecting to evidence

Where there is a jury, an objection to evidence is usually made in the absence of the jury. A person objecting to evidence may say: **18.02.17**

"At this point there is a matter of law on which I would seek leave to address you and I feel it would be more appropriate if it were canvassed in the absence of the jury."

An objection to evidence should be made with care, see **18.01.10**. It may be made as follows:

(a) The party identifies the evidence to which an objection is taken.
   If the coroner indicates that he is prepared to hear the objection:
(b) The party gives reasons for the objection and refers to any relevant law.
(c) Reply by any other party at the invitation of the coroner.
(d) Response by the party, dealing with any new points raised by the other parties or the coroner but not repeating the submissions in (b).
(e) Decision by the coroner.
(f) Jury recalled.

Other witnesses attending court including police witnesses

18.02.18   The coroner will usually be assisted in the inquiry by the police. The attendance of police witnesses does not, of itself, indicate that the inquest is an inquiry into criminal liability. The police may have prepared plans and/or taken photographs (if appropriate), see **18.02.08** or may simply attend court as witnesses.

The coroner may also call evidence from other eye witnesses to the incident.

Documentary evidence

18.02.19   The coroner may admit documentary evidence (for example, a written statement).

The coroner will usually introduce the evidence in order that any party may object to its admission before it is read, see also **18.02.17**.

Medical evidence

18.02.20   The coroner will usually call medical evidence after evidence of fact (although the distinction between expert evidence and evidence of fact is blurred in cases involving death in hospital or whilst undergoing treatment).

However, there may be some cases where it is preferable to call the medical evidence first or where, as a matter of convenience to professional witnesses, the order is changed.

The extent of the medical evidence, other than that of the pathologist, will depend upon the nature of the case. For example, different considerations will apply between:

(a) Cases of immediate death.
(b) Serious injury subsequently followed by death.
(c) Industrial disease or other long standing illness followed by death while being treated.
(d) Suicide (where psychiatric evidence might be called).

Basic research into the areas of expertise involved will assist in cross-examination.

The coroner may call the pathologist, who is sworn: **18.02.21**

> **"Your full name is (***name***) and your address is (***address***). You are a consultant pathologist at (***name of hospital***) and on (***date***) you carried out a post mortem examination on the body of (***name of deceased***)?"**

> **"And do you now produce exhibit (–) which is your report on the findings of the post mortem examination in which you found the cause of death to be (***state cause***)?"**

The pathologist may then set out his findings as to the physical condition of the body and expand upon his reasons as to the cause of death.

Applications may be made after the conclusion of the evidence, or at   **18.02.22**
any appropriate time during the inquest. The following, **18.02.23–25**, are examples:

Application to call evidence

Although it is usually expected that the coroner will have gathered   **18.02.23**
together all relevant information and made use of it at the inquest, an advocate may wish to apply to the coroner to call further evidence, for example:

> **"With your leave, I would ask that (***name***) be called to give evidence in relation to (***state reason***)."**

Application to adjourn (part heard)

> **"(***For example***) With your leave, I would respectfully make   **18.02.24**
> application that in the light of the evidence of (***name***), and the implications thereof, the inquest be adjourned whilst further**

evidence is sought (and that it is thereafter reconvened to be heard with a jury)."

Application for a view

18.02.25   An application for a view will usually be made at **18.02.03** although it may be made at a later stage (if appropriate), for example:

> "**At this stage, I would respectfully make application for an order that there be a view of** (*state place of death, for example, factory*)."

Conclusion of the evidence

18.02.26   After all the evidence has been called, the coroner may ask those assembled whether any other person has relevant evidence to give.

Address to the coroner on law only

18.02.27   On completion of the evidence and any applications, no one is permitted to address the coroner or jury on the facts in evidence at the inquest.

An interested person may address the coroner on relevant matters of law.

18.02.28   Where there is a jury, it will be excluded during legal submissions, see **18.02.17**, particularly if the submissions concern the summing up to the jury and the law on any appropriate verdict, for example:

> "**There are certain matters of law on which I would seek leave to address you before:**
> **(a) You sum this case up to the jury, and I feel it would be more appropriate if these matters were canvassed in the absence of the jury.**
> **(b) You give your decision in this matter** (*if the coroner sits alone*)."

18.02.29   It is unusual for the coroner to invite submissions if he is sitting alone but an advocate may seek leave to address him on the law, whether or not there is an invitation to do so.

Summing up (with jury)

18.02.30   On completion of the evidence and any legal submissions, the coroner will, if sitting with a jury, sum up the evidence to the jury and direct them on any points of law. The coroner should:

(a) Warn against adding any riders to the verdict.
(b) Explain the scope of the inquest.
(c) Warn against any comments exceeding the scope of the inquest.
(d) Advise the jury to limit themselves to the facts of the case.
(e) Advise the jury only to answer the questions in the inquisition, see **18.02.35**.
(f) Advise the jury as to the various verdicts that they are entitled to return.
(g) Advise the jury that they are free to return any verdict available to them, subject to their obligation not to frame their verdict in a way which attributes civil or criminal liability to any named person.
(h) If there is a likelihood of an open verdict, the jury should be asked to agree as far as possible on registrable particulars, see **18.02.35 (para. 5).**

Summing up (without jury)

If the coroner is sitting alone, it is not necessary for him to sum up the evidence although, in practice, the coroner may refer to it briefly. The coroner will usually state in public the verdict he has reached. **18.02.31**

Returning the verdict

After summing up, if there is a jury, they will retire to consider their verdict with any plans, photographs or exhibits. The coroner's officer will take the appropriate jury oath. **18.02.32**

The jury may return any verdict available to them, see **18.02.36**. **18.02.33**

If, after a "reasonable period" the jury cannot agree, the coroner should direct, in open court that, if after a further attempt the jury cannot agree, he will accept a majority verdict (maximum of two dissenters). **18.02.34**

If the jury still cannot agree, the coroner will discharge the jury and hold a new inquest.

Questions in the inquisition

A verdict is returned by the coroner or the jury answering the questions in a document known as the inquisition which consists of the following paragraphs: **18.02.35**

Para.(1)   The name of the deceased.

Para.(2)   The injury or disease causing the death.

Para.(3)   The time, place and circumstances in which the injury was sustained/disease contracted, etc.

Para.(4)   The conclusion as to cause of death (the verdict), see **18.02.36.**

Para.(5)   The registrable particulars of the deceased:

     (i)   Date and place of death

     (ii) Full name of the deceased

     (iii) Maiden name of a married female

     (iv) Date and place of birth

     (v) Occupation and usual address.

The verdict

18.02.36   The conclusion as to cause of death is known colloquially as the verdict whereas, in fact, the whole inquisition is "the verdict". It is usually the most important finding at an inquest. The following standard verdicts are available:

(a) Natural causes.

(b) Industrial disease.

(c) Dependence on drugs/non-dependent abuse of drugs.

(d) Want of attention at birth.

To (a)–(d) the following words may be added (if appropriate): "and the cause of death was aggravated by lack of care/self neglect".

(e) Killed himself (while the balance of his mind was disturbed).

(f) Attempted/self induced abortion.

(g) Accident/misadventure.

(h) Execution of sentence of death.

(i) Killed lawfully.

(j) Open verdict.

(k) Killed unlawfully.

(l) Stillbirth.

An open verdict may be returned where there is insufficient evidence to return any other suggested verdict.

18.02.37   This is a complicated part of the law, much discussed in recent Divisional Court cases. At the present time, matters are far from clear. The advocate is advised to consult the standard texts and the Justice of the Peace Reports which publish most applications to quash inquests in the Divisional Court, see also **13.02**.

The jury/coroner may make recommendations to the appropriate **18.02.38** authorities so as to avoid future fatalities.

After the verdict it might be appropriate for the advocate to express **18.02.39** condolences or sympathy to the family of the deceased on behalf of his client(s) (without admitting liability).

Treasure trove

Treasure trove is hidden treasure. If a jury determines that the treasure **18.02.40** (which must be gold or silver) was hidden, it will belong to the Crown who, by convention, restores it to the finder (unless required by a museum, etc). If it is determined that it was lost or abandoned, it will usually belong to the owner of the land if the true owner is unknown.

Costs

Applications for costs are not made in the coroner's court. **18.02.41**

Conclusion

The inquest is formally closed. Usually the coroner's officer will call **18.02.42** for silence and ask those present to stand as the coroner leaves court.

If the coroner is to start immediately with another inquest, the coroner's officer may simply advise those present that the inquest is over and that those connected with it may depart (but see **23.01.05–07**).

CHAPTER 19

Consistory Court

1. INTRODUCTION

Introduction

19.01.01   Each diocese of the Church of England (and the Church in Wales) has a court of the bishop, which is known as the consistory court. The judge of this court is known as the chancellor of the diocese.

In the diocese of Canterbury the court is known as the Commissary Court and the judge as the Commissary General, but his jurisdiction is the same as that of a chancellor in any other diocese.

The Chancellor

19.01.02   The Chancellor is appointed by the Bishop of the diocese by letters patent.

It is possible, in the letters patent, for the bishop to reserve to himself the right to hear causes alone or with the chancellor. This is considered a regrettable anomaly and there are no current examples of such letters patent.

The Registrar

19.01.03   Each diocese will also have a Registrar of the consistory court who is also the bishop's legal secretary.

The Registrar is very similar to a High Court master, in that he deals with all proceedings in ecclesiastical matters up to the hearing.

He is normally present in court for the hearing (unlike a master), sitting as a court clerk or associate. He is also responsible for providing the necessary staff to administer the consistory court.

Faculty applications

The consistory court deals with all matters of canon law at first instance but its main business and purpose is dealing with faculty applications. **19.01.04**

Church buildings are exempt from ordinary planning and listed building legislation but changes in their use or ordering may not be made without a faculty granted by the consistory court.

In effect, a faculty application is similar to a planning application, except the practice at the hearing will follow the practice in a trial in the High Court, see **9.06**.

The consistory courts are a regular part of the judicial system and the practice in them follows the traditional adversarial pattern and is not inquisitorial except that the chancellor has wider powers than any other judge to summon witnesses, see **19.02.11–14**. **19.01.05**

Parties

A person may be a party to proceedings before the consistory court if he has a personal interest in the faculty application or if he is a parishioner of the parish concerned or a member of its electoral roll. **19.01.06**

A great deal of preparation and prior consultation is necessary before a faculty hearing. This should be researched in the usual textbooks. **19.01.07**

The petition

The petition is the first pleading. This is lodged by the party or parties seeking the grant of a faculty who have a sufficient interest in the subject matter of the suit. **19.01.08**

A petition could cover anything from a simple memorial plaque on a wall to the entire renovation, refurbishment or reordering of the church.

The party or parties presenting the petition are known as the petitioners.

The citation

Once the petition has been lodged with the court, the Registrar lays it, together with any plans or other supporting documents, before the Chancellor, who will then issue a general citation. **19.01.09**

349

19.01.10   The citation announces the works to be done in the petition.
        The petition and any necessary and supporting plans must be pub-
licly displayed by the incumbent and church wardens in various places
in the parish for a continuous period of not less than 10 days including
two Sundays.

19.01.11   The citation requires all persons who have (or claim to have) a lawful
interest in the subject matter of the petition to send to the registrar a
notice of objection within a required time limit if that person wishes to
object to any of the proposed works.

Notice of objection

19.01.12   The service of a notice of objection is the equivalent of entering an
appearance in High Court proceedings.

Act on petition

19.01.13   An objector who wishes to pursue his objection must serve particulars of his objection, within the required time limit (specified in the
citation). This pleading is known either as the particulars of objection or
act on petition.
        By lodging this pleading an objector becomes a party to the proceed-
ings and is known as a party opponent and becomes liable for an order
for costs.

19.01.14   If no objection is lodged but the Chancellor thinks it appropriate that
there should be a hearing and that the petitioners should be put to proof
of their case, he may invite the archdeacon to enter an appearance,
either to put the petitioners to proof or by way of outright opposition to
their petition.
        When this course is adopted the archdeacon will enter an act on
petition which may be a neutral pleading or may make points of
objection.

Answer

19.01.15   After an act on petition has been lodged the petitioners have the right
to a further pleading called the answer which should be lodged within
14 days.

19.01.16   Further pleadings may be necessary but are unusual and are regu-
lated by the Registrar.

Summons for directions

All contentious hearings will require a summons for directions and this can either be heard by the Registrar or by the Chancellor himself in chambers. **19.01.17**

2. PRACTICE AT THE HEARING

Introduction

Right of audience

Barrister, solicitor, interested party or parties in person. **19.02.01**

Dress

Barristers and solicitors are robed. An interested party should be respectably dressed. **19.02.02**

Church representatives should be respectably dressed but do not have to wear the robes of their orders.

Mode of address

The court is referred to as the **Venerable Court**. **19.02.03**

The Chancellor is addressed as **Worshipful Sir** or **Sir**. He is referred to in the third person as the **Worshipful Chancellor**.

Most dioceses have a mace for the Chancellor to symbolise his authority. It is carried in and out of court in front of the Chancellor and placed before him during the hearing. The officer who carries the mace is known as the apparitor. **19.02.04**

Practice

Introduction

The Registrar will usually stand and read out the name of the case. **19.02.05**

The petitioner may then introduce the parties to the court, as follows: **19.02.06**

"I appear for the petitioner(s). My (learned) friend appears for the (party/parties opponent/archdeacon) (*name(s)*)**."**

Proving the case

19.02.07   The burden of proof is on the petitioners, but strictly speaking there is no particular standard of proof in an ecclesiastical case.

The Chancellor gives such weight as he considers appropriate to individual items of evidence. The grant or withholding of a faculty is in his discretion (which must be judicially exercised).

After the introduction of the parties, the hearing proceeds in the same way as a trial in the high court, see:

- Preliminary applications   **9.06.36**
- Petitioner's opening   **9.06.46–49**

Evidence in support of the petition

19.02.08   The petitioner calls evidence in support of the petition. The evidence must be given orally, although the Chancellor has power of his own motion to direct that all or some of the evidence may be given before an examiner or by affidavit.

A written statement may be admitted in evidence under the Faculty Jurisdiction Rules.

19.02.09   The usual rules of evidence apply and witnesses called to give evidence for the petitioner(s) are then subject to cross-examination by the party (or parties) opponent or archdeacon, if he has intervened, see **19.01.14**.

- Evidence in support of the petition   **9.06.50–69**

The case for the party opponent or archdeacon

19.02.10   The party (or parties) opponent, may then open the case to the court and call evidence in the same manner as the petitioner.

- Evidence in the case of the party or parties opponent
  or archdeacon   **9.06.76–81**

Judge's witnesses

19.02.11   Thus far, the proceedings are almost identical to High Court civil proceedings but before the evidence is closed there is one very important difference in the consistory court namely that the Chancellor may call judge's witnesses.

19.02.12   The judge's witnesses are likely to be representatives of the Central Council for Churches or the Diocesan Advisory Committee or some other diocesan official whom the Chancellor thinks can assist the proceedings.

The judge has to give 7 clear days notice in writing of his intention to **19.02.13** call a witness and the nature of the evidence that the witness is being called to give.

Any witness called by the judge is liable to cross-examination by all **19.02.14** the parties and then to re-examination by the judge.

A view of the locus in quo

The consistory court usually sits in the church in question. This has **19.02.15** obvious advantages for the parties to view the *locus in quo*.

However, some chancellors, either through age or infirmity or other indispostition, prefer not to sit in church but at some other location. This course almost inevitably means that a view of the *locus in quo* will be necessary, see **9.06.67–68**.

Speeches

When the evidence is completed, the parties may make submissions **19.02.16** to the court on the law and the evidence, see **22.03**, as follows:

(a) Party (or parties) opponent.
(b) Petitioner(s).

● Speeches   **9.06.83–86**

Judgment

The Chancellor will then give his judgment. In most cases this will be **19.02.17** reserved in order that he can consider the matters he has heard and seen and to view the church, if he has not already done so.

If the Chancellor allows the petition, he will direct the issuing of a **19.02.18** faculty which is the court order allowing for the particular works to be carried out.
● Judgment   **9.06.87–89**
● Judgment order   **9.06.90–91**

Costs

The Chancellor also provides in his judgment for the costs to be paid. **19.02.19** Unlike other courts, one of the parties is also ordered to pay the costs of the court.
● Costs   **9.06.96**

Appeal

19.02.20 An unsuccessful party is entitled to appeal as of right. Appeal lies, in the Province of Canterbury, to the Court of the Arches or, in the Province of York, to the Chancery Court of York.

If the proceedings are certified by the Chancellor (on the application of either party) to involve a matter of doctrine, ritual or ceremonial, appeal lies to the Court of Ecclesiastical Causes Reserved.

19.02.21 The time limits for appeal are 28 days after the date of judgment of the consistory court or 14 days after the date of the Chancellor's certificate, whichever period last expires.

CHAPTER 20

Costs

1. INTRODUCTION

Introduction

Costs are any "fees, charges, disbursements, expenses and remune-   **20.01.01**
ration incurred by a party in or incidental to the conduct of
proceedings."

The order

The court may award costs to either party usually on finding for that   **20.01.02**
party, (the usual order), or the court may make an order for costs to be
assessed and announced at the close of proceedings, in either case
without agreement between the parties; or the court may make an order
for costs which have been agreed between the parties.

Bases of taxation

The amount of the costs allowed will be taxed on either: **20.01.03**

(a) The *standard basis*: Where an order for costs is made in a criminal
case and in most civil cases costs will be allowed on the standard
basis, namely "a reasonable amount in respect of all costs
reasonably incurred" and "any doubts are to be resolved in
favour of the paying party"; or

355

(b) The *indemnity basis*: In some civil cases costs may be allowed (in the discretion of the court, on application) on the indemnity basis, namely "all costs except an unreasonable amount or those unreasonably incurred" and "any doubts are to be resolved in favour of the receiving party".

Costs in criminal cases, see **20.02.**

20.01.04   An order for costs against the defendant must be assessed at the time of or before sentence, see **7.03.25**. It is likely to be less than the true costs of the case and will usually be measured by the defendant's ability to pay, see **20.02.15**.

An order for costs against the prosecution or out of central funds is made by the court in the usual way and will be taxed on the standard basis (or, exceptionally, costs may be agreed).

Costs in civil cases, see **20.03.**

20.01.05   An order for costs is likely to "follow the event", see **20.03.03**, (except in interlocutory applications, see **20.03.07–19**) and (unless otherwise specified) will be taxed on the standard basis or costs may be agreed, or costs may be assessed (usually an amount pre-set by the court) for convenience.

2. COSTS IN CRIMINAL CASES

Introduction

20.02.01   This section provides a brief guide to the award of costs in the courts of criminal jurisdiction, namely:

The magistrates'/youth court, the Crown Court, the Court of Appeal (Criminal Division) and the Divisional Court of the QBD.

20.02.02   The following are considered in this section:
Prosecution costs:
     20.02.05–08:   Prosecution costs out of central funds
     20.02.09–19:   Prosecution costs against the defence
Defence costs:
     20.02.20–27:   Defence costs out of central funds
     20.02.28–30:   Defence costs against the prosecution
Wasted costs order (against a party's legal representatives):
     20.02.31–32.

As a general rule, the award of costs in the youth court follows the rules in the magistrates' court subject to certain procedural and financial limits. **20.02.03**

Central funds

Central funds are maintained by the government. As a general rule, a party making an application for costs will usually apply for costs out of central funds. **20.02.04**

Prosecution costs out of central funds

An order for the payment of the prosecution's costs out of central funds is rare because it may not be made in favour of the following: **20.02.05**

(a) The Crown Prosecution Service or other public authority.
(b) Any person acting on behalf of (or in his capacity as an official of) the CPS or other public authority.

An order for the payment of the prosecution's costs out of central funds is, in practice, limited to a private prosecution. **20.02.06**

A court may order that the prosecution's costs (or such amount as the court considers reasonable) be paid out of central funds in: **20.02.07**

(a) Any proceedings before the magistrates'/youth court, Crown Court, Court of Appeal (Criminal Division) or Divisional Court of the QBD in respect of an indictable offence.
(b) Any proceedings before the Divisional Court of the QBD in respect of a summary offence.

The amount

The court has complete discretion in the award of costs out of central funds. The amount is usually taxed or assessed by the court, see **20.01.03**, or it may be specified (if agreed) by the court. **20.02.08**

Prosecution costs against the defendant

Magistrates'/youth court and Crown Court

A magistrates'/youth court or Crown Court may order that (a contribution towards) the prosecution's costs be paid by the defendant (or the parents of a juvenile defendant) where: **20.02.09**

357

(a) The defendant is convicted by the magistrates'/youth court.
(b) The defendant is convicted by the Crown Court.
(c) The Crown Court dismisses the appellant's appeal against conviction and/or sentence.

20.02.10   The prosecution may say, see **7.03.25:**

> **"There is an application for costs of** (*amount, and, where an explanation is called for:*) **made up as follows** (*state how the amount is calculated*)**."**

Or (in a case where it is unlikely that the court will make an order for costs):

> **"Would you/the court consider the question of costs?"**

Court of Appeal

20.02.11   The Court of Appeal may order that (a contribution towards) the respondents costs be paid by the appellant if the appeal or the application for leave to appeal is dismissed by the full court.

Divisional Court

20.02.12   The Divisional Court has the power to award costs *inter partes* on:

(a) An application for judicial review of a decision of the magistrates' court or the Crown Court, see **13.02.20.**
(b) An appeal by way of case stated (from the magistrates' court), see **13.04.16.**

The amount

20.02.13   The amount of costs must be specified in the order. Unlike **20.02.08 & 28** there is no provision for the subsequent taxation of costs against the defendant.

20.02.14   The court should take into consideration the means of the defendant as well as the nature of the case and/or the conduct of the defence when exercising it discretion to award costs against the defendant.

20.02.15   As a rough rule of practice, the court will not usually make an order for costs together with any other financial penalty which, in the opinion of the court, is more than the defendant could pay in one year.

Remission of legal aid contribution

A defendant may be represented under a legal aid order accompa- **20.02.16**
nied by a contribution order (usually with periodic payments).

If the defendant is convicted, the court may remit any payments
which have not fallen due, usually where a custodial sentence is
imposed or where the rough rule of practice in **20.02.15** applies.

The defence may say:

> **"The defendant is on legal aid with a contribution of £(–), of
> which £(–) is still outstanding. Would you remit that sum?"**

Appeal of an order for costs from the magistrates'/youth court to the Crown Court

A defendant, against whom an order to pay part or all of the **20.02.17**
prosecution's costs has been made, may appeal against conviction and/
or sentence to the Crown Court.

Where the appeal is allowed the Crown Court may also review the
order for costs.

Where the appeal is dismissed, see **20.02.09(c)**.

A defendant may not appeal an order for costs against him on its own **20.02.18**
except where the court improperly exercised its discretion in making
the order. In this case the appeal is to the Divisional Court of the QBD.
The defendant must obtain leave, see **13.02.04–07**.

Appeal of an order for costs from the Crown Court to the Court of Appeal

A defendant against whom an order to pay part or all of the **20.02.19**
prosecution's costs has been made may appeal the order on its own to
the Court of Appeal.

The defendant must obtain leave, see **11.01.17–20**.

Defence costs out of central funds

Defendant's costs order

A defendant's costs order is a payment out of central funds to a **20.02.20**
defendant of such amount as the court considers reasonably sufficient
to compensate him for any expenses properly incurred by him in the
proceedings.

20.02.21   A defendant's costs order is made in respect of expenses actually incurred by the defendant.

If the defendant is legally aided, payments made by the legal aid fund are disregarded. If the defendant is not legally aided, a defendant's costs order may also include the costs of his representation.

20.02.22   A defendant's costs order may be made in the magistrates'/youth court, Crown Court, Court of Appeal and Divisional Court of the QBD:

(a) Where the prosecution offer no evidence or otherwise discontinue the proceedings.

(b) Where the defendant is found not guilty on a trial or, on an appeal, the conviction (or part of it) is set aside, or a less severe punishment is imposed.

In the Crown Court, Court of Appeal or Divisional Court of the QBD the order may include the defendant's costs in the court below (or, of the first trial, on a re-trial).

(c) In the magistrates' court, where the defendant is discharged in committal proceedings.

The amount

20.02.23   The amount will be:

(a) Assessed or taxed by the court, see **20.01.03**, or may be,

(b) Specified (if agreed) by the court.

20.02.24   The court has a complete discretion in making a defendant's costs order. As a general rule, the court will make a defendant's costs order if the defendant is entitled to one except where:

(a) The defendant brought suspicion on himself. (The advocate should be prepared to argue this exception as it is often overworked).

(b) The defendant was acquitted on a technicality.

20.02.25   When making the application for a defendant's costs order, the defence may say:

"Would you make a defendant's costs order?"

"The defendant is legally aided. He has incurred out of pocket expenses of £(–) namely (*state nature of expenses, usually travelling*) **in these proceedings. And I would ask for an order in that sum."**

or

"The defendant is not legally aided. He has personally incurred the cost of his representation in these proceedings. And I would ask for an order for costs to be taxed."

Return of legal aid contribution

A defendant may be represented under a legal aid order accompan- **20.02.26**
ied by a contribution order (usually with periodic payments).
  If a defendant is acquitted or discharged, the court will usually:

(a) Remit any payments which have not fallen due.
(b) Remit any payments which have fallen due but not been paid.
(c) Order that some or all of the payments which have been made be returned.

The defence may say: **20.02.27**

"The defendant is on legal aid with a contribution of £(–). Would you order that his legal aid contribution be returned?"

Defence costs against the prosecution

Magistrates'/youth court, Crown Court, Court of Appeal

The defendant's costs will usually be paid out of central funds. **20.02.28**
However, the court may order either party (in this case, the prosecution) to pay costs incurred as a result of an unnecessary or improper act
or omission.

The court will usually indicate whether it is of the opinion that an **20.02.29**
order for costs should be made against the prosecution, for example:

"There is no reason that the prosecution should not pay the costs thrown away."

The prosecution may then address the court.

Divisional Court

See **13.02.20** and **13.04.16**. It is not necessary to satisfy the court of **20.02.30**
any impropriety.

Wasted costs order

20.02.31   Where costs have been wasted because of default by a party's legal representative (solicitor or counsel), the court may award costs against that representative.

20.02.32   Before making such an order the court shall specify the costs that are to be met and (at its discretion) direct an investigation by a taxing officer. The legal representative has the right to be heard. The procedure of the hearing is in the court's discretion.

3. COSTS IN CIVIL CASES

Introduction

The effect of an order for costs

20.03.01   In the civil courts, the costs of an action may often exceed the claim. Therefore it is important that the parties should attempt to keep an approximate running total of the costs incurred to date for the purposes of considering settlement of the action.

The advocate should also be prepared to warn his client that civil litigation is not cheap; it is a gamble and, no matter how meritorious the claim, there is very rarely the certainty of winning.

20.03.02   The following are considered in this section:
20.03.03–06: The "usual order" for costs.
20.03.07–21: Orders for costs (usually in interlocutory proceedings).
20.03.22–27: Certificate for counsel.
20.03.28:   The final order.
20.03.29–30: Wasted costs order (against a party's legal representatives).

The general principles

Costs "follow the event"

20.03.03   Costs are in the discretion of the court but will usually "follow the event" (which means that the successful party will obtain his costs against the unsuccessful party).

Exceptions to 20.03.03

(a) Costs of an amendment to pleadings, without leave, are borne by   **20.03.04**
the party making the amendment.

(b) Costs of an application to extend time limits are borne by the
applicant.

(c) Costs of proving facts, where a party on whom a notice to admit
facts has been served, see **9.06.64**, has refused to admit the
specified facts, are usually borne by the party refusing to make the
admission.

(d) Costs of discovery before action against a party are borne by the
applicant.

Note: The general rule does not necessarily apply in the Family
Division.

Costs are recovered by order of the court

A party is not entitled to recover the costs of any proceedings from   **20.03.05**
any other party to the proceedings except by order of the court.

Exceptions to 20.03.05

A party is entitled to his costs without an order of the court, where: **20.03.06**

(a) The action against that party is withdrawn without leave.

(b) The party accepts a payment into court in satisfaction of his
claim.

(c) The party successfully defends a summons to set aside the
proceedings on the ground of irregularity.

Costs in interlocutory proceedings

The issue of costs often arises in interlocutory proceedings because the   **20.03.07**
proceedings are not a final determination of the issues between the
parties and there is no "event", as such, for costs to follow. See **9.02.01**
and interlocutory applications generally, and **9.03** Summary judgment,
9.04 Directions and **9.05** Discovery.

The usual orders for costs are:

Costs in the cause

Costs in the cause means that on the final determination of the issues   **20.03.08**
between the parties, the costs of the proceedings will follow the event.

20.03.09   An order for costs in the cause is usually made on an interlocutory application of an administrative nature or by agreement. Either party may say, for example:

> **"I ask for costs in the cause. (This is not a suitable time to adjudge the costs of this application)."**

Costs in any event

20.03.10   Costs in any event means that the party in whose favour the order for costs is made, is entitled to his costs of those proceedings regardless of the final determination of the issues between the parties.

20.03.11   An order for costs in any event is usually made against a party whom it appears to the court has incurred costs wastefully. The successful party may say, for example:

> **"I ask for the costs of this application in any event. This application should never have been made/opposed."**

Costs thrown away

20.03.12   Costs thrown away means that where proceedings (or any part of them) have been ineffective or set aside, the party in whose favour the order for costs is made, is entitled to his costs of the proceedings regardless of the final determination of the issues between the parties.

20.03.13   An order for costs thrown away is often made in similar circumstances to an order for costs in any event. The successful party may say, for example:

> **"I ask that the costs be costs thrown away. The plaintiff/defendant refused to consent to this application and has now failed to attend for the hearing, I ask that the costs be costs thrown away."**

Costs reserved

20.03.14   Costs reserved means that the question of who should be liable for the costs of the proceedings will be determined on the final determination of the issues between the parties (although the costs will usually follow the event unless the court orders otherwise).

20.03.15   An order for costs reserved is often made on an interlocutory application. Either party may say, for example:

"I would ask that today's costs be reserved in order that they can be resolved at trial/on a later date."

No order as to costs

No order as to costs is frequently made in cases where both parties are legally aided and an apportionment of costs would be inappropriate.   **20.03.16**

Either party may say: **20.03.17**

"I would ask that there be no order for costs save legal aid taxation (*see* 20.03.20). Both parties are legally aided with nil contributions."

Costs not to be enforced without leave

A legally aided party is not normally liable for the other side's costs unless he can be shown to have assets.   **20.03.18**

If a party wins against a legally aided opponent he may obtain an order for costs not to be enforced without leave. This will enable him to return to court at a later date, if the legally aided party is found to have assets, to make an application for costs to be paid by that party. The successful party may say: **20.03.19**

"I ask for judgment as prayed and costs. As the (*name of party*) is legally aided but (*for example*: in employment/has disclosed certain means), I would ask for costs to be awarded but not to be enforced without the leave of the court (after proper investigation of his means)."

Legal aid taxation

In order for a solicitor instructed by a client on legal aid to be able to have his fees paid out of the legal aid fund, it is necessary for him to have an order for legal aid taxation if the case is not finished.   **20.03.20**

A party may ask for legal aid taxation at each stage of the proceedings although the district judge/judge/master may decline to grant the order. If in doubt, a party should ask for legal aid taxation, for example: **20.03.21**

"I ask that there be no order for costs save for legal aid taxation of the plaintiff's/defendant's/both parties costs."

Certificate for counsel

20.03.22   If counsel is instructed in certain interlocutory matters, see **9.02.11(a) & 25**, a certificate for counsel is required if his fee is to be allowed on taxation of costs.

As a general rule, a certificate for counsel is required for applications in chambers. It will only be given where the court is of the opinion that the expense of instructing counsel is justified.

20.03.23   A certificate for counsel is often thought to be needed for legal aid cases only. This is incorrect as it can be relevant on the taxation of costs between privately funded parties where one was represented by a solicitor and the other by a barrister.

20.03.24   A certificate for counsel is never required on the full trial of an action.

20.03.25   After an application for costs, a party may apply for a certificate for counsel as follows:

> **"And I would ask for a certificate for counsel for the plaintiff/ defendant/both parties."**

20.03.26   If the court is reluctant to grant a certificate for counsel, the party may draw the court's attention to:

(a) The complexity of the case.
(b) The issues of law.
(c) Any matters (including (a) and (b)) which may have been raised but for agreement between the parties.
(d) The time saved.

20.03.27   If it is not clear whether the application is an appropriate application on which to grant a certificate for counsel, a party may say:

> **"I am unsure whether a certificate for counsel is required. In order to avoid any doubt, perhaps I might have a certificate for counsel in any event?"**

Final order

20.03.28   The final order for costs may be for:

- Costs to be taxed, see **20.01.02**.
- Assessed costs of £(–), (in certain cases, usually in the county court or, if the parties agree) see, for example **8.07.10**.
- Costs to be taxed, if not agreed.

Wasted costs order

Where costs have been wasted because of default by a party's legal **20.03.29** representatives (solicitor or counsel), the court may award costs against that representative.

Before making such an order, the court shall specify the costs that are **20.03.30** to be met and may (at its discretion) direct an investigation by a taxing officer. The legal representative has the right to be heard. The procedure at the hearing is in the court's discretion.

CHAPTER 21

Examination of Witnesses

1. EXAMINATION IN CHIEF, CROSS-EXAMINATION AND RE-EXAMINATION

Introduction

21.01.01 The purpose of examination (asking questions) of a witness is to obtain answers.

In practice, a party should not ask a witness questions if he does not need the witness' answers.

21.01.02 The party examining a witness should:

(a) Ask short, straightforward and easily understood questions.
(b) Ask the witness only questions which are relevant to the issues between the parties.

21.01.03 The party examining a witness should not ask the witness questions of which that party has little or no idea of the answer.

Examination in chief

21.01.04 The purpose of calling a witness (with certain exceptions) is to obtain evidence from that witness in support of the case (or part of the case) of the party calling that witness.

The party calling the witness should first identify the witness to the court or tribunal, as follows: **21.01.05**

"Are you (*name*) **of** (*address*)**?"**

or

"What is your name? What is your address?"

The witness may then be asked to describe his relationship to the party calling the witness and/or the case, for example: **21.01.06**

"Are you the employer/wife/neighbour of (*name of party*)**?"**

Or, the witness may be asked his occupation (if relevant to the case).   **21.01.07**

In examination in chief, the witness should be asked questions in such a way that, without the answer being suggested to him, the witness tells the court that which the party calling the witness wants the court to know.   **21.01.08**

The party calling the witness should: **21.01.09**

(a) Examine the witness only on matters relevant to the purpose of calling the witness.
(b) Examine the witness from a statement or proof of evidence made (and preferably signed) by the witness before the witness is called to give evidence.

The party calling the witness should not ask leading questions (*i.e.* questions suggesting the answer) unless all parties agree this may be done. The party should make this agreement clear, for example: **21.01.10**

"I have the agreement of (*name of party or* **all parties) to lead this witness (on this part of his evidence)."**

Even if a party is permitted to lead, the evidence of a witness will usually sound better if it is unprompted. In practice, the essential part of the evidence of that witness is better adduced in the usual way.

Cross-examination

The purpose of cross-examination is to test the accuracy of evidence given by the witness against the party who has not called the witness and/or to obtain evidence from the witness favourable to that party.   **21.01.11**

The party cross-examining a witness may ask leading questions.   **21.01.12**

21.01.13   The party should:

(a) Put his case on the relevant issues to the witness. If it is the party's case that the witness is either mistaken or untruthful he should make either allegation clear.

(b) As a general rule, cross-examine only on the issues which are in dispute between the parties.

21.01.14   The party cross-examining a witness should not ask repetetive questions either, to emphasise an answer made by the witness which is favourable to that party or, to persuade the witness to change an answer made by the witness which is unfavourable to that party (although different questions may be asked).

Re-examination

21.01.15   The purpose or re-examination is to attempt to reinstate any part of the evidence of the witness rendered less cogent by cross-examination and to clarify any points raised in cross-examination that were not raised in examination in chief.

21.01.16   The general rule in **20.01.01** should be carefully considered by a party considering re-examination.

21.01.17   The party re-examining a witness should ask questions only on matters arising out of cross-examination. The party is not permitted to introduce new matter.

21.01.18   The party re-examining a witness should not:

(a) Ask leading questions.
(b) See **20.01.14**.

Releasing a witness

21.01.19   After re-examination, a party calling a witness may invite the court to release the witness. The party may say:

> **"Unless there is any objection, perhaps this witness (and any other witness) could be released."**

The court may then invite the observations of all parties as to whether **21.01.20** the witness or any other witness should be released and, if so, whether the witness(es) should be available to be recalled if necessary.

2. REFRESHING THE MEMORY

Introduction

A witness may wish to refresh his memory in the witness box from a **21.02.01** document made at the time. The witness is often a police officer although it may be any other witness who has made a contemporaneous or near contemporaneous document or note.

"Refreshing the memory" means what it says. The witness should not (but, often does) read verbatim from the document.

Practice

The party calling the witness may say: **21.02.02**

> **"Do you wish to refresh your memory from** (*state nature of document/note*)**? When did you make** (*the document/note*)**?"**

If the document/note was not made at the time: **21.02.03**

> **"How long after the events recorded in** (*the document/note*) **did you make** (*the document/note*)**? When you made** (*the document*) **were the events still fresh in your mind?"**

If the document/note was not made by the witness: **21.02.04**

> **"When did you see** (*the document/note*)**? Did you check the contents of** (*the document/note*)**? and/or Did you sign** (*the document*)**?**
>
> **When you saw/checked the contents of** (*the document/note*) **were the events recorded in** (*the document/note*) **still fresh in your mind?"**

The party may then say to the court: **21.02.05**

> **"Could** (*name of witness*) **be allowed to see/refresh his memory from** (*the document/note*)**?"**

The document/note (or a copy) should be made available to the party **21.02.06** or parties against whom the witness is called.

21.02.07   A witness may also refresh his memory before giving evidence from a document/note which may not have been made at the time.
The party calling the witness should:

    (a) Inform the other party or parties that the witness has refreshed his memory from the document/note, and
    (b) Make available the original or a copy of the document/note.

3. EXPERT EVIDENCE

Introduction

21.03.01   An expert witness is a person with expert knowledge, whose opinion on any matter in which he has expert knowledge will be admitted in evidence.
It is for the court to decide whether the witness is an expert witness.

Practice

21.03.02   The party calling the witness should prove the witness' expert knowledge and/or qualifications, after the witness has been identified, as follows:

> **"Are you** (*state occupation of witness and/or area of expertise, for example*: **a pyschiatrist, a consultant toxicologist, a surveyor with specialist knowledge of** (*curtain walls*)**).**
> **How long have you been a** (*repeat above*)**? What are your qualifications?**
> **Do these qualifications/Does your** (*state area of expertise*) **enable you to give evidence of** (*state purpose of calling witness*)**."**

21.03.03   The party may then address the court, as follows:

> **"Unless there is any objection I intend to ask** (*name of witness*) **about** (*state purpose of calling evidence*)**."**

21.03.04   The party should then establish the manner in which he intends to adduce the expert evidence. He may ask the witness to define any specialist terms used or describe any special tests.

21.03.05   The party may then examine the witness in the usual way.

4. PRODUCING DOCUMENTS/EXHIBITS

Practice

A party may, during the course of examination in chief or cross-examination (but only exceptionally in re-examination) invite a witness to produce a document/exhibit, for example: **21.04.01**

> **"Could you look at this/Could the witness be shown this** (*state nature of exhibit, for example,* **document/contract/letter/object)?"**

The witness should then be asked to identify the document/contract/letter/object, for example: **21.04.02**

> **"Have you seen** (*the document/exhibit*) **before? When/where? (Is that your signature?) What is it?**
>   **Do you now produce** (*the document/exhibit*)**?"**

- OMIT **20.04.03–05** where there is no argument as to admissibility.

In almost all civil cases, where there has been an order for discovery (and most criminal cases), a witness should not be asked to produce (without leave) any document/exhibit which has not been disclosed.   **21.04.03**
A party taken by surprise may object, as follows:

> **"This document has not been disclosed and I would invite** (*the court*) **to exclude it."**

A witness should not be asked to produce a document/exhibit with which he has no connection (prior to the hearing of the case).   **21.04.04**

The parties may then argue the admissibility of the document/exhibit.   **21.04.05**

If the document/exhibit is admitted, the party may then say to the court: **21.04.06**

> **"(***To the court***) Could that** (*the document/exhibit*) **be produced? Could** (*the document/exhibit*) **be marked exhibit number (–)? (***The document/exhibit***) is at page (–) in the bundle."**

5. TENDERING A WITNESS

Introduction

21.05.01 If a witness gives corroborative evidence the party calling him may tender that witness for cross-examination on all or part of his evidence (as appropriate).

Practice

21.05.02 After identification of the witness the party may say:

> **"Were you present with** (*name of witness*) **and are you therefore able to give evidence of** (*state nature of corroborative evidence*)**? Have you had the opportunity of reading/considering/hearing the statement/report/proof of evidence/evidence of** (*name of witness*)**? Do you agree with** (*the evidence*)**?**
>   (*In the case of a joint document/note*) **Did you make that** (*document/note*) **with** (*name of witness*)**?"**

21.05.03 The party may then say:

> **"I tender this witness for cross-examination."**

6. AFFIDAVIT EVIDENCE

Introduction

21.06.01 A party wishing to rely on affidavit evidence should serve the affidavit and exhibits on the parties and the court (depending on the nature of the hearing) a reasonable time before/within a specified time of the hearing.

21.06.02 A party will not usually be permitted, except in interlocutory proceedings, to rely on an affidavit (in the absence of agreement between the parties) unless the witness attends court to be cross-examined on it.

Practice

The witness giving affidavit evidence is sworn and identified. The party **21.06.03** may then say:

> **"Do you recognise this as an affidavit sworn by you on (*date*) for use in these proceedings? Did you read it through before you signed it and check that the contents were true?"**

The party may then say to the court: **21.06.04**

> **"Has (*the court*) read the affidavit?"**

The court will either require the party to indicate the relevant passages or read the affidavit.

The party may then say: **21.06.05**

> **"I intend (with your leave) to tender this witness for cross-examination on his affidavit, but first, there are certain matters on which I would seek to examine this witness."**

The party may then examine, see **21.01.04–10**, the witness on:

(a) Any matter that has arisen since the affidavit was sworn.
(b) Any matter which was not material at the time the affidavit was sworn (for example, if the affidavit was served for the purpose of an interlocutory application).

The witness may then be cross-examined and re-examined on his **21.06.06.** affidavit in the usual way.

CHAPTER 22

Speeches and Submissions

1. PREPARATION AND PRESENTATION OF SPEECHES AND SUBMISSIONS

Purpose of opening and closing speeches and submissions

22.01.01 As a general rule, in a hearing before any court, tribunal or inquiry:
The opening speech *prepares*:
The purpose of opening is to assist the court, tribunal or inquiry to assimilate and understand the evidence it is about to hear.
The closing speech *persuades*:
The purpose of closing is to win the support of the court, tribunal or inquiry for that party on the basis of the evidence it has heard.

Preparing submissions

22.01.02 The Court of Appeal and, to a certain extent, the High Court requires the use of skeleton arguments and chronologies; and an increasing number of courts (including the Crown Court), tribunals and inquiries are encouraging their use.

If properly prepared, they can be very persuasive because they enable the judge/tribunal/inspector to identify the arguments and assist the advocate in organising them effectively in oral submissions.

376

Skeleton arguments

A skeleton argument should: 22.01.03

(a) Briefly identify the facts upon which (if proved) that party relies in support of the argument.
(b) Identify (not argue) any point of law, with reference to authorities in support.
(b) (Appeals only): Identify any finding of fact in the transcript or notes of evidence and state briefly the basis on which it is contended that the court can interfere with that finding of fact.

Chronologies

A chronology should list in chronological order events which are   22.01.04
relevant to the matters referred to in the skeleton argument.

As part of the chronology, in a complex case, a party may also list in   22.01.05
alphabetical order the persons, companies, bodies etc. who are relevant to the matters referred to in the skeleton argument, with a brief biography, for example:

Anderson, John   **Director of** (name of) **company, 01.07.92–01.01.93.**

Lists of authorities

Whether or not a skeleton argument is used, the parties should   22.01.06
exchange lists of authorities in advance of the hearing in order that each party can properly prepare his argument(s).

Where possible, the advocate should refer to the report of the case in   22.01.07
the reports (or practice manuals) which are preferred by that particular court.

Service of skeleton arguments/chronologies/lists of authorities

The parties should serve on the court the lists of authorities and   22.01.08
skeleton arguments and chronologies, if required, (in some cases, up to a number of weeks) in advance of the hearing and, in any event, not later than the close of business on the day before the hearing or, sometimes, up to 10.00 am on the day of hearing.
In the High Court, the close of business is said to be 5.00 pm, but this may be earlier in the county court and in some tribunals.

Presentation of submissions

22.01.09   In submissions to the judge, the advocate should take care not to appear to express his own opinion. The use of the phrase: **I think that**, should be avoided.

An expression of opinion can be avoided by the use of the phrases:

> **"I would submit that: or I would seek to persuade** (*the court*) **that:"**

Referring to cases

22.01.10   A party referring to a case should do so as follows:

Donoghue v. *Stevenson* [1932] A.C. 562

> **"The case of Donoghue and Stevenson, which is reported in the Appeal Cases for 1932 at page 562."**

Price v. *Strange* [1977] 3 W.L.R. 943

> **"The case of Price and Strange, which is reported in the third volume (*or* volume 3) of the Weekly Law Reports for 1977 at page 943."**

R v. *Galbraith* (1981) 73 Cr.App.R. 124, C.A.

> **"The (Court of Appeal) case of (the Queen and) Galbraith, which is reported in volume 73 of the Criminal Appeal Reports for 1981 at page 124."**

22.01.11   The "v" in the title of a case is almost always "and", although sometimes (usually in criminal cases) it may be "against". It is never "versus".

22.01.12   If the advocate is referring to a criminal case and is unsure whether it is the **"Queen"** or the **"King" and . . . ,"** he may say **"the Crown and . . ."**

Referring to statutes

22.01.13   A party referring to a statute should do so as follows:

Civil Evidence Act 1968, section 2(1):

> **"Section 2, subsection 1 of the Civil Evidence Act, 1968."**

or

"The Civil Evidence Act, 1968, section 2, subsection 1."

The advocate should avoid referring to the subsection first, followed by the section of an Act because it presents difficulties to a person keeping a note.

22.01.14

Authorities against a party

If the advocate is aware of a legal authority against him which has not been referred to by the other party, he should draw the authority to the attention of the court, tribunal or inquiry and attempt to distinguish it (usually on the facts), for example:

22.01.15

> **"There is an authority which is against me, namely** (*state authority*) **to which the court has not been referred. I would submit that it does not apply in this case for the following reasons** (*state reasons*)."

Assessing the length of and content of speech/submission

The advocate should always measure his submissions to the court, tribunal or inquiry that he is addressing; for example, a High Court judge will not need to be reminded of the standard of proof in civil cases or, the chairman of a tribunal of his jurisdiction (which is usually defined in the same statute under which the chairman was appointed).

22.01.16

The advocate's submissions may be as long or as short as necessary to cover all the points that need to be made (without unnecessary repetition), except see, for example, **9.02.15**.

22.01.17

Decision by the judge during submissions

If the judge has reached a decision by the end of all the submissions, apart from the party having the right to address him last and, if the decision is in that party's favour, he may say:

22.01.18

> **"I need not trouble you** (*name of party*)."

2. SPEECHES AND SUBMISSIONS IN CRIMINAL CASES

Introduction

The prosecution and the defence may open and close their cases to the jury, but see **22.02.15** and **5.04.62- 64**.

22.02.01

379

During the course of the trial, the prosecution or the defence may also make legal submissions, see **22.01.02–18**.

Speeches and submissions

22.02.02   There is obviously a distinction between speeches to the jury and submissions to the judge, but there will also be a distinction between speeches to a jury and those to a bench or board. An advocate may consider it necessary to address a jury on the burden and standard of proof (the so-called "golden thread" speech) but a bench, for example, should only need reminding of it briefly.

Addressing the jury

22.02.03   In speeches to the jury, the advocate should take care not to appear to express his own opinion. The use of the phrase: **I think that/I am sure that**, should be avoided.
    An expression of opinion can be avoided by the use of the phrases:

    "You may think that: *or* **It is a matter for you but:"**

Prosecution opening speech

22.02.04   The prosecution is entitled to make an opening speech.

22.02.05   The prosecution should prepare his opening speech carefully. It is usually the prosecution's best opportunity to pre-dispose the court and/ or jury in his favour.
    The prosecution may read from an opening note.

22.02.06   In many respects, the speech of the party opening the case is similar in both civil and criminal cases. The speech will prepare the court for the evidence it is about to hear.

22.02.07   The prosecution's opening will usually contain:

    (a) An explanation of the nature of the case.
    (b) An outline of the evidence upon which the prosecution intends to rely.
    (c) An explanation of the nature of the charges (in jury trials and, where appropriate in the magistrates' court, for example, where the offence alleged is technical or complex).
    (d) An explanation of the burden and standard of proof (in jury trials).

(e) An invitation to the court or jury to draw the inference, on the evidence, that the defendant is guilty.

Submission of no case to answer

Introduction

With the courts becoming increasingly reluctant to allow a submission of no case to answer, actually making the submission is becoming more difficult.   **22.02.08**

Except where there is a "legal submission" at half time, a submission is only likely to succeed where there is virtually no evidence at all. In this case, the defence will usually point to those parts of the case where the evidence is extremely weak and, in doing so, give those parts a significance which they do not deserve.

It is usually the case that both the defence and the prosection have little time to prepare their submissions; and with judges now allowing any evidence, no matter how weak, to go to the jury, it is important that they should consider first what is or is not in evidence.   **22.02.09**

For example, the defence may have put certain matters in cross-examination (which he later hopes to prove in evidence) with which the witness has disagreed. The defence should remember that only the answers given by a witness in cross-examination are evidence. The questions put in cross-examination are not evidence.   **22.02.10**

On the other hand, the prosecution may have called a witness who has not "come up to proof". This means that what the witness has said in evidence is not what he said in his statement to the police.   **22.02.11**

In responding to a submission of no case to answer, the prosecution should address the court on the evidence as it was given in court and should not, as a general rule, direct the judge to the statement of the witness of which part, only, is in evidence.

After having addressed the court on what is (or is not) in evidence, the manner in which the defence develop the submission will depend on how effectively he measures the sympathy of the court at that stage.   **22.02.12**

Practice

In practice, the order of submissions is as follows: **22.02.13**

(a) The defence should identify the evidence to which he refers and direct the judge to any relevant law.

(b) Reply by the prosecution.

(c) Response by the defence dealing with any new points raised by the prosecution or the court but not repeating the submissions in (a).

(d) Decision.

(e) Jury (or board, in a court martial) recalled.

Defence opening speech

22.02.14 In the magistrates' court and youth court, the rule is: one speech each.
In the Crown Court and court martial, the defence may make an opening speech where the defence are proposing to call other evidence of the facts (whether or not the defendant gives evidence).

22.02.15 The defence may not make an opening speech where:

(a) The defendant only is giving evidence and the defence are not proposing to call other evidence of the facts.

(b) The defence is calling character evidence only.

(c) The defence is not calling any evidence on behalf of the defendant.

22.02.16 The defence will usually confine the opening speech to an outline or explanation of the defence case although this is not strictly necessary and the defence may criticise the prosecution's case.

22.02.17 As a general rule, the defence opening speech prepares the court or jury for:

(a) The defence evidence, and/or

(b) Any observations the defence intends to make in his closing speech.

22.02.18 The defence opening speech may also be used to explain to the jury the purpose of questions put in cross-examination of the prosecution witnesses if it is not, at that stage, obvious or apparent and it is to be proved in evidence.

Prosecution closing speech

22.02.19 In the magistrates' court and youth court, the rule is: one speech each.
In the Crown Court and court martial, the prosecution will usually make a closing speech except where:

(a) The defence called no evidence.

(b) The defence called evidence but the case lasted only a short time.

The purpose of the closing speech is to draw together all the relevant **22.02.20** evidence in the case to demonstrate to the court/jury/board how, on that evidence, the court/jury/board is entitled to draw the inference that the defendant is guilty of the offences charged.

Defence closing speech

The defence closing speech is usually the only opportunity that the **22.02.21** defence has to address the court/jury/board.

Despite the literature on the subject of defence speeches to the court **22.02.22** (usually, to a jury), the defence should not feel intimidated by a closing speech.

The defence advocate should feel comfortable with his style. **22.02.23** Although style will come with experience, a good rule is to "be natural". If the advocate is not accustomed to illustrating his day to day conversation with anecdotes or jokes, he should not do so in his speech to the jury.

The defence advocate should also remember that a jury (or court) is **22.02.24** made up of individual people. He should consider what he would say to each one of them individually if he addressed them on behalf of his client.

The defence should prepare his closing speech carefully. The speech **22.02.25** should be properly ordered in a series of simple points and propositions which are relevant to the defendant's case.

The defence may find it useful to write down each point and proposition in advance for ease of reference.

The defence should address the court on each point, explaining the **22.02.26** significance of the evidence, the proposition the defence makes on that evidence and how it will assist the court in finding the defendant not guilty of the offence(s) charged.

If the defence follows these simple points and propositions, he will **22.02.27** avoid making an unstructured speech. An unstructured speech will almost certainly be either too long or too short because its length will not be measured by the points that the defence should make.

The defence will usually conclude the closing speech by emphasis- **22.02.28** ing the burden and standard of proof.

3. SPEECHES AND SUBMISSIONS IN CIVIL CASES

Opening speech/submissions

22.03.01   The party having the burden of proof will usually be entitled to make an opening speech (although, in some cases, both parties may make an opening speech).

22.03.02   As a general rule, the party having the burden of proof is the party who has brought the case or is making the application. That party will have done so for a reason. Therefore, a party opening the case, in addition to explaining the nature of the case, should also explain the reason(s) why he is entitled to the order or judgment sought.

22.03.03   The party making an opening speech should prepare it carefully. It is usually that party's best opportunity to pre-dispose the court, tribunal or inquiry in his favour.

22.03.04   The party making an opening speech may prepare and serve on the court and the other parties the following:

(a) A skeleton argument, see **22.01.03**.
(b) A chronology of events, see **22.01.04–05**.

22.03.05   If the party making an opening speech is proposing to refer to authorities, he must prepare and serve a list of authorities on the court and the other parties, see **22.01.06–07**.

22.03.06   The opening speech will usually contain:

(a) An explanation of the nature of the case.
(b) An outline of the evidence upon which that party intends to rely.
(c) A brief statement of the order or judgment sought.
(d) The reason(s) why that party is entitled to the order or judgment sought.

Submission of no case to answer

22.03.07   In practice, a submission of no case to answer is very rarely made because the court will usually "put the defendant (or the party not having the burden of proof) to his election". This means that the court will only hear the submission of no case to answer if the defendant elects not to call evidence in support of his case.

The practice of the judge or court should be clarified, see **9.06.72–73**.

In practice, if a submission of no case to answer is made, the order of   **22.03.08** submissions is as follows:

(a) The defendant (or party not having the burden of proof) should identify the evidence to which he refers and direct the judge to any relevant law.
(b) Reply by the plaintiff.
(c) Response by the defendant, with the leave of the judge.
(d) Decision.

Closing speech/submissions

As a general rule, a closing speech may be made by either party.   **22.03.09**

The closing speech will be that party's last opportunity (and, usually,   **22.03.10** the only opportunity of the party not having the burden of proof) to persuade the court why he is (or, the other party is not) entitled to the order or judgment sought.

The party should not repeat the evidence, although he should draw   **22.03.11** the court's attention to any important and relevant part(s) of it.

The closing speech will usually contain: **22.03.12**

(a) A summary of any important and relevant part(s) of the evidence.
(b) A summary of any relevant agreed facts (if appropriate).
(c) An explanation of any relevant evidence in dispute which is consistent with that party's case.
(d) An explanation of the relevant law, see **22.03.04–05**, consistent with that party's case, but see **22.01.15**.
(e) The reason(s) why that party is (or, the other party is not) entitled to the order or judgment sought.

Law and facts in opening and closing speeches/submissions

A party may refer to any relevant law during the course of his opening or   **22.03.13** closing speech or in any submissions where, on the evidence adduced (or about to be adduced), it is relevant.

22.03.14   A court, tribunal or inquiry may need to be persuaded on the law but, in most cases, it will need to be persuaded on the facts. As a general rule, the advocate should address the court, tribunal or inquiry on the facts before referring to the law.

22.03.15   It is sometimes an indication that a party has a weak case on the facts if he addresses the court, tribunal or inquiry on the law first or refers to numerous and/or obscure authorites.

CHAPTER 23

Etiquette

Introduction

The judge/bench/board/tribunal/inspector/coroner

When the judge, magistrate(s), tribunal, inspector or coroner (person(s) hearing the case) enter the room in which the hearing is to be held, all persons present should stand (and advocates will usually bow).

23.01.01

The parties should not sit until the person(s) hearing the case are seated.

During the hearing

When the court, tribunal or inquiry is sitting, a party should enter/leave/move about the room without causing a distraction and, in particular:

23.01.02

(a) A party should not walk immediately in front of the person(s) hearing the case if any other route is available.
(b) A party should not walk between the person(s) hearing the case and the party addressing them.
(c) A party in criminal proceedings should not walk between the defendant and the judge/bench/board when pleas are being taken or the defendant is being sentenced.

All parties should observe silence and avoid any act which may distract the witness or the court, tribunal or inquiry when a witness is taking the oath.

23.01.03

If a witness (or party to the proceedings) is being cross-examined and the court adjourns, the advocate who called the witness may recall the

23.01.04

witness when the court resumes (although this rule is now considered old fashioned), for example:

> **"(*Name*), could you return to the witness box, please. You are being cross-examined by** (*name of party*)**."**

The advocate will then sit down and the opposing advocate will continue his cross-examination.

After the hearing

23.01.05   In open court, an advocate should never leave the person(s) hearing the case sitting unattended *by an advocate*. This is called "dressing the court".

If the advocate's case is the last case in which any party attending before the court, tribunal or inquiry is represented the advocate should sit in the court/hearing room until released.

23.01.06   The judge may say:

> **"Please don't wait/There's no need to stay, (*name*)."**

23.01.07   In the magistrates' court and in some tribunals and inquiries this rule is often honoured in the breach. The advocate (and sometimes the court/tribunal/inquiry) is often even not aware of it.

However, it is a matter of courtesy and the advocate should sit in the hearing room until released, or he may say:

> **"There are no other represented cases before you today/this morning/this afternoon. Could I have your permission to leave?"**

INDEX

Costs—*cont.*
prosecution costs—*cont.*
industrial tribunal, in,
14.03.35−36
judgments, appeal from,
8.04.20
judicial review, 13.02.20
Lands Tribunal, in,
16.03.19−21
liquor licensing appeal,
5.09.08
magistrates' court, in,
1.06.52, 20.02.09−10,
20.02.17−18, 20.02.28−29
meaning, 20.01.01
order for, 20.01.02
planning inquiries, in,
17.03.51−53
possession actions, 8.07.10
Queen's Bench Division, in,
13.04.16
small claims arbitrations, in,
8.08.16
Social Security Appeal
Tribunal, in, 15.03.23
taxation of
indemnity basis, 20.01.03
standard basis, 20.01.03
youth court, in, 2.02.24,
20.02.09-10, 20.02.17−18,
20.02.28−29
County court
chambers
in court room
conduct in, 8.01.07
seating in, 8.01.06
dress in, 8.01.03
judge's room
admission of public,
8.01.09
order of presentation,
8.01.10
seating and conduct in,
8.01.08
Court of Appeal Civil Division,
appeal to, 8.06.28
discovery, in, 8.03.15−18,
9.05.14−15

County court—*cont.*
district judge
appeal from
in small claims arbitration,
8.04.21
to judge, 8.04.01−21
interlocutory matter
appeal in
appellant's case,
8.04.06−08
costs, 8.04.12
generally,
8.04.01−03
respondent's case,
8.04.09
submissions to the
judge, 8.04.10−11
applications to, 8.02.07,
8.02.08−19
interlocutory applications,
8.02.07
parties, attendance of,
8.02.10−11
practice
appeal, 8.02.19
appointment, 8.02.15−16
hearing, 8.02.17−18
preparation, 8.02.12−14
dress in, 8.01.03
family proceedings in, *see*
Family proceedings
final orders, appeal from,
8.04.13−20
High Court, relationship to
8.01.01
interlocutory applications,
8.02.01−02.02, 8.06.03
affidavits, 8.02.06−07
applications on notice,
8.02.04
district judge, to, 8.02.07
ex parte, 8.02.03
judge, to, 8.02.07
notice of application,
8.02.05
judge
see also seeing the judge
below

395